Two week loan

Please return on or before the last date stamped below.
Charges are made for late return.

ANDREW M. GREELEY

The Persistence of Religion

SCM PRESS LTD

First published 1973
By SCM Press Ltd
56 Bloomsbury Street London

© Schocken Books Inc. 1972

Typeset in the United States of America
Printed in Great Britain by
Redwood Press Ltd
Trowbridge, Wiltshire

Contents

Acknowledgments

For permission to reprint excerpts in this volume, grateful acknowledgment is made to the following:

The Antioch Review and Clifford Geertz for excerpts from "Ethos, World-View and the Analysis of Sacred Symbols," from *The Antioch Review*, Vol. 17 (Dec. 1957). Copyright © 1957 by The Antioch Review, Inc. Reprinted by permission of the editors.

The Atlantic Monthly and William C. Martin for excerpts from "The God-Hucksters of Radio," copyright © 1970 by The Atlantic Monthly Company, Boston, Mass. Reprinted by permission. *The Atlantic Monthly* and Ernst van den Haag for excerpts from "One Man's Mead, Another Man's Poison" (originally entitled "Margaret Mead Falls into the Generation Gap") copyright © 1970 by The Atlantic Monthly Company, Boston, Mass. Reprinted by permission.

Beacon Press for excerpts from "The Symbol of Virginity" by Herbert Richardson from *The Religious Situation: 1969*, edited by Donald R. Cutler. Copyright © 1969 by Beacon Press; and for excerpts from "Modern Secularity" by Guy A. Swanson from *The Religious Situation: 1968*, edited by Donald R. Cutler. Copyright © 1968 by Beacon Press. Reprinted by permission of Beacon Press.

Bishop Museum Press for the Polynesian creation myth from E. S. Craighill Handy, *Polynesian Religion*. B. P. Bishop Museum Bulletin 34, p. 11, 1927, Honolulu.

The Bobbs-Merrill Company, Inc. for excerpts from *Naming the Whirlwind: The Renewal of God-Language*, copyright © 1969 by Langdon Gilkey, reprinted by permission of the publisher, The Bobbs-Merrill Company, Inc.

George Braziller, Inc. for excerpts from *The Two Hands of God* by Alan W. Watts. Copyright © 1963 by Alan W. Watts; and for excerpts from *Alpha: Myths of Creation* by Charles Long. Copyright © 1963 by Charles Long. Reprinted by permission of the publisher.

Doubleday and Company, Inc. for excerpts from *A Rumor of Angels* by Peter Berger. Copyright © 1969 by Peter L. Berger; for excerpts from *Protestant, Catholic, Jew* by Will Herberg. Copyright © 1955 by Will Herberg; for excerpts from *From Fertility Cult to Worship* by Walter Harrelson. Copyright © 1969 by Walter Harrelson. Reprinted by permission of Doubleday & Company, Inc.

Evans Brothers Ltd. for excerpts from *The World Year Book of Religion 1968*, and *The World Year Book of Religion 1969*. Reproduced by kind

Herbert W. Richardson, *Toward an American Theology*, published as *Theology for a New World*, SCM Press 1968
John A. T. Robinson, *Christian Morals Today*, now included in *Christian Freedom in a Permissive Society*, SCM Press 1970
Theodore Roszak, *The Making of a Counter Culture*, Faber 1970
Giorgio de Santillana, *Hamlet's Mill*, Macmillan 1969
Stephen Toulmin, *Foresight and Understanding*, Hutchinson 1967

1. Introduction

LET US BE CLEAR at the beginning: this is a volume of dissent. It rejects most of the conventional wisdom about the contemporary religious situation. It does so on the grounds of sociological research and theory. The dissent is not merely from the conventional wisdom of the popular journals, divinity schools, and the self-defined "relevant" clerics and laymen. It dissents from the pop sociological-religious analysis which has become part of the American intellectual preconscious. It dissents from the assumption of most sociologists who do not specialize in the sociology of religion. It dissents from the official sociological model of what has been happening in the modern world—though, as I hope to show, the official model is to some considerable extent a misinterpretation of the thought of the fathers of the sociological tradition. It does not, I think, dissent from the position of a considerable number of scholars specializing in the sociology of religion, though I am certain that this book will push the thought of men like Clifford Geertz toward conclusions which they themselves have not yet articulated.

The thesis of the book, bluntly, is that the basic human religious needs and the basic religious functions have not changed very notably since the late Ice Age; what changes have occurred make religious questions more critical rather than less critical in the contemporary world.

In other words, when I am told by the enthusiastic admirers

of Dietrich Bonhoeffer that the "world has come of age" and that what is now needed is a "religionless Christianity" I become profoundly skeptical. That the world has changed is clear enough, but it does not follow that man has changed so very substantially that he can be said to have "come of age," by which, I take it, is meant that he can dispense with the Ultimate.

Lest there be any doubt as to the position I'm taking, let me cite five statements of what I take to be the conventional wisdom to which I am opposed. While the citations are not chosen exactly at random, they are, nonetheless, representative of many more similar quotations which one can find with almost no effort in many commentaries on contemporary religion.

In the introduction of his *Toward a Reconstruction of a Religion,* Eugene Fontinell observes:

> That institutional religion is in deep crisis is beyond dispute, though the nature of and the reasons for that crisis may be expressed in diametrically opposite language. Some would hold that the term "crisis" is too mild to do justice to the reality of the situation in which religion finds itself: *collapse,* understood as a functional breakdown or an existential irrelevance, would be a more accurate description. There is no universal agreement on the degree and permanence of this collapse but there is a significant convergence in descriptions of it by psychologists, sociologists, philosophers and theologians of every major religious tradition. I agree with those who see religion as in a state of collapse—it is only against such a background that the necessity for the effort which is urged in this work can be understood. Despite my negative evaluation of the present state of religion, I hope that this undertaking will be seen as a positive effort.
>
> My hypothesis, stated starkly and simply, is that only a radically reconstructed religion can enable religion at once to survive and to serve man. This last is redundant, since there can be no *significant* survival that is not also a human service.[1]

My position is diametrically opposed to Professor Fontinell's. I do not think religion is in a state of collapse, and none of the empirical data that I have available lead me to believe that it is. I think that Professor Fontinell is talking about a situation which

is limited to his colleagues on university faculties and their counterparts in the mass and not-so-mass media. The fallacy of
equating what goes on in the intellectual community—and only
a segment of that—with the whole of society is one that has been
so long enshrined among academics, that he who questions it is
viewed as just a little odd. Nonetheless, I will assert here (and
develop at length later) the proposition that the religious crises
of the intellectual community by no means reflect the religious
situation of the mass of the people. "Western man," "modern
man," "technological man," "secular man" are to be found, for the
most part, only on university campuses, and increasingly only
among senior faculty members, as the students engage in witchcraft, astrology, and other bizarre cultic practices.

My good friend Professor Marty speaks of "the Modern
Schism":

> During the middle decades of the nineteenth century (from
> approximately 1830 to 1870), the Western nations went "over
> the hump of transition" towards a new ethos of industrial enter-
> prise, urbanization and nationalism, accompanied by locally vary-
> ing programmes or creeds like liberalism, evolutionism, socialism,
> or historicism. These and other "isms" helped constitute the
> modern world and made up what Robert Binkley once called
> "the pitiless and persistent" rivals of the twentieth-century
> Church. . . .
> The Modern Schism affected most the inherited religion
> of the West, Christianity. Its upheaval may be compared to the
> effects of a geological "fault" on glacial terrain.[2]

I would argue against Professor Marty that liberalism, evolutionism, socialism, and historicism, if they have been pitiless
and persistent rivals of religion, have also been extremely unsuccessful rivals.

And John Cogley, in his *Religion in a Secular Age,* says:

> In times past the "modern" response to the experiences of
> life was also the "religious" response if only because the average
> man's thought patterns were molded by the basic concepts of

his faith. Even though it is probably true that the ordinary man at no point in history could be classified among the devout (and if one takes seriously the perennial complaint of preachers that their particular times were the worst ever, it would seem to be so), still, most cultures, East and West, have been faithful mirrors of dominant religious attitudes. Even in Western Europe, sometimes in the same nations, one still finds notable differences in outlook arising from either the Protestant or the Catholic interpretation of Christianity. But each year such differences seem to be fading as contemporary science, technology, and the influence of the mass media cross geographical lines. The process sometimes has been called Americanization, though it might more accurately be termed modernization—the United States was simply the first and most skilled in putting modernity to mass use.

As modernity takes hold, however, social institutions and popular attitudes often seem to become more of a threat to, than a sustaining force for, religious belief. Consequently, for millions in the West and growing numbers elsewhere, modernity and religion are now regarded almost as antonyms rather than as complementary social forces.[3]

But I would argue against Mr. Cogley that vastly more millions are able to harmonize religion and modernity without feeling any notable personality strain in the process.

Ramon Echarren, writing in the 1970 pastoral issue of *Concilium,* said:

> Mankind today is changing profoundly. Physical data, the organization of society, social relations, systems of communication and ways of thinking are altering radically. Humanity has entered an era in which change has become the norm, and adaptation to change a fundamental value. Our highly socialized society has given man a new vision of his position in the world; of what his relations with other men are, could and should be; of the value of solidarity; of the requirements of a morality in which "other people" must in some way be taken into account; and of the need to find fulfillment through co-operative effort, i.e., through teamwork. This greater dependence of men upon each other effects a new relationship between the individual and society in which numerous counterbalancing factors play an im-

portant part: a democratic outlook; the supreme value attached
to the dignity of the person; the desire for emancipation from
every form of authoritarianism, formal or informal; the rejection of tradition as a limitation on the autonomy of one's own
decisions; the insistence on the total respect of personal privacy;
the right of the individual to speech, thought and opinion that
are free in the sense of being without all coercion, social pressure,
and so on.[4]

I would argue, in response to Professor Echarren, that mankind is not changing profoundly. Some of the circumstances of
human life have changed but, as I shall attempt to explain in
this volume, relying heavily on the thought of Robert Nisbet,
fixity is far more characteristic of the human condition than
change. And Professor Peter Berger, in his *Rumor of Angels*, says:

> Whatever the situation may have been in the past, *today* the
> supernatural as a meaningful reality is absent or remote from
> the horizons of everyday life of large numbers, very probably of
> the majority, of people in modern societies, who seem to manage
> to get along without it quite well.[5]

Against Peter Berger I would contend that there is no real
reason to believe that the supernatural is any more absent or
remote from the horizons of everyday life of most people today
than it was six thousand years ago. Primitive societies have their
share of atheists or agnostics (or the functional equivalent
thereof) every bit as much as does modern society, and there is
no reason to think that enthusiastic religious commitment is any
more unfashionable today than it was among neolithic men.

By now it will be clear how complete and systematic my
disagreement with the conventional wisdom is. In the next chapter I will attempt to analyze the sources of the conventional
wisdom and show how its errors are rooted in profoundly inadequate assumptions about modern society. In the subsequent
chapters, I will attempt to analyze what I take to be five of the
essential human needs to which religion provides a response.
Since the average reader is already convinced that I am wrong,

I must ask him to suspend his judgment at least until he has heard what I have to say. One may dissent from many different varieties of the conventional wisdom and find not only an open-minded, but an enthusiastic audience, but to challenge the conventional wisdom on religion is to challenge a system of convictions which has taken on a special, indeed even a mythological, aura of its own. Unless one's listeners are willing to make a special effort to listen carefully to what is being said, they are likely to spend most of their time and energy trying desperately to find holes in the argument.

I would also like to believe—though it is perhaps foolish of me to do so—that the labels "optimist" and "conservative" which were attached to my *Religion in the Year 2000* might be held in abeyance in the consideration of this volume. An optimist I surely am not. By temperament I am a morose and melancholy Celt; by religious conviction I am a man of hope. But neither temperament nor conviction must be permitted to interfere decisively in social analysis. To say that religion survives may seem optimistic to churchmen, though it should not, because the obvious conclusion of the present volume is that it has survived in most instances despite the church leaders and not because of them. It may also seem extremely pessimistic to those who view mythological religion as residue of an unenlightened past. I would like to persuade both the churchmen and the modernists that my description is realistic; that is to say, it describes a religious reality which both must acknowledge is not likely to vanish from the scene in any sort of future situation that we can now imagine.

I am not able to understand why one is thought "liberal" if one sees religion falling apart and "conservative" if one expresses doubt about the demise of religion. Politically and ecclesiastically I am a liberal; educationally, I am a radical; as a social analyst, I would like to think that I am a skeptic. If I don't believe Martin Marty, Peter Berger, Ramon Echarren, John Cogley, and Eugene Fontinell, it is not because I have ideological differences with any of them but simply because they do not offer evidence that convinces me.

My efforts in this book are *sociological,* and they begin with two empirical observations:

1. The available statistical data simply *do not* indicate a declining religiousness in the United States.
2. The resurgence of bizarre forms of the sacred on the secular university campus has now persisted long enough that it cannot simply be written off as a passing fashion.

My analysis proceeds primarily from a sociological viewpoint, and I rely for the most part on authors who are sociologists, although I will not exclude such commentators on religious phenomena as Paul Ricoeur or Langdon Gilkey, who may not, technically speaking, be social scientists.

It is to be noted that I have my own personal religious commitments, but I do not think these commitments are such as to make me naive as a social analyst. If my analysis did indeed indicate that religion was losing its importance as a response to human needs in the modern world. I could easily say—as Peter Berger does in fact say—so much the worse for the modern world. However, my analysis does not put me in a position where I must make that kind of decision.

One of the principal assumptions of the present volume is that one does not analyze contemporary religiousness by limiting oneself to the university campus. Such a statement seems to be so obviously true as to be unnecessary, and yet most essays on contemporary religion have not looked at the religiousness of what one could call, using the currently fashionable phrase, "the silent majority." If substantial segments of the population are still involved in religious activity, they are dismissed either as a residue of the past or as engaging in some sort of "culture religion" which results from "social pressures" and is not "authentic." But it is one of the elementary principles of the sociology of religion that all religion is cultural, all religion involves social forces, and all religion labors through the difficulty of being something less than authentic. It is the sheerest sort of snobbery to reject the religion of the majority of the population as irrelevant to the analysis of contemporary religion. While this snobbery is common enough to members of the intellectual ethnic group, it still is not good social analysis to define as modern man the academic and his colleague in the media and to write off the rest of the population as irrelevant residues of the tribal past. Such snobbery becomes even less justifiable when tribalism reappears on the university campus with a vengeance. One would be much better advised to ask why religion has persisted in the masses when some of the elite have seen fit to reject it. One must also ask why religion is so popular once again, especially in its stranger forms, among the students of this intellectual elite. And one must finally ask whether the elite themselves might possibly have some kind of functional substitute for religion.

It is, first of all, necessary that we turn to the data. In my book *Religion in the Year 2000* I discuss at some length the available statistical material on religious practice. For the present it is enough to summarize the data contained in Chapter III of that book.[6]

Perhaps the most striking way of beginning to present the data is to cite Guy A. Swanson's consideration of the question of whether "religious institutions or interactions with the sacred order are on the wane." Swanson's method is a clever one: he admits that no comparisons can be made with religious behavior of the past; therefore, he argues that what we might well do is compare religious behavior in the present with political behavior in the present. He points out that "almost every informed student of the subject seems to believe that the American political system is vital and effective." Does religion, then, fall below politics in its vitality and effectiveness? Here I quote a "sample" of his comparisons:

ITEM: Approximately 60 per cent of the American electorate votes in national elections. Approximately 68 per cent of the adult population attends religious services in any given four-week period and 79 per cent claims church membership.

ITEM: 76 per cent believes that the churches are doing a good or excellent job in its area of the country; 80 per cent believes that national or state governments are doing that well.

ITEM: 27 per cent of the electorate reports it discussed politics with others prior to an election; 90 per cent of the people in the Detroit area, the only geographic source of data on this point, reports discussing religion with others during the month just past.

ITEM: Fourteen out of every hundred Americans have written or wired a congressman or senator, 7 out of a 100 have done so more than once. 24 per cent of the population has called on someone to invite his membership in a church. 88 per cent of the population prays frequently or every day; 40 per cent read from the Bible in the month just past and between 60 per cent and 65 per cent read from it during the past year. In metropolitan Detroit, 65 per cent of all adults are self-exposed to religious programs on radio or television and 75 per cent to reports of religion in the newspapers.

ITEM: Approximately five families in every 100 made a financial contribution to a political party or candidate in 1956. At least 40 in every 100 made a financial contribution to a religious body; three in every 100 tithe.

ITEM: The major Protestant denominations once again have an ample supply of ministers in service and also of candidates for the ministry, despite growth of church membership (and of members of local churches) far in excess of the rate of growth of the national population and despite sharply higher standards of training and ability required of students entering ministerial curricula. Positions in state and federal governmental service are going begging for lack of suitable applicants.

ITEM: Only 7 per cent of all respondents says it has no strong feelings about its religious beliefs. Although there seem to be no dependable national estimates, the proportion of the electorate that declares itself indifferent to political positions and issues is always greater than 7 per cent.

ITEM: 51 per cent of the American people correctly name the first book of the Bible. That is about the proportion that knows the number of senators from its own state—and that can spell "cauliflower."

ITEM: 95 per cent does not know what the initials IHS represent, just about the number which does not know that all members of the House of Representatives are elected every two years.

ITEM: 95 per cent knows the name of the mother of Jesus. That is the proportion that can state the term of office of the President of the United States and correctly locate Texas or California on a blank map.

ITEM: Only 34 per cent can correctly identify the Sermon on the Mount or can give the name of the current United States senators from its state.

ITEM: About the same percentage of the population knows that there are new editions of the Bible as knows that the President can override a Congressional veto. The respective figures are 64 per cent and 67 per cent.

As Swanson concludes:

. . . there is no point in continuing; the comparison can be multiplied at great length and with the same result. In the absence of good, longitudinal information, we cannot be certain of the meaning of the statistics on religion, but in the presence of comparable information from contemporary politics, I believe that the religious data require our being cautious indeed concerning assertions of the present irrelevance of religion for the personal lives and the institutional commitments of most Americans.[8]

One can add a number of "items" to those listed by Swanson: *Item:* Gerhard Lenski, in his study of Detroit, found that the religious variable was at least as powerful a predictor of attitudes and behavior as social class.[9] In ordinary social research, social class is only less important as a predictor than age and sex, thus, religious affiliation is still an extremely important "sociological factor."

Item: In the only available longitudinal research on religious attitude and behavior (the Ben Gaffin-Gallup studies of 1952 and 1965) almost no change was observed in the religious attitudes and behavior of American gentiles between 1952 and 1965.[10]

TABLE 1
CONTINUITIES AND CHANGES IN
RELIGIOUS BELIEFS AND BEHAVIOR
(Per cent)

Religious Beliefs and Behavior	1965			Change from 1952		
	Protestant	Catholic	Jewish	Protestant	Catholic	Jewish
Continuities:						
Believing in God	99	100	77	0	0	−21
Believing Christ is God	73	88	—	−1	−1	—
Believing in Trinity	96	86	—	−2	−1	—
Believing in prayer	94	99	70	0	0	−19
Praying three times a day or more	23	25	5	+2	−3	−4
Believing in life after death	78	83	17	−2	−2	−18
Believing in heaven	71	80	6	−4	−3	−15
Active church member	75	80	62	0	+3	+12
Changes:						
Believing religion important in own life	74	76	30	−2	−7	−17
Attending church weekly	67	33	4	+5	+8	−8
Attending church at all	67	87	61	—	—	+17
Believing Bible inspired	85	82	17	0	−6	−28
Reading Bible at least once weekly	47	37	31	+7	+15	+17
Number of cases	(3088)	(1162)	(128)			

Item: In the same longitudinal research there were no striking differences between those under twenty-five and those over twenty-five. Indeed, Catholic young people were, if anything, more orthodox than their predecessors.

TABLE 2

RELIGIOUS ATTITUDES OF RESPONDENTS UNDER TWENTY-FIVE AND OVER TWENTY-FIVE IN RESPECTIVE GROUPS (IN 1965)

(Per cent)

Religious Attitudes	Catholic		Protestant	
	18–25	Over 25	18–25	Over 25
There is a God	100	99	100	97
Bible is inspired	76	83	74	86
Pray	99	99	90	94
Life after death	85	81	72	77
Heaven	84	79	68	70
Hell	76	70	57	54
Against mixed marriage	62	62	65	74
Birth control	21	38	17	18
Divorce wrong	37	36	12	10
Church member	87	90	62	76
Clergy not very understanding	59	43	58	50
Sermons not "excellent"	93	70	76	68
Church too concerned about money	23	16	12	15
Number of cases	(135)	(1027)	(259)	(2829)

Item: In the ongoing National Opinion Research Center (NORC) study of the religious behavior of June 1961 college graduates, church-attendance levels remained high, with no evidence of drift away from organized religion in the decade after college graduation.[11]

Item: In the same research, two-thirds of the graduate students and the arts and science faculties of the top twelve American graduate schools describe themselves as having religious affiliation, 47 per cent of the Protestants attended church at least once a month, as did 87 per cent of the Catholics, while 60 per cent of the Jews said that they attended at least once a year.[12]

TABLE 3
CHURCH ATTENDANCE OF GRADUATE STUDENTS
BY RELIGION (ORIGINAL RELIGION)
(Per cent)

Church Attendance	Protestant	Catholic	Jewish
Weekly	21	78	1
2 or 3 times a month	14	4	3
Monthly	12	5	7
2 or 3 times a year	26	9	38
Yearly	12	0	14
Never	15	4	38
Total	100	100	101
Number of cases	(510)	(158)	(180)

Item: The studies currently being done at the American Council on Education by Alexander Astin and his associates show no changes in the religious-affiliation patterns of college students in the late 1960's from those studied by NORC in the early 1960's.

Item: Surveys in Scandinavia, Italy, the Low Countries, Czechoslovakia, and Great Britain report that between 80 per cent and 85 per cent of adults are believers.

Item: A German poll reports that 68 per cent said they were certain there was a God, but 86 per cent admitted to praying.

Item: David Martin reports that in contemporary England "a total of 85–90 per cent [believe] in God," and "over 90 per cent are buried with religious rites, some 80 per cent are baptized, and some 70 per cent married in church. . . ." [13]

Survey researchers like myself would consider the evidence afforded in the above items to be overwhelming. However, there is strong humanist bias against survey data, a bias which is not altogether absent even among sociologists. Let it be noted at this point, therefore, that I am merely arguing from the data that religion has managed to persist in the modern world, in some fashion or the other, despite forces of secularization and change which are alleged to be working with great vigor. The data then serve merely as a point of departure for this book. Anyone concerned with contemporary religion must, at a minimum, be held to explain the survival of religion in the midst of the crisis which is alleged to have been destroying it in the past decade or, depending upon the observer, century. The attitudes and behavior described above can indeed be labeled "residual," but they are mighty big residues. The persistence of religious attitudes and behavior would suggest that there may be strong countervailing forces at work which if they do not negate, at least weaken somewhat, trends toward secularization and change.

"But," Peter Berger once remarked in a conversation, "something must have changed!"

Something, indeed, has changed and it is one of the purposes of this book to determine what, precisely, has changed, in the hope that precision about the nature of change may help explain the paradox of the persistence of high levels of religious involvement in the midst of a supposedly scientific and secular technological society.

It seems to me that five "changes" ought to be acknowledged:

1. Religion has no direct influence over the large corporate structures which have emerged in the last four hundred years. Big Government, Big Business, Big Labor, Big Military and Big Education are not directly influenced either by religion or by church. I will argue that while the emergence of the large corporate structures provides a serious challenge to religion's interpretive and communal functions, it does not weaken the importance of these functions.

2. A considerable number of phenomena which once received a directly religious interpretation now can be explained by rational science. I will argue that as long as rational science cannot cope with the basic questions religion is designed to cope with, this is of itself essentially a trivial change, at least as far as religion is concerned.

3. Man's development of his capacities for abstract thought and expression means that myths are no longer self-sufficient and must be interpreted. I will argue that although this is an extraordinarily important religious development with profound strategic

and tactical implications for religion, the fact that the myths must be interpreted does not mean that man can do without myths. Indeed, I will maintain in this book that one of the profound religious and human crises of our time has been the failure of the scientific and technological society to understand that rational scientific thought is not a substitute for man's mythopoetic needs and capacities, but a complement.

4. Religion is a more explicit and individual matter now than it has ever been in the past. While the individual is by no means free from the power of the group, he still has a good deal more elbowroom for making religious decisions than he ever did in the past.

5. Religious commitment is, at least to some extent, a matter of free choice. Within social, cultural, and linguistic contexts a man may be able to play the role of a consumer in the supermarket of religions. Even if most men do not in fact exercise the option of choosing a religion very different from that which they inherited, they are at least aware of the possibility of choice and, as Clifford Geertz points out, this is an extraordinary change.

These last two changes are of great importance because they make the matter of religious meaning system and religious community more explicit and conscious than it has ever been before. I will argue that with the possibility of option there comes the immense burden of decision, but the need to *decide* about religion makes religion a more central and explicit question than it has ever been before. Insofar as an ever-increasing number of people must, in some fashion or the other, face the religious issues as explicit and central, it is legitimate, I think, to argue that the present era is *more religious* than any one of the past.

All of these changes are very important for the religious dimension of human life. The broader social changes of which these are but the religious manifestations make the world a different place from what it was in the age of Cro-Magnon man. I do not for a moment deny social and technological change, nor do I deny that these changes have implications—powerful and pervasive implications—for man's religious behavior, but what

I am asserting in this volume is that however much the context. has changed, the basic functions religion plays in human life are essentially the same:

1. Religion provides man with a "faith" or, to use the sociological terminology, a meaning system, which enables him to cope with the question of the Ultimate.

2. Religion provides man with some feeling of belonging with the communal group whose members share ultimate commitments and through that sharing provide strong basic support for one another.

3. Religion strives to integrate with the rest of human life the profound and disturbing forces of human sexuality.

4. Religion offers man a channel for coming into intimate contact with the Powers that are real, a contact which is frequently mystical and even ecstatic.

5. Religion provides man with certain leaders whose role is to provide both comfort and challenge when man attempts to wrestle with the Ultimate.

I am not arguing that all men experience these needs in any very powerful way, save at certain times in their lives, nor am I denying that some men apparently experience none of these needs in a particularly vigorous fashion. What I am asserting is that these needs are inherent in the human condition and that there is no reason to believe that they are any less widespread or less powerful today than they were among the prehistoric painters of France. What we know of primitive tribes in the modern world permits us to be profoundly skeptical about the notion that religious needs were any more highly developed among prescientific peoples than they are in the modern world.

In the next chapter I will attempt to explain the intellectual origins of the conventional wisdom with which I am in disagreement, and in subsequent chapters I will attempt to discuss the five basic functions of religion in such a fashion as to show that they are inherent in the human condition insofar as we know it.

2. New Myths and Old

THE STARTING POINT of our inquiry is the inability of the conventional wisdom to cope adequately with the empirical data showing that most men are still religious—at least in some fashion or other. An explanation which dismisses as "residual" or "inauthentic" the behavior and attitudes in which seven-eighths of the population in advanced industrialized countries engage is something less than an adequate mode. Yet the model persists relatively unchallenged. It is therefore necessary to investigate the assumptions of the model so that we can understand its persistence in the face of data which seriously question its adequacy.

David Matza, at the beginning of his study of a similar phenomenon in criminology, observes:

> Since assumptions are usually implicit, they tend to remain beyond the reach of such intellectual correctives as argument, criticism, and scrutiny. Thus, to render assumptions explicit is not only to propose a thesis; more fundamentally it is to widen and deepen the area requiring exploration. Assumptions implicit in conceptions are rarely inconsequential. Left unattended, they return to haunt us by shaping or bending theories that purport to explain major social phenomena. Assumptions may prompt us to notice or to ignore discrepancies or patterns that may be observed in the empirical world. Conceptions structure our inquiry.[1]

I propose to argue in this chapter that there are two basic assumptions on which the conventional wisdom of religious crisis depends:

1. The assumption of organic evolution.
2. The assumption of gesellschaft replacing gemeinschaft.

These two assumptions are related; indeed, the second could be considered an application and specification of the first. They are widespread and represent the official, if implicit, model of social change currently reigning in the social sciences.

Some time ago, I had begun to question the validity of both assumptions as the result of my study of religious and ethnic groups. In the context of these two assumptions, religious and ethnic groups ought to be declining, but in fact both kinds of collectivities seemed to be prospering, even in the most advanced industrialized society in the world. At that point, I happened to read two books by Professor Robert Nisbet, *Social Change in History*[2] and *The Social Bond*,[3] and discovered that Professor Nisbet was questioning the same assumptions in a much more sweeping and generalized fashion—and, I might add, with a great deal more erudition than is at my command.

There are two pictures which seem to me to be inadequate in the conventional wisdom of religious crisis and decline. The first is "secular" man; that is to say, man who has "come of age." He is so confident that he has solved all the mysteries of the universe, that he can dispense with a sense of mystery and with all questionings about the Ultimate. Secular man can do without the sacred. His first cousin is technological man, who not only understands the universe but dominates it with his scientific knowledge and his technological skills. Both men are able to cut themselves off from the primordial ties of faith, consciousness of kind, and common land which bound men together in the past. The relationships which they enter are determined by the functional requirements of the corporate structures that they have built up to understand and dominate the universe. They are both members of Professor Warren Bennis' "temporary society." They have, it is alleged, developed such capacities for intimacy, that they need have no roots in one place, or one organization, or one community. They need not even have only one sexual partner. They are men on the move, ready on only something more than an instant's notice to go to whatever end of the earth the corporate technostructure requires them to. And upon arriving at that end, argues Professor Bennis, they quickly sink roots and initiate a new set of intimate relationships which are intense, satisfying, and destined to be terminated whenever the technostructure requires.

But the point is that I don't know very many such people, and I don't think anybody else does. The man who can do without the sacred, without the primordial, and without roots exists, if he exists at all, in the great secular universities.*

Even among the university faculties, secular, mobile, technological man does not seem quite as happy, quite as satisfied, quite as well integrated as his own mythology would have him believe he ought to be. And his students, much to his dismay, seem bent upon proving how nonsecular, nontechnological, and nonmobile they really are. The intellectual heir of the secular, scientific man on the university faculty is the young commune member, alternately reading tarot cards and going on psychedelic trips. It is foolishness to expect us to take as a model of contemporary man someone who represents only a tiny minority of the population, and whose own offspring fiercely reject the model he stands for.

Yet the model persists. Its persistence is rooted in the faith—and here I use the word advisedly—that secular man and technological man are the inevitable result of an evolutionary process which cannot be resisted. It is Professor Nisbet who both describes and demolishes this faith. I can do no more in the present volume than summarize his argumentation. But since *Social*

---

* The "wanderer" can also be found among the very poor. Thus, a lower-class Negro can move from St. Louis to Chicago to Indianapolis to Memphis to Atlanta with a great deal of ease, but unlike the mobile university professor or technocrat, his move is generally facilitated by the fact that he has relatives in each of the cities to which he moves. Frequently he moves precisely so as to be with his relatives.

Change in History and *The Social Bond* are two of the most important books in contemporary social science, the reader would be well advised to read into them himself.

A good place to begin is with Nisbet's version of Professor Elting E. Morison's story about the British military.

> During World War II in Britain when armaments were becoming scarce and use of manpower critical, time and motion studies were made of gun crews in the artillery. It was hoped that the speed of operation of each gun could be increased. In one such study of a gun crew numbering five men, a peculiar act was noted. At a certain point, just before the firing of the gun, two of the men simply stood at attention for three seconds, then resumed the work necessary to the next firing. This was puzzling. The men themselves could not explain it; it was a part of the technique they had learned in gunnery school. Neither the officers nor the instructors at gunnery school could explain it either. All anyone knew was that the three-second standing at attention was a "necessary" part of the process of firing the highly mechanized piece of artillery. One day an old, long-retired artillery colonel was shown the time and motion pictures. He too was puzzled at first. He asked to see the pictures again. Then his face cleared. "Ah," he said when the performance was over. "I have it. The two men are holding the horses." [4]

Nisbet goes on to comment on the story:

> Not for close to half a century had horses drawn artillery, but they once had—holding the horses while the gun fired was necessary. The horses disappeared from the artillery, but the way of behavior went on. We laugh, and say the story is one more illustration of military inertia and add to it the familiar stories of military opposition to the introduction of tanks in World War I, to the introduction of aircraft ("it will frighten the horses"), and so on. But the history of the academic, legal, medical, and engineering professions is not different, except in details. Nor is the rest of society different. Once "control" is gained through some kind of habit or institutionalization of behavior, no effort ordinarily will seem too great to protect that

form of control, to avert the possibility of its being dropped or significantly changed. The appeal of habit is the possibility it affords to *suspend conscious thought,* to transfer thought elsewhere to spheres not yet reduced, or easily reduced, to habit. The consequence is that few of us can be said to welcome change—at least in those primary spheres where we feel most deeply identified—family, work, religion, and others.[5]

This story beautifully illustrates what I take to be the first of the three principal criticisms Nisbet levels at the model of evolutionary social change. As he says,

Despite the abundance of phrases in both popular and learned thought attesting to the omnipresence, the constancy, the timelessness of change, all empirical evidence suggests that in the history of any specific mode of behavior, persistence occupies a formidable place.[6]

He then proceeds to analyze a number of different institutions: the university, the family, the calendar, science, and literature; and illustrates how in each of these institutional structures, fixity is more real than change. The University of South Dakota today is different from the University of Bologna in the thirteenth century. Indeed, the University of Bologna today is different from the University of Bologna in the thirteenth century. *What* is taught is very different, but the way things are taught is strikingly similar.

Now, as then, we find the university organized in terms of colleges, faculties, institutes; we find its work parceled out in the forms of curricula, courses, and lectures. Today, as then, the prime protagonists are groups called faculty and students. And as surely today as eight hundred years ago, the permission of the faculty is required before a student may receive what was then and is now called a degree or license. The norms of academic consensus remain much the same, as do the criteria of advancement, whether faculty or student advancement.
    Even the conflicts reveal a striking similarity. . . . Violations by students of the civil (and canonical) order were com-

monplace, frequently violent, met by attacks in the form of reprisal by outraged townspeople and, occasionally, by censure or excommunication by the chancellor or bishop.[7]

Nisbet notes, somewhat tartly, that the university is an institution which, given its commitment to pursue the intellectually new, is the place where one would most likely expect to find dramatic structural changes; and yet, on the contrary, the structures persist.

> If such conservatism or fixity of type is apparent in an institution dedicated to the search for the new in knowledge, it is easy to understand these same conditions in institutions such as the church, family, caste, and village community. For in these the preservation of the old takes on calculated, even ritualistic, status.[8]

The family has certainly persisted remarkably unchanged.

> Deviations from the norm of monogamous marriage have always been present in the form of evasions—some of which have been sanctioned evasions, some not. But the norm of monogamy, like the structure of monogamy with its roles and statuses, goes on century after century. . . . Innumerable "proofs" are fashioned of the "bankruptcy" of marriage, of its all too evident lack of relation to the sexual needs of male and female, and of instabilities made manifest by desertion and divorce rates. But the monogamous marriage, like Ol' Man River, keeps rolling along.[9]

The university and the family are important realities. The calendar is relatively unimportant. Calendar reformers have pointed out for decades and even centuries that the calendar which we use "is not merely built upon the names of now-forgotten pagan religious figures, but far worse, it is built upon conceptions of time that are as needless today as they are obsolete." [10] Yet the last calendar reform was imposed on a very unwilling world by Pope Gregory in 1582. Even though the Gregorian calendar was immensely superior to the Julian calendar, it took several centuries before the Protestant world adopted it, and some of the Greek Orthodox world has yet to adopt it.*

Nisbet comments, "Rarely is change desired. . . . Surely, one would expect change to be a way of life in that area of human culture most committed by its norms to incessant change—science." [11] Relying on the work of Thomas Kuhn in his *The Structure of Scientific Revolutions* and Robert K. Merton in his sociological studies of the scientific system, Nisbet concludes: "Science . . . can suffer from the kind of conventionalization of the old and hostility to the new that we are more accustomed to thinking of in areas of politics, religion, or life styles." [12] And turning to the work of the literary historian John Livingston Lowes in his *Convention and Revolt in Poetry*, Nisbet reports, "even in the supposed haven of the incessantly creative and, hence, change-inducing mind, routinization, conventionalization, and downright conservatism of type are very common, with genuine change rare. In literature and in science, as in religion, fixity is real." [13]

Professor Nisbet's case is devastating. Change, of course, does occur, but basic changes in structures occur rarely, and the persistence and fixity of structures is one of the givens of the human condition. To argue in the opposite direction is to blind oneself to the empirical data on grounds of ideology and of faith. In *Social Change in History,* Nisbet examines in great detail the development of the idea of organic evolution in human structures. However attractive the theory is, he concludes: *"Change cannot be deduced or empirically derived from the elements of social structure."* [14] The social evolutionists of the present may claim that their doctrine is rooted in Darwinism, but Nisbet argues, on the contrary, it is rooted in Aristotelianism.

---

* In the very secular city of Chicago in the 1960's the Catholic Ukrainian Church was split wide open on a controversy about the celebration of Easter according to the Gregorian calendar. The young and progressive Catholic bishop attempted to change the celebration from the Julian to the Gregorian, but ran into resistance; and, at the time of the present writing, this disagreement has become for all practical purposes a schism.

It is frequently claimed, in justification of these functionalist and growth theories, that they represent the application of the insights of modern biological evolutionary theory to the study of society. They do not. There is not the slightest substantive relation between the conclusions, much less the methods, of the theory of evolution in contemporary biology and the conclusions regarding the nature of change reached by those sociologists who work with abstract universals such as social systems. The latter come directly from a view of developmentalism that is very old in Western society, that goes back indeed to Greek preoccupation with the life cycle of the organism as the key to the understanding of all change in the universe. The contemporary biological theory of evolution, on the other hand, rises directly from the highly empirical studies of post-Darwinian biologists, particularly those in the field of genetics. One does not find here reliance upon any model of self-contained growth, upon assumed patterns of differentiation, or upon hoary concepts of stages, immanence, and cumulative variation.[15]

According to Nisbet, then, the evolutionary model of human social structure is rooted in a metaphor which originated in Greek philosophy. Social structure may be compared to the human body; its growth continuous and genetic as is the growth of the human body. It is useful, Nisbet argues, as a metaphor, but it has nothing to do with the facts of social reality.

To argue that *change* is continuous is to argue not merely that change goes on constantly but that it reveals in its successive manifestations some kind of *genetic linkage* of these successive manifestations. It is to argue that each discrete change that we identify in the record literally emerges from a preceding change in a series of changes, that one change engenders another by virtue of some potentiality it has for "giving birth" to another change. And to argue that change is continuous is to argue, finally, that in this genetic linkage of changes something akin to organic growth is present from the start, with each later stage drawn cumulatively from prior stages, as so plainly occurs in the succession of changes any organism reveals in its growth.

But in the study of social behavior over time, in an identifiable area, with full attention given to what actually happens (in contrast to what might be drawn from some abstract model or constructed social system), we find none of these arguments capable of demonstration. For in fact change is *not* continuous, and the successive changes which are manifest in the record do *not* emerge genetically one from the other. Nor is there any evidence of the continuous accumulation of small or microchanges into the large or macrochanges that is so evident in organic growth or that might properly be inferred from some process over which a single intelligence presides from start to finish— as when one "develops" an idea into a large idea or policy.[16]

Just as fixity and persistence are more common than change, so when change occurs, discontinuity is the rule of life: "genetic continuity does not exist from change to change or event to event." [17] Whatever genetic continuity there is in human history is put in by the observer, Nisbet notes. There was absolutely nothing in the social structure of England that generated the Norman invasion and the immense impact that it had on the rest of the development of the Anglo-Saxon world. Events—discrete, sometimes random, generally unpredictable—create the warp and woof of human history, not organic evolution.

The idea of "necessary" historical evolution is rooted in the secularized version of St. Augustine's understanding of history.

It is *necessary*, wrote Marx and Engels, that mankind everywhere evolve from primitive communism to slavery to feudalism to capitalism. And it is *necessary* that this same succession culminate eventually in universal communism. It is *necessary*, wrote Comte, that human knowledge pass everywhere from a condition characterized by religious belief alone to one based upon metaphysics and, in due time, to a final condition reflecting the triumph of positive science. It is *necessary*, wrote the anthropologist Lewis Morgan (whose work was used by Engels), that the family, property, and the state each develop through a series of stages that can be authoritatively described.

Necessity in this sense is plainly an act of faith, a dogma, a means of living with present uncertainties and deprivations. It is not even certain that human beings, for the most part at least, could live without such dogmas, religious or secular. In them are to be found the sinews of hope and purpose. We should not depreciate them. But, whatever their value and our need for them religiously or metaphysically, they have nothing to do with the scientific or critical understanding of change in social behavior—that is, finite, empirical social behavior in time and place. Here no necessity is to be found, no irreversibility, no iron determinism.[18]

Change, then, is neither constant nor genetically induced nor continuous. Finally, it is not directional. Even though historians like Spengler may argue that each culture has its childhood, youth, manhood, and old age; in fact:

> We cannot speak of genesis, development, maturation, decline, and fall when we deal scientifically or objectively with human history, as we assuredly can when the object is a plant or another organism in nature. When we consider human history, all we can objectively ascertain are the facts of continuation of peoples marked by persistence, changes, and events. There were, in the Italian peninsula, people known as Etruscans (and perhaps others before them), followed by Romans, and then many others in all degrees of intermixture. They lived, produced children, died; they maintained ways of behavior; they changed ways of behavior. That is all. The rest is interpretation.[19]

Directionality in social change is not in the event but in the mind of the beholder. Nisbet concedes, of course, things are different today than they were at a previous time in history. We may say that Paris is large today and it was small in the thirteenth century. We may say that there are more gesellschaft relationships now relative to the number of gemeinschaft relationships than there were in the thirteenth century; but to see a necessary, continuous, and directional process in this growth is to ignore the fact that other cities the size of Paris and even larger did not, in fact, grow in the same direction. The differences between, let us say, Paris and Bruges are differences that are to be explained in terms of events and not internal cause, necessity, or directionality.

One must view skeptically, therefore, those reconstructions of the past in the forms of cycles or trajectories. By arbitrarily accepting some data and excluding much other data, some kind of cycle can no doubt be discerned in the history of, for example, the Roman people. Or, if one insists upon conceiving civilization as a single great whole, one can deal with it in terms of some assumed direction in time. Civilization, we say, has moved from the homogeneous to the heterogeneous, or from the communal to the individualistic, or from handicraft to computer technology, or from the original goodness of the Golden Age to present corruption and misery. We can say any of these things, and we do. The question is, do we mean anything when we say them? I repeat, in any concrete, empirical, substantive sense, "civilization" or "mankind" can only be taken to mean the vast, nearly incommensurable totality of ways of living of all the peoples who have ever existed on earth. How does one make an entity out of this far-flung and diversified conglomerate of peoples and acts? The answer is, we cannot. What we do is define "civilization" (usually with great advantage to ourselves) as a cluster of certain traits, material and immaterial, and trace this imaginary cluster from the simple aborigines of Australia or Tierra del Fuego to the complexities and splendor of, for example, Harvard University. Thus, we conclude triumphantly, civilization has progressed, or civilization has developed constantly through ever greater differentiation.[20]

Nisbet concludes his argument against directionality and the claim that with directionality one can forecast the future, with a characteristically acid comment.

There are few who cannot say with Tennyson, "I dipt into the future, far as human eye could see, Saw the Vision of the world, and all the wonder that would be." Some do it well, others badly; none can do it scientifically.[21]

The essential theme of Robert Nisbet's brilliant analysis of Western intellectual theory is that history and human social structure are not organisms like an animal or a human body. While the organic may be useful to provide a framework upon which we can hook the collections of data that we have hoarded together, it is a dangerous and heuristic model. How dangerous and how deceptive can be seen in Nisbet's example of Professor Marion Levy's analysis of social change in China, which purports to explain China at the end of the last century in terms of tension within the Chinese family structure, quite independently of the events of the invasion of China by the great powers of the Western world. But Nisbet's analysis, for all its brilliance—a brilliance that can only be hinted at in the present brief summary —will not be easily accepted. One suspects that he is under no illusions that it will. Nor has Professor Matza's devastating attack on the conventional wisdom about delinquency theory been readily accepted. Change itself, Nisbet would be the first to acknowledge, is something that we all dread, particularly when it affects matters of deeply held faith, and the model of organic social evolution is, indeed, just such a matter.

If we admit that the historical evolutionary model is a tacit and frequently unconscious assumption, then the conventional wisdom about crisis and decline in religion is obviously in deep trouble. The conventional wisdom presumes dramatic change, continuous change, and directional change; and it assumes it, be it noted, as a matter of faith. The empirical data which we cited previously can be much more easily accounted for in an explanatory model that accepts Nisbet's dictum that fixity and persistence are more typical than change. What one would have to explain about contemporary religion is not the persistence of religions from the past, for this is to be taken for granted. The challenge would be to describe and explain, so far as one can, the religious changes that *have* occurred.

The reader may not wish to accept Nisbet's thesis, though he would be well advised to examine both *The Social Bond* and *Social Change in History* with extreme care before he rejects the thesis. But he at least should be aware that the conventional wisdom about religious crisis and decline makes precisely those assumptions about social change which Nisbet calls into question. Only if Nisbet can be refuted does the conventional wisdom stand in a position where it can make any a priori claim to validity. If Nisbet cannot be refuted, then the purveyors of the conventional wisdom will have to collect empirical data to support their position—*overwhelming empirical data*. Because if Nisbet is correct, his assumption denying a major change in basic human social structures remains until powerful contrary evidence is produced.

My own problems with the conventional wisdom can be expressed at a much lower level of generalization than Professor Nisbet's. I do not believe that society is evolving from gemeinschaft to gesellschaft. It is first of all necessary, then, that we define these two phrases which are used so readily by social scientists, frequently without any precise meaning. Once more I fall back on Professor Nisbet for definitions.

When we refer to groupings of a *Gemeinschaft* character, we have in mind relationships encompassing human beings as full personalities rather than the single aspects of cohesion, communality, and duration in time. The most obvious and historically persistent types of *Gemeinschaft* are kinship groups, village communities, castes, religious organizations, ethnic groups, and guilds. In each of them the claims of the social unity upon the individual tend to be nearly total. *Gemeinschaft* types of social aggregates may spring from personal or territorial attributes, be religious or secular, small or large. What is essential is the quality of strong cohesiveness of persons to one another and the quality of rooted, persisting collective identity. The kinship group serves as the archetype of *Gemeinschaft*. It is by all odds the oldest form, and its spirit, its sense of communal membership, even its nomenclature, tend to become the image of other, nonkinship types of *Gemeinschaft*. In any genuinely *Gemeinschaft* type of social grouping there is a profound ethic of solidarity, a vivid sense of "we *versus* they," and of commitment of the whole self to the *Gemeinschaft*.

If we speak in moral terms, it would be a great mistake to label *Gemeinschaft* as necessarily "good." Bear in mind that examples of genuine *Gemeinschaft* include the ethnic ghetto as well as the village community, the totalitarian nation as well as the family, extreme social caste (as in India) as well as the guild or religious parish. *Gemeinschaft* is a neutral, descriptive term so far as ethical preference is concerned. *Gemeinschaft* cannot be subsumed under any of the types of social aggregate we have thus far considered, for it may be either small or large, open or closed, personal or territorial. Like each of these, it is a distinctive perspective for examining social behavior and a social order.

Gesellschaft may also be either small or large, open or closed, personal or territorial. What is crucial to this type of aggregate, irrespective of anything else, is the fact that, whether small or large, personal or territorial, it engages the individual in only one of the aspects of his total being, or, at most, only a few aspects. From the individual's point of view his relationship with others in *Gesellschaft* is more tenuous, loose, and less deeply rooted in his allegiances or commitments. *Gesellschaft* is commonly founded around a few specific interests or purposes, whether religious, economic, recreational, or political. In contemporary Western society there is a vast abundance of *Gesellschaft* types of relationship among individuals, types in which human beings are to be found linked more or less casually or else contractually, in terms of some specific interests. Such types do not and, by their nature, cannot command depths of loyalty or become the focus of motivation, as do those in *Gemeinschaft* groupings.[22]

That there are more relationships which involve only a part of one's personality at the present time than there were a hundred and fifty years ago is self-evident. The basic insights of the great sociologists of the nineteenth and twentieth centuries, such as Tönnies' and Max Weber's, about the shift in the style of human relationships stand at the very core of the sociological tradition. But it is merely a step from saying that there are more gesellschaft relationships to saying that gemeinschaft relationships are disappearing. None of the sociological giants would have argued in such a fashion, though it is fairly easy to misinterpret them and arrive at such a conclusion. However, I do not think it is an exaggeration to say that an implicit assumption of much contemporary serious sociology and practically all "pop" sociology is that in fact gemeinschaft is disappearing and gesellschaft is replacing it.

There is, I should like to observe, no real evidence that this is occurring. Man's primordial ties persist and persist vigorously. The fallacy of assuming that they are on the wane is based on the rather quaint notion that there are only a limited number of relationships possible for a human being. If he has more gesell-schaft relationships than his father or his grandfather, then it is concluded he will have fewer gemeinschaft relationships. How-ever, what in fact has occurred, if one departs from one's philo-sophical assumptions long enough to inspect the data, is that there are simply more relationships. A vast network of gesell-schaft relationships has become a superstructure based on an infrastructure of persisting gemeinschaft relationships. It is not my intention to deny that there is stress and strain between these two structures, or to argue that there are no tendencies toward dehumanization and depersonalization in much of gesellschaft society. I am simply saying that the large corporate structures which constitute the gesellschaft technological society represent *additions* to the pool of human relationships and not substitu-tions for the old relationships.

The critical question for social analysis ought to be how these two kinds of relationships affect one another in a society which has truly grown far more complex than it was centuries ago. However, the myth of mass society and of mass man isolated from primordial ties and living in an impersonal, dehumanizing world is so powerful that such analysis has not been pursued with any particular diligence. The critics of the mass society and its prophets (such as Harvey Cox in his *Secular City*) are in agreement upon one thing: society has evolved from gemein-schaft to gesellschaft. The optimists see this as a liberating, humanizing experience, and the pessimists see it as a degrading, mechanizing experience. Neither side has bothered to ask whether it has actually happened.

It is *the* great theme of classical sociology that in the last centuries Western society has moved from gemeinschaft to gesell-schaft, from community to association, from primary group to secondary group, from mechanical solidarity to organic solidarity, from traditional authority to bureaucratic authority, from primordial drives to contractual drives. Weber, Durkheim, Tönnies, Troeltsch, and Talcott Parsons have merely arranged different orchestrations on this architectonic theme. Under the impact of rationalization, bureaucratization, industrialization, and urbanization, it is argued, the old ties of blood, faith, land, and consciousness of kind have yielded to the rational structural demands of the technological society. In the conceptual framework of Professor Parsons' famous pattern variables, the immense social changes of the last two centuries have moved the race, or at least the North Atlantic component of it, from the particularistic to the universal, from ascription to achievement, from the diffuse to the specific. And other observers see a shift from the mythological to the religionless, from the sacred to the profane, from the folk to the urban. In other words, in the organized society at the present time, it is the rational demands of the organization itself—or the organizations themselves—which provide the structure that holds society together. Non-rational and primordial elements, if they survive at all, survive in the "private sphere" or in the "interstices." The old primordial forces may still be somewhat relevant in choosing a wife or a poker or bridge partner, but they have no meaning in the large corporate structures—business, labor, government, education, or even, for that matter, church. In the private sphere and in the interstices, the nonrational and primordial ties are seen as everywhere in retreat. Ethnic groups are vanishing, religion is losing its hold, men and women are becoming so mobile that they need no geographic roots. Professor Bennis argues that there is emerging a "temporary society" made up of those members of the social elite for whom geographic, institutional, and interpersonal stability are no longer necessary. These men, according to Professor Bennis, move from place to place, occupation to occupation, and relationship to relationship without feeling any sense of personal or physical dislocation. Wherever they go, they are immediately able to relate intensely to their fellows, and when the time comes to terminate a set of relationships, they then enter into a new set equally intense but equally transitory. There is some suggestion in the *Temporary Society* that members of this new elite might even be capable of temporary marriage relationships. Whatever is to be said about the merits—moral, biological, or aesthetic—of the temporary society, it is certainly the ultimate in the pilgrimage from gemeinschaft to gesellschaft. The lives of the denizens of the temporary society are completely shaped by the functional necessities of technological industrialism.*

In this official model of classical sociology, then, the primordial is to be seen as on the way out. There may be some disagreement as to the speed of the evolutionary process, but nonetheless, secular man, technological man, religionless man, temporary man is seen as the man of the future. He is the one who occupies the critical positions in the government, in the media, in the university faculties, in the large corporate businesses. He needs little in the way of roots, nothing in the way of transcendental faith, and, as far as the technostructure is concerned, precious little in the way of emotion. Professor John Schaar ironically describes the cognitive ideology of such a man. "Reality is that which is tangible, external, measurable, capable of being precisely conveyed to others; everything that is left over—and some might think that it is half of life—becomes curiously unreal or epiphenomenal. If it persists in its intrusions on the 'real' world, then it must be treated as trouble and those whose acts or motives are imbedded in the unreal world are treated as deviant cases in need of repair or reproof." [23]

Even if one does not wish to go quite that far in describing the pilgrimage from community to association, one still must admit that the implicit basic premises of most contemporary social analysis assume that the "public sphere" is the real world, that what goes on in the corporate structures is that which holds society together and that the primordial or the tribal are limited

---

* To make my own biases in the matter perfectly clear, if I had to choose between the temporary society and a commune, I wouldn't have much difficulty choosing the latter.

to certain reactionary segments within the society and will even there be eradicated by a generation or two of college education.

The Old Right and the New Left may disagree, but I think that an implicit value premise runs through much of this analysis: the rationalized society is not only the way things are but the way things should be. The primordial or prerational ties are seen as "unenlightened" and "reactionary." One need not discuss the current resurgence of interest in white ethnic groups very long without realizing that among many liberal academics there is a strong moral revulsion against ethnic groups. The term "white ethnic racist" is used much the same way as "damn Yankee" is used in the South. It becomes one word and indeed an epithet. An official of a national social-work organization inviting me to give a speech at a meeting on the subject noted that "as far as I'm concerned, these people [white ethnics] are simply a barrier to social progress, though I suppose they have their own problems, too." And at the same conference a panel discussion about white ethnics labels them as "social conservatives." Serious discussions are held under the sponsorship of government agencies or private foundations in which the white ethnic "problem" is discussed as something about which "something must be done," and one cannot speak to an academic group on the subject of ethnicity without some timid soul rising in the question period and wondering whether it might not even be immoral to discuss the question of ethnic groups, since ethnicity stresses the things which separate men and we ought to be concerned about those things which unite them. The bias in these reactions is apparent: the survival of the primordial is a social problem. The evolution from the nonrational to the rational, the sacred to the profane, the primordial to the contractual, the folk to the urban is seen not merely as a useful analytic model, but as a profoundly righteous moral imperative. As some people have not yet completed their pilgrimage through this simple evolutionary model, obviously they are a social problem and "something must be done about them," such as, for example, seeing that their real income goes up at the rate of five per cent a year or providing day-care centers for their neighborhoods. If one does enough such things for them, maybe then they, or at least their children, will someday become more enlightened and be just like us.

It is certainly not my intention to deny the great utility of the official model of classical sociology. Obviously, a great transformation has come over the North Atlantic world since 1750. I need only to visit Ballendrehid, County Mayo, Ireland, to know that it is rather different from Chicago, Cook County, Illinois. The insight of the greats of the sociological tradition is extraordinarily valuable, but the trouble with it as an analytic model is that there is a strong temptation either to ignore or to treat as residual phenomena whatever can't be made to fit the model. I would be prepared to contend that it is the very elegance of the official model of classical sociology which has blinded us to an incredibly vast range of social phenomena which must be understood if we are to cope with the problems of contemporary America.

I would suggest, then, that there is another model which must be used either in conjunction with the official one or as the component of a more elaborate model which will integrate the two. According to this model, the basic ties of friendship, primary relationship, land, faith, common origin and consciousness of kind persist much as they did in the Ice Age. They are the very stuff out of which society is made, and in their absence the corporate structures would collapse. These primordial, prerational bonds which hold men and women together have of course been transmuted by the changing context. The ethnic group, for example, did not even exist before the last of the nineteenth century. It came into existence precisely in order that the primordial ties of the peasant commune would somehow or other be salvaged through the immigration experience. But the fact that the primordial ties have been transmuted does not mean that they have been eliminated. It simply means that they operate in a different context and perhaps in a different way. They are, according to this second model, every bit as decisive for human relationships as they were in the past. In fact, a strong case could be made that one primordial relationship—that of marriage—has in one respect become far stronger than it ever was in the past, because the ties of interpersonal affection are now required more rather than less by marriage partners; and while they may appear structurally tenuous, such ties of affection can be far more demanding on the total personality than were the structural ties of the past.

To the extent that this model has validity, we have not witnessed a simple, unidimensional, and unidirectional evolution from gemeinschaft to gesellschaft. What has happened, rather, has been a tremendous complexification of society, with vast pyramids of corporate structures being erected on a substratum of primordial relationships. Since the primordial ties tend to be the infrastructure, or at least to look like the infrastructure to those who are interested primarily in corporate bureaucracies, it is possible to ignore them or attribute to them minimal importance. One does not, after all, think about the foundation of the Empire State Building when one sees it soaring into the air above Manhattan Island—at least not unless one happens to be an engineer.

To the extent that this second model has any validity, one would be forced to conclude that the persistence of primordial bonds is not merely a social problem, but also a social asset. Communities based on consciousness of kind or common faith or common geography would be seen in this model not merely as residues of the past, but rather as basic subcomponents of the social structure. Membership in such communities would be seen as providing personal identity and social location for members, as well as making available a pool of preferred role opposites whose availability would ease stress situations at critical junctures in modern living. In other words, collectivities grouped around such primordial bonds would be seen not merely as offering desirable cultural richness and variety but also as basic pillars of support for the urban social structure. A city govern-ment would view itself as fortunate in having large and diverse ethnic groups within its boundaries because such collectivities would prevent the cities from becoming a habitat for a "lonely crowd" or a "mass society." Psychologists and psychiatrists would be delighted with the possibilities of ethnic-group membership providing support and self-definition as an antidote to the "anomie" of the mass society. Or, another way of putting the same matter would be to say that to the extent the second model is a valid one, the lonely crowd and the mass society do not really exist.

But to what extent does the second model have any validity? My inclination would be to say that, if anything, much more research data can be fitted into the second model than into the first one. This book is not the appropriate place to review in great detail all the available evidence on the survival of the primordial, but I can at least list the principal research efforts. The now classic Hawthorne experiments of Elton Mayo and his colleagues demonstrated how decisive in the supposedly rationalized and formalized factory was the influence of informal friendship groups. Ruby Jo Reeves Kennedy proved in the early 1940's that there had been no change in patterns of religious intermarriage for a half century, and thirty years later the research done at NORC on young college graduates indicates that denominational (which includes Baptists, Lutherans, Methodists, etc., as separate denominations) intermarriage is still not increasing in the United States. *The American Soldier,* studies by Samuel Stouffer and his colleagues, showed how decisive personal loyalty was in holding together the combat squad. The work of Morris Janowitz and Edward Shils proved that the Wehrmacht began to fall apart only when the rank-and-file soldier began to lose faith in the paternalistic noncom who held his unit together. The voting studies of Paul Lazarsfeld and his colleagues proved that voting decisions were not made by isolated individuals but rather by members of intimate primary groups; and the similar studies of Elihu Katz and others on marketing decisions and the use of innovative drugs showed how such decisions were strongly influenced by informal personal relationships. Will Herberg's classic *Protestant, Catholic, Jew* suggested a model explaining that religion is important in the United States precisely because it provides self-definition and social location. James Q. Wilson's study of police discovered that sergeants of different ethnic groups have different administrative styles, and the work of Edward Levine and others on the Irish as politicians have made clear—to those who are yet unaware of it—that the Irish have a highly distinctive political style (a political style, be it noted, that assumes the persistence and importance of primordial groups).

Manpower research done at NORC indicates that ethnicity is a moderately strong predictor of career choice. (Germans go into science and engineering, Jews into medicine and law, Irish into law, political science and history, and foreign service.) Studies of hospital behavior show that different ethnic groups respond differently to pain in hospital situations. (The Irish deny it and the Italians exaggerate it.) The Banfield and Wilson school of political science emphasizes urban politics as an art of power brokerage among various ethnic and religioethnic groups. More recent research at NORC has shown that there is moderately strong correlation between ethnicity and a number of behavioral and attitudinal measures—*even when social class has been held constant.* Other research studies suggest that in large cities professional practice—medical, dental, real estate, construction—tends to be organized along religious or ethnic lines, and yet other studies indicate that some groups choose to create a form of self-segregation, even in the suburbs. Louis Wirth was right; there would indeed be a return to the ghetto, but the ghetto would not be in Douglas Park, it would be in Skokie and Highland Park.

One could go on, but it hardly seems necessary. Weep not for gemeinschaft; it is still very much with us. On the contrary, the burden of evidence ought to be on those who claim to see it vanishing. When it is argued that at least among the social elites secular, technological, religionless man seems to dominate, we need only point out that the offspring of precisely these elites seem presently most interested in re-creating the tribal in the world of the psychedelic, neosacral communes. The model of classical sociology obviously is not to be abandoned, but it must be freed from a simpleminded, evolutionary interpretation. Furthermore, it is even more necessary to divest the model of the moralistic overtones which it has acquired, certainly in the world of pop sociology and, if I am not very much mistaken, also in the world of professional sociology. To assume that religious or ethnic or geographic ties are unenlightened, reactionary, or obscurantist is to make a moral judgment for which there are no grounds in serious social analysis.

The issue of the two models is not by any means just a theoretical one, for if one uses only the first model, then the angry white ethnic groups are seen basically as a social problem. But if one also uses the second model, one might conclude that ethnic loyalty could be a strong, positive force which might make available vitality and vigor for the preservation and enrichment of urban life for all members of the city. Thus, I would hypothesize that if one takes as a dependent variable the propensity to desert the city, one would find in a strongly ethnic neighborhood a much lower score on that variable than one would in a cosmopolitan neighborhood. I would even go further and suggest that in an ethnic neighborhood under "threat" there would be less inclination to desert the city than there would be in a cosmopolitan neighborhood which was less threatened. And I have been told that in one study of his first election in Gary, Indiana, it was discovered that Poles who are more strongly integrated into the Polish community were more likely to vote for Mayor Hatcher, a Negro, than Poles who are less integrated into the ethnic community (though, obviously, in any absolute numbers still not very likely to vote for him). There has been so little positive research done on the subject of white ethnic groups, that one is hesitant to state conclusively that at this point in time ethnic identification and loyalty might be a positive asset for promoting social change in the city. Unfortunately, the rigid theoretical limitations of the official model have made it difficult to persuade funding agencies that such research might be appropriate. We are now faced with the rather bizarre situation in which many funding agencies are almost pathetically eager to do something about "the white ethnic problem," without ever having established that it is in fact a problem, and when it might be, rather, a distinct advantage.

If the second model has any utility at all, one could also call into question much of the romantic criticism and equally romantic utopianism of contemporary American society. It may turn out that there is, after all, rather little anomie. It may be that the mass society does not exist beyond Los Angeles and the university campuses around the country. It may be that the young who are seeking to create new clans, new tribes, or new communes could achieve the same goals by moving back into their grandparents' neighborhood—an experiment which would also have the happy advantage of revealing to them that intimate communities can be narrow, rigid, and doctrinaire, and, in many instances, quite intolerant of privacy, creativity, and diversity. If such romantic utopians would at least spend some time in their grandparents' neighborhood, they would be a bit more realistic about the problems that they will encounter in the Big Sur or along the banks of the Colorado River.

It should be clear by now that I entertain a good deal of skepticism about the so-called rapid social change which we have allegedly witnessed for the last two centuries (or, alternately, the last two decades). It is also probably clear that I was equally skeptical on the subject of whether this social change has been evolutionary and, indeed, unidirectional in its movement. Social change there has been; presumably, at this point we are willing to see that some of it has been good and some of it has been bad. Some of it has enriched human living and some of it has polluted the human environment. I have no desire to go back to Ballendrehid, County Mayo, Ireland. I think, on the whole, we are far better off than our ancestors, but to say that we are far better off is not to say that we are all that much different from them; and because we know more than they did, it does not necessarily follow that we are either morally or intellectually superior to them. If one abandons—at whatever pain—a simpleminded, easy-directional, melioristic, evolutionary model of social change, then one is put in a position where one will not at all be surprised at the survival of primordial groups in an industrial society. One might even be grateful that they survived. In any event, one would be far better able to understand how the Irish have been able to govern the large cities of the country for so long.*

The conventional model assumes that the human race has been evolving sociologically as well as biologically; that this evolution is continuous, pervasive, and directional; that in recent years it has been evolution from gemeinschaft to gesellschaft in which the primordial, intimate ties of faith, family, friendship, common origin, and common land have been reduced to a residue; and, finally, that as part of this process, man has lost his need and capacity for the sacred, and, therefore, religion has come upon a period of crisis and decline. Relying in part on Professor Nisbet, I argue that these assumptions are doctrinaire and dogmatic and not rooted in observable, verifiable, empirical fact. Religion may be in crisis and may be in decline, but the crisis and decline cannot be proved by a priori assumptions, in particular, the assumption of organic social evolution.

Another way of approaching the issue of social change is to look briefly at the work of the European intellectual historian Friedrich Heer, one of whose basic themes is the persistence of the archaic tradition in the face of the modernizing tendencies of Western society. Speaking of the first millennium of Christian history, he says:

> Throughout this European millennium, the world of archaic thought and communal culture was defended and preserved in the folk-culture of the village, in pre-Reformation monasticism, in the clergy and in the old aristocracy. Together they fought

* Be it noted that an Irish political leader would not think that someone who managed to win 42 per cent of the vote and alienate two or three of the major ethnic groups of the city was a particularly successful politician.

against reform and against foreign ways, defending themselves fiercely against invasion from above and outside. There is an abundance of evidence in European folklore that pagan festal customs, cults of the dead, ways of resorting to the other world in legal matters, primitive magic and techniques, persisted in the villages of many parts of Europe until the middle of the nineteenth and often into the twentieth century. The Merseburg incantations, in their ninth-century wording, were in use near Vienna about 1930, and at about the same time, a procession at Maria in Lavant included the sacrificial ram which excavations show to have been offered in sacrifice at that very spot three thousand years ago. Various games and customs at different seasons of the year, Masonic lodges, initiation rites (like those practised a century ago by French seafarers), preserved, in a reduced form, the festal calendar and festal culture which lasted until the new mechanical techniques and ways of work broke up the ancient concept of the world.[24]

Heer sees the history of the Western world as a gigantic dialogue between archaic civilization and modernizing civilization, with the archaic managing not only to survive but to influence "the high culture, every bit as much as it was influenced by it."

Archaic society was the substructure of European civilization. Western culture, technology and religion had roots in its great unities, connections, identities and relationships. It maintained itself down to the nineteenth century by a network of inter-relationships. Visible and invisible threads tied folk-culture, the monasteries, the towns, the ancient nobility, the companies, fraternities and guilds together. This world and the world above; nature and supernature; God and man; freedom and fate; perception and reason; life and death; soul and body; inanimate and animate; individual and collective; "I, thou and it" all formed a series of dialectical identities. In the matter-of-fact popular view of things this meant a system of unions and alliances which needed to be renewed, strengthened and reaffirmed through the ritual and rhythm of the cults of feast and holiday, of working life and of the dead. In the majority of cases, European popular speech (and for a long time the people's languages were, in a sense, only dialects of the one common language of archaic society and its people) had no words at all for these dualities and mental distinctions.

These problematical questions belonged to the foreign world of the higher culture. They lacked words for them, because their own problems and questions lay elsewhere. Only towards the end of the fourteenth century, relatively late in European history, did the seamless universe begin to tear apart. The people's speech began to be used in theology and philosophy. For a long while, vernacular poetry (saga and legend, song and epic), in close connection with customary law, was the expression of this folk-wisdom and its conception of cosmos and chaos. A truly comprehensive intellectual history of Europe would have to bring to light the struggle between these two worlds throughout our European millennium. It would have to reunite what history has arbitrarily divided and study both cultures as one: Alcuin's semi-Pelagian court philosophy, and the Song of Hildebrand and Hadubrand; the pomp and circumstance of the humanism of Lupus of Ferrières, and Godescalc's doctrine of grace; Hugh of St. Victor's humanist cosmos and the *Nibelungenlied*; the fairy stories and the spiritualist philosophy of the eighteenth century.

The struggle between the two cultures generally assumed three forms:

(a) An open battle on the part of the higher culture and its governmental order against the folk-culture, which could never be entirely vanquished. The higher culture hurled its prohibitions and enactments of councils, curias, parliaments, universities, academies and faculties against the upthrust and undertow from below. Such definite acts from above were historically clear-cut events occurring at particular moments, and they often provoked rebellion from below (peasants' revolts, heretics' wars, etc.).

(b) Parallel with this state of open conflict, a manifold process of assimilation and accommodation took place. The dress, fashions, architecture, music and dance of the aristocracy and the towns sank down to the level of the people, but so did thoughts, ideas and mental attitudes. Distortion of these ideas occurred frequently and produced bizarre responses among the people. Revolutions and heresies often arose out of misunderstandings of words, concepts, ideas and emotions. Mutilation of an idea often had a strange power to unleash explosive forces in the lower sphere. The migrations along the roads of Europe transmitted the ideas from group to group. The people scavenged in the palace of culture built by those who ruled them and picked up bits of theologies and ideologies and scraps of systems of thought and belief.

(c) Within the great creative personalities a constant psychological dialogue went on between the two worlds. Dreams, visions, and childhood experiences of the lower culture fused with their philosophical and theological systems. At the same time, the personal underground of the subconscious mind fed their conscious work from below. At its deepest level their intention was always reconciliation: reconciliation of the upper world, the world of order and government, with the lower world; reconciliation of time (something imposed from above) and eternity, which flows along in the time in flux, time asleep.[25]

The only point on which we might differ with Heer is whether the archaic tradition has finally been definitively routed. The persistence of interest in astrology, for example, and its recent resurgence on the university campuses along with a whole host of other survivals from the archaic tradition make one dubious as to whether the underground really vanished or simply went deeper underground. Indeed, it is altogether possible that it did not go further underground at all, but was simply ignored by sociologists and historians whose dogmatic assumptions blinded them to its existence. David Martin calls this blindness "unilateralist history."

Unilateralist history is an unwillingness to look at history apart from the heuristic devices employed to make its superabundant data manageable. I mean that a sociologist looking at a Hogarth cartoon of church life in London is somehow disinclined to query whether such an age was more religious than our own. Broadly, he handles his perceptions in terms of a handy historical tripod, one leg in the present, one in the nineteenth century and one in the twelfth. So far as religion is concerned the leg in the twelfth rests firmly in official Catholicism as then but recently formalized, and the other legs rest firmly on trends in the empirical religious practice of the last 100 years. Any deviation from the official norms of the twelfth century then counts as secularization, just as does any decline from practice in mid-Victorian England: an easy solution to old problems.

This is linked with a version of creeping epiphenom[en]alism in the following way. Twelfth-century religion was—it must be assumed—firmly Catholic, and was powerful, either in being at that time the womb of progressive forces and ideas which were later to turn against it, or in being the focus of man's most potent alienation from himself. Nowadays, however, religion is a spent force, growing steadily weaker.[26]

Martin ironically notes:

I even asked one theologian just how many examples of modern secular man were extant. "What," he said, "in a percentage?" Yes, I replied, confirming his worst suspicions.

The incident confirmed mine as well. Theologians never lose their habits, not anyway their habits of *mind*. They know modern man exists *de fide*. Who is so gross a sceptic as not to believe in modern man? In a style reminiscent of Marxist theology all who do not conform to the thesis or agree with its proponents are suffering from 'false consciousness': they are just behind.[27]

At this point my case is clear enough, even if the reader is not persuaded. The religious crisis and the religious decline are matters of dogma rooted in doctrinaire assumptions about the nature of history and social change. Neither the crisis nor its assumptions can be substantiated by empirical fact.

There are two minor mythical assumptions that must also be dealt with. The first is what I would call the "literary myth." According to this myth one may write of a society in terms of the ideas generated by its intellectuals and philosophers, and having done so, one can then be presumed to have adequately described the social processes of the society. Professor Martin Marty seems at least somewhat guilty of subscribing to this myth in his *The Modern Schism*,[28] in which he discusses the so-called secularization process in England, France, and Germany in terms of the relationship between the social structures of these three societies, the historical context, and the ideas of authors such as John Stuart Mill, Jeremy Bentham, Ludwig Feuerbach, and Albrecht Ritschl.

It is not at all my intention to deny the importance of these men, or even to deny that they had some influence on the society of which they were a part; but to suggest that their ideas about religion and the sacred accurately reflected the ideas of the general population or had any serious impact on the ideas of the general population is merely to state a testable hypothesis and not an inevitable conclusion. Most people in the Germany, England, and France of their time—or even of this time—not only had not read Marty's authors but had not even heard of them. If there is one fact that ought to be self-evident, it is that disbelief in the university does not create disbelief in the larger society— or, as it turns out, even among most university students. Intellectuals are, of course, not unimportant, but neither are they the whole human society, however much they may seem to themselves to be the most forward and progressive elements within the society.

Finally, we must do battle with the really intolerable myth that the present generation is the hinge of history, and that modern man is the only man who has ever thought rationally or operated scientifically. Historians such as William D. Stahlman, who specialize in the history of archaic science, are severely critical of

> modern man's reveling in his own denial that ancient myth has truth value. He is so self-deluded that he finds it impossible to believe that his ancestors could have played the game of life by rules different than the rules he knows. Preconditioned by his science-saturated milieu, he tends towards impatience when myth is not immediately translatable into scientific terminology. . . . The new prehistorians, then, have no other choice than to make a gradual, convincing approach towards uncovering what is surely science in a large body of myths ranging from Finnish runes to Altaic legend. The hope is to demonstrate that myth terminology (everyday language with special meanings) was coined by what we should rightfully call "archaic scientists."

One basic assumption in this new literature is that archaic man was capable of highly abstractive thought long before he acquired the tool called writing. This assumption will not be popular with those who have totally misunderstood Darwinian evolution and have forgotten its biological origin. Fashionable historians of archaic times have found it convenient to hide behind the ideas of cultural evolution. Through ignorance of or lack of interest in science—in astronomy in particular—they have simply assumed that preliterate man was *naturally* ignorant of any science, however loosely that term might be defined. Confusing biological evolution with histories (and prehistories) and cultures, these historians have succeeded in blinding themselves to essential clues to an understanding of the very essence of culture. Following what appear to be the logical requirements of positivism, they grasp at the biological seedbed of evolution only to misuse it in a mistaken concreteness. They embrace the simplistic notion that all awareness, all sensitivity, all fields of knowledge simply evolved (and this miraculously in the course of several millennia).[29]

Stahlman and others (to whom we will return in a later chapter) insist that for thousands and tens of thousands of years before the capacity for abstract writing had been developed man very carefully studied, recorded, and passed on to his successors a host of what can only be called scientific observations, particularly about the stars; observations which enabled him to predict such phenomena as the precession of the equinoxes, and to create such works of genius as Stonehenge.[30]

Claude Lévi-Strauss argues that Neolithic man was, in fact, an extraordinary, ingenious scientist.

It was in neolithic times that man's mastery of the great arts of civilization—of pottery, weaving, agriculture and the domestication of animals—became firmly established. No one today would any longer think of attributing these enormous advances to the fortuitous accumulation of a series of chance discoveries or believe them to have been revealed by the passive perception of certain natural phenomena.

Each of these techniques assumes centuries of active and

methodical observation, of bold hypotheses tested by means of
endlessly repeated experiments. . . . To transform a weed into
a cultivated plant, a wild beast into a domestic animal, to produce, in either of these, nutritious or technologically useful
properties which were originally completely absent or could
only be guessed at; to make stout, water-tight pottery out of
clay which is friable and unstable, liable to pulverize or crack
(which, however, is possible only if from a large number of
organic and inorganic materials, the one most suitable for re-
fining it is selected, and also the appropriate fuel, the tempera-
ture and duration of firing and the effective degree of oxidation);
to work out techniques, often long and complex, which permit
cultivation without soil or alternatively without water; to change
toxic roots or seeds into foodstuffs or again to use their poison
for hunting, war or ritual—there is no doubt that all these
achievements required a genuinely scientific attitude, sustained
and watchful interest and a desire for knowledge for its own
sake. For only a small proportion of observations and experiments (which must be assumed to have been primarily inspired
by a desire for knowledge) could have yielded practical and immediately useful results. There is no need to dwell on the working of bronze and iron and of precious metals or even the
simple working of copper ore by hammering which preceded
metallurgy by several thousand years, and even at that stage
they all demand a very high level of technical proficiency.

Neolithic, or early historical, man was therefore the heir of
a long scientific tradition. However, had he, as well as all his
predecessors, been inspired by exactly the same spirit as that of
our own time, it would be impossible to understand how he
could have come to a halt and how several thousand years of
stagnation have intervened between the neolithic revolution
and modern science like a level plain between ascents. There
is only one solution to the paradox, namely, that there are two
distinct modes of scientific thought. These are certainly not a
function of different stages of development of the human mind
but rather of two strategic levels at which nature is accessible
to scientific enquiry: one roughly adapted to that of perception
and the imagination; the other at a remove from it. It is as if
the necessary connections which are the object of all science,
neolithic or modern, could be arrived at by two different routes,
one very close to, and the other more remote from, sensible
intuition.[31]

Lévi-Strauss insists that it is a mistake to think that these are two stages or phases in the evolution of knowledge. Quite the contrary, both approaches are equally valid. Indeed, he goes so far as to suggest that contemporary science may actually be seeking to recapture and reintegrate the insights that come through imagination.

> Physics and chemistry are already striving to become qualitative again, that is, to account also for secondary qualities which when they have been explained will in their turn become means of explanation. And biology may perhaps be marking time waiting for this before it can itself explain life. Mythical thought for its part is imprisoned in the events and experiences which it never tires of ordering and re-ordering in its search to find in them a meaning. But it also acts as a liberator by its protest against the idea that anything can be meaningless with which science at first resigned itself to a compromise.[32]

One can only add to Professor Lévi-Strauss's observation the comment that both sociology and psychology also seem quite interested at the present time in recovering the qualitative—a recovery all the more important because their attempts to model themselves after the physical sciences, or rather what they thought the physical sciences were, have turned out to be singularly unsuccessful.

Our ancient ancestors, then, were not naive simpletons. They lacked some of the intellectual tools we have: writing, mathematics, skill at abstract rationalization. But the fact that we take their scientific achievements so much for granted does not make the achievements any less great. Our arrogant assumption that we are among the first scientists and that our ancestors were imprisoned by ignorance and superstition is simply one more assumption which is not in accordance with concrete historical facts.

We are not nearly so advanced as we thought we were, and our predecessors not nearly so backward as we thought they were. They made great scientific discoveries, and we currently live in a world where most people still accept the sacred. Whether we are any more *scientific* than they and they any more sacral than we is a question for which the available research evidence does not provide any easy answer. But it is safe to say that they were far more scientific and we are far more sacral than the simple ethnocentrism allows us to perceive. Ethnocentrism, it turns out, can be temporal as well as geographic.

But to repeat Professor Peter Berger's protest, "Something must have changed!" It is not the purpose of this chapter to prove nothing by proving too much. There have been a number of extremely important changes in the human condition since the late Ice Age. These conditions have transformed both the physical conditions of human life and also the social structure, though I would argue that the social structure has been transformed not so much by destroying old relationships as by expanding both the number and variety of possible relationships. First of all, there has been the immense change that has come from the discovery of writing and mathematics and the utilization of both these skills in improving man's capacity for abstract thought and his utilization of that capacity. Secondly, there is the process of "rationalization," that is, the attempt to organize human social structures and human thought according to values drawn directly from human reason. Nisbet chooses to use the word "secularization" to describe this process, though he says Max Weber's word "rationalization" is every bit as appropriate.

> I have in mind here the kind of change that is associated with the rise of critical rationalism, as in ancient Greece and again in the Western Renaissance, and also the rise of systematic science, as in the seventeenth century in England and France.[33]

In Nisbet's view of things, the process is going on constantly in human behavior, though only at certain times in history does it become so strong that it is able to influence enough men so that a definitive break may take place—however temporarily—with the traditional.

It is outweighed in significance by the fact that there are certain ages in which secularization reaches a high point of intensity, elicits the creative attention of minds of highest quality, and leads to an unwonted emphasis on individual reason rather than mere obedience to tradition. The process of secularization results in the novel respect for values of utility rather than of sacredness alone, control of environment rather than passive submission to it, and, in some ways most importantly, concern with man's present welfare on this earth rather than his supposed immortal relation to the gods.[34]

Rationalization, then, is not something that is unique to our own time; but the cumulative effects of rationalization—interrupted by the triumphs of conventional wisdoms which are frequently nothing but the ritualization of new insights—have been great.

This leads to the third important change that must be noted, a change which is a direct result of the first two: man's technology has become dramatically more sophisticated and more powerful. This change can be measured by the tremendous increase in the amount of energy available for human use. From the wheel, the horse, and the sailboat to the jet engine and the atomic reactor is an immense change, and I am fully prepared to concede it as progress, though it is currently fashionable among the critics of the technological society to denounce such progress. Most such critics, however, would not be alive were it not for technological progress.

The fourth change is one that we have already hinted at: the complexification of human relationships. In most human societies man's relationships have been with his wife, his children, his parents, his relatives, his neighbors, other members of his tribe, his chief, and his priest; but progress in abstract thought and the use of this abstract thought to organize the production of energy has led to the emergence of large corporate structures: the state, the business corporation, the labor union, the national or supernational church, and the giant educational system. Man does not, thereby, at least in my view of things, abandon his relationship to his family, his friends, his neighbors, his chief (though now he may be called the precinct captain), or his priest; but he does take on a whole new set of relationships. His life becomes richer, more complicated, and, quite possibly, more confusing, and, be it noted also, much more healthy and comfortable.

Finally, there is a process which Nisbet calls "individualization."

> By "individualization" I mean the complex set of elements involved when we speak of the release of the individual from the ties and constraints of community. Admittedly there is a certain degree of exaggeration involved in the word "release." . . . There is no behavior in social context that is not bound in some degree to social authority, role, and status. Therefore we have to consider it release in somewhat relative terms. But however we consider it, the phenomenon of sudden individualization, or release of considerable numbers of individuals from the ties—suddenly perceived as restraints—of old, deeply fixed social codes and communities is a real one in the history of human society. If the word "individualism" had not taken on (as it has in the United States) extraneous ideological connotations, we could summarize the process in one phrase, "rise of individualism." [35]

With the combination of increased availability of energy, the complexification of social relationships and the increase in the exercise of the capability for abstract thought, man is "more on his own" than he ever has been in the past. This is not to say that he is completely autonomous, but it is to say that he must make more decisions and must exercise more choices than he ever had to before. He must, as we shall argue later on in the book, be far more personally involved in choosing his religious values than he would have had to be even a half century ago. This is not to say that he chooses his religious values completely independent from the culture, social class, ethnic group, and geographic environment in which he finds himself, but that he enjoys relatively more freedom vis-à-vis these background factors than his predecessors did. This freedom, however, as we shall note in subsequent chapters, brings with it a very considerable burden.

Important though they may be, none of these changes is necessary, continuous, genetically induced, or directional. Abstract thought, complex social relationships, immense increase in the availability of energy, relative increase of the exercise of freedom of choice can make for a better, richer human life. Indeed, they probably have done so on balance, but they can also create immense human suffering. In either case, they by no means indicate a crisis for or a decline in religion.

One frequently hears it said that either religion will adjust to the changed society or people will abandon it! We would suggest that this is an absurd statement. Men make their own religion and they will remake it one way or another to fit the new situation in which they find themselves. The statement might be modified to say that the churches must change to meet the new social situations or men will abandon them in favor of new religious institutions. Such a statement would be unexceptionable so long as one understands that the changes in human society, however dramatic they may be, do not mean that contemporary man's religious needs are totally different from the needs of his predecessors. More knowledge, more power, a more complex society, and relatively more freedom do not, it seems to me, eliminate man's need for faith, community, meaningful sexuality, the sacred, or religious leadership. If anything, indeed, the changes aggravate the need for all of these religious functions because they make the need more explicit, more conscious, and more subject to choice. The churchman, then, who accepts the injunction that he must change to mean that he must come up with something totally new, and that he must abandon everything from the religion of the past, is likely to find that he has surrounded himself with a small coterie of secular men, men who believe as religiously as he does that they are the wave of the future and that the evolutionary process assures their triumph as the most advanced and most progressive—and, yes, let's say it—

the fittest of their species. They would do well to attend the meeting of the local witchcraft coven that their students have formed.

The work of these first two chapters has been essentially negative. We have argued that the conventional wisdom about contemporary religion is inadequate to explain vast amounts of empirical data, and we have found that this inadequacy is based on doctrinaire and a priori assumptions about the nature of human social change. These assumptions imply a simpleminded unidirectional, organic, evolutionary model which was initially merely descriptive but quite quickly became normative: not only has religion declined, not only is it in crisis, but the decline and the crisis are things that *ought* to be because they represent a triumph of enlightenment and rationality over the obscurantism, ignorance, and superstition of the past.

But to turn Sportin' Life back on himself, "It ain't necessarily so!"

3. Religion and Faith

RELIGION IS an explanation of what the world is all about. The most critical link in the chain of argument I am formulating in this volume is the contention that man (by which I mean most men at many times of their lives) need some sort of ultimate explanation. In attempting to deal with this question of religion as a meaning system, I will rely very heavily on the work of my friend and colleague Professor Clifford Geertz, who on the basis of the breadth of his knowledge and the elegance of his style must certainly be granted the title of the most distinguished social scientist of religion currently practicing.

In Professor Geertz's thought, religion is a cultural system; that is to say, one of the various systems of meaning and explanation by which men order and interpret their lives. "Culture denotes an historically transmitted pattern of meaning embodied in symbols, a system of inherent conceptions expressed in symbolic form by means of which men communicate, perpetuate and develop their knowledge about and attitudes towards life." [1]

Men cannot exist without culture. They would not be the clever savages of Golding's *Lord of the Flies*, relying on the wisdom of animal instincts,

nor would they be "nature's noblemen of Enlightenment primitivism," or even, as classical anthropological theory would imply, intrinsically talented apes who had somehow failed to find themselves. They would be unworkable monstrosities with very few useful instincts, fewer recognizable sentiments, and no intellect: mental basket cases. As our central nervous system—and most particularly its crowning curse and glory, the neocortex—grew up in great part in interaction with culture, it is incapable of directing our behavior or organizing our experience without the guidance provided by systems of significant symbols. What happened to us in the Ice Age is that we were obliged to abandon the regularity and precision of detailed genetic control over our conduct for flexibility and adaptability of a more generalized, though of course no less real, genetic control over it. To supply the additional information necessary to be able to act, we were forced, in turn, to rely more and more heavily on cultural sources—the accumulated fund of significant symbols. Such symbols are thus not merely expressions, instrumentalities, or correlates of our biological, psychological, and social existence; they are prerequisites of it. Without men, no culture, certainly; but equally, and more significantly, without culture, no men.[2]

Meaning symbols by which we communicate, perpetuate, and develop our knowledge about an attitude toward life are built into the human condition.

We are, in sum, incomplete or unfinished animals who complete or finish ourselves through culture—and not through culture in general but through highly particular forms of it: Dobuan and Javanese, Hopi and Italian, upper-class and lower-class, academic and commercial. Man's great capacity for learning, his plasticity, has often been remarked, but what is even more critical is his extreme dependence upon a certain sort of learning: the attainment of concepts, the apprehension and application of specific systems of symbolic meaning. . . .

We live, as one writer has neatly put it, in an "information gap." Between what our body tells us and what we have to know in order to function, there is a vacuum we must fill ourselves, and we fill it with information (or misinformation) provided by our culture. The boundary between what is innately controlled and what is culturally controlled in human behavior is an ill-defined and wavering one. Some things are, for all intents and purposes, entirely controlled intrinsically: we need no more cultural guidance to learn how to breathe than a fish needs to learn how to swim. Others are almost certainly largely cultural: we do not attempt to explain on a genetic basis why some men put their trust in centralized planning and others in the free market, though it might be an amusing exercise. Almost all complex human behavior is, of course, the vector outcome of the two. Our capacity to speak is surely innate; our capacity to speak English is surely cultural. Smiling at pleasing stimuli and frowning at unpleasing ones are surely in some degree genetically determined (even apes screw up their faces at noxious odors); but sardonic smiling and burlesque frowning are equally surely predominantly cultural, as is perhaps demonstrated by the Balinese definition of a madman as someone who, like an American, smiles when there is nothing to laugh at. Between the basic ground plans for our life that our genes lay down—the capacity to speak or to smile—and the precise behavior we in fact execute—speaking English in a certain tone of voice, smiling enigmatically in a delicate social situation— lies a complex set of significant symbols under whose direction we transform the first into the second, the ground plans into the activity.[3]

Man without culture and without meaning is not man.

Becoming human is becoming individual and we become individual under the guidance of cultural patterns, historically created systems of meaning in terms of which we give form, order, point and direction to our lives. . . . To be human . . . is thus not to be Everyman; it is to be a particular kind of man, and of course men differ. . . . "Other fields," the Javanese say, "other grasshoppers." [4]

Our meaning systems enable us to put pattern and order into our lives.

They are extrinsic sources of information in terms of which human life can be patterned—extrapersonal mechanisms for the perception, understanding, judgment, and manipulation of the world. Culture patterns—religious, philosophical, aesthetic, scientific, ideological—are "programs"; they provide a template or

blueprint for the organization of social and psychological processes, much as genetic systems provide such a template for the
organization of organic processes. . . .

The reason such symbolic templates are necessary is that,
as has been often remarked, human behavior is inherently extremely plastic. Not strictly but only very broadly controlled
by genetic programs or models—intrinsic sources of information
—such behavior must, if it is to have any effective form at all,
be controlled to a significant extent by extrinsic ones. Birds learn
how to fly without wind tunnels, and whatever reactions lower
animals have to death are in part innate, physiologically pre-
formed. The extreme generality, diffuseness, and variability of
man's innate response capacities mean that the particular pattern his behavior takes is guided predominantly by cultural
rather than genetic templates, the latter setting the over-all
psychophysical context within which precise activity sequences
are organized by the former. The tool-making, laughing, or lying
animal, man, is also the incomplete—or, more accurately, self-
completing—animal. The agent of his own realization, he creates
out of his general capacity for the construction of symbolic
models the specific capabilities that define him.[5]

Man is therefore a symbolizing, conceptualizing, meaning-
seeking animal, not by choice, but by absolute biological necessity. His culture, and the meaning that the culture provides, is
not an option for him. Quite the contrary, man creates and
operates according to his "meaning templates" whether he wants
to or not. Man is *driven* to the search for meaning.

In his various writings, Geertz has so far analyzed in greater
or lesser detail five meaning systems: common sense, ideology,
science, art, and religion. The "common sense" mode of seeing is

a simple acceptance of the world, its objects and its processes,
as being just what they seem to be. . . . In the pragmatic mode
we wish to act upon the world so as to blend it to one's practical purposes, to master it or, so far as that proves impossible,
to adjust to it. . . . This everyday world is the established scene
and the given object of our actions. Like Mt. Everest it is just
there and the thing to do with it, if one feels the need to do
anything with it at all, is to climb it.[6]

Science, on the other hand, moves beyond everyday reality. "Deliberate doubt and systematic inquiry, a suspension of the pragmatic mode in favor of disinterested observation, the attempt to analyze the world in terms of formal concepts whose relationship to the informal conceptions of common sense becomes increasingly problematic. These are the hallmarks of the attempt to grasp the world scientifically." [7]

In the artistic perspective, on the other hand, one chooses to go in the opposite direction. Instead of trying to go behind the meaning of experience, the artist attempts to dwell purely on appearances.

> Instead of questioning the credentials of everyday experience, that experience is ignored in favor of . . . an engrossment in surfaces, an absorbance in things, as we say, in themselves. . . . It is the artist's skill which can produce those curious quasi-objects, poems, dramas, sculptures, symphonies which, dissociating themselves from the solid world of common sense, take on the special sort of elegance that only sheer appearance can achieve.[8]

Ideology is an attempt to interpret political reality, particularly when both common sense and religion fail to provide adequate interpretations for what goes on in political reality.

> The differentiae of science and ideology as cultural systems are to be sought in the sorts of symbolic strategy for encompassing situations that they respectively represent. Science names the structure of situations in such a way that the attitude contained toward them is one of disinterestedness. Its style is restrained, spare, resolutely analytic: By shunning the semantic devices that most effectively formulate moral sentiment, it seeks to maximize intellectual clarity. But ideology names the structure of situations in such a way that the attitude contained toward them is one of commitment. Its style is ornate, vivid, deliberately suggestive: By objectifying moral sentiment through the same devices that science shuns, it seeks to motivate action. Both are concerned with the definition of a problematic situation and are responses to a felt lack of needed information. But the informa-

tion needed is quite different, even in cases where the situation is the same. An ideologist is no more a poor social scientist than a social scientist is a poor ideologist. The two are—or at least they ought to be—in quite different lines of work, lines so different that little is gained and much obscured by measuring the activities of the one against the aims of the other.

Where science is the diagnostic, the critical, dimension of culture, ideology is the justificatory, the apologetic one—it refers "to that part of culture which is actively concerned with the establishment and defense of patterns of belief and values." That there is a natural tendency for the two to clash, particularly when they are directed to the interpretation of the same range of situations, is thus clear; but that the clash is inevitable and that the findings of (social) science necessarily will undermine the validity of the beliefs and values that ideology has chosen to defend and propagate seem most dubious assumptions. An attitude at once critical and apologetic toward the same situation is no intrinsic contradiction in terms (however often it may in fact turn out to be an empirical one) but one sign of a certain level of intellectual sophistication. One remembers the story, probably *ben trovato,* to the effect that when Churchill had finished his famous rally of isolated England, "We shall fight on the beaches, we shall fight on the landing grounds, we shall fight in the fields and in the streets, we shall fight in the hills . . ." he turned to an aide and whispered, "and we shall hit them over the head with soda-water bottles, because we haven't any guns." [9]

But religion is not concerned, at least not basically, with the political situation or with abstract matters of reality, or with disembodied appearances of reality, or even with the givenness of reality. It is concerned with the Ultimate on which reality rests.

The religious perspective differs from the commonsensical in that, as already pointed out, it moves beyond the realities of everyday life to wider ones which correct and complete them. Its defining concern, moreover, is not action upon those wider realities but acceptance of them, faith in them. It differs from the scientific perspective in that it questions the realities of everyday life, not out of an institutionalized scepticism which dissolves the world's givenness into a swirl of probabilistic hypotheses, but in terms of what it considers wider nonhypothetical truths.

Rather than detachment, its watchword is commitment; rather than analysis, encounter. And it differs from art in that, instead of effecting a disengagement from the whole question of factuality, deliberately manufacturing an air of semblance and illusion, it deepens the concern with fact and seeks to create an aura of utter actuality.[10]

With these matters of definition and comparison serving as a context, we are now able to give Geertz's definition of religion as a meaning system, a definition which we propose to make our own in this book. A religion is

(1) a system of symbols which acts to
(2) establish powerful, pervasive, and long-lasting moods and motivations in men by
(3) formulating conceptions of a general order of existence and
(4) clothing these conceptions with such an aura of factuality that
(5) the moods and motivations seem uniquely realistic.[11]

The critical phrase in the definition is "formulating conceptions of a general order of existence." Man turns to his religious symbols not merely to provide him with interpretation but also to help him cope with the critical question of interpretability. His dependence upon symbols is so great that if interpretability is threatened chaos is perceived as lurking just around the corner. According to Geertz, chaos threatens man in three sets of circumstances: when he finds himself

at the limits of his analytic capacities, at the limits of his powers of endurance, and at the limits of his moral insight. If they become intense enough or are sustained long enough, bafflement, suffering, and a sense of intractable ethical paradox are all radical challenges to the proposition that life is comprehensible and that we can by taking thought, orient ourselves effectively within it. Any religion, however "primitive," which hopes to persist must attempt somehow to cope with these challenges.[12]

The most important of these three problems is the problem of bafflement.

> But it does appear to be a fact that at least some men—
> in all probability, most men—are unable to leave unclarified
> problems of analysis merely unclarified, just to look at the
> stranger features of the world's landscape in dumb astonishment
> or bland apathy without trying to develop, however fantastic,
> inconsistent, or simple-minded, some notions as to how such
> features might be reconciled with the more ordinary deliver-
> ances of experience. To explain those things which cry out for
> explanation, man has an explanatory apparatus—the complex
> of received culture patterns (common sense, science, philo-
> sophical speculation, myth) that one has for mapping the em-
> pirical world. Any chronic failure of one's explanatory apparatus
> tends to lead to a deep disquiet.[13]

Nor is bafflement necessarily abstract or metaphysical. Geertz
tells the story of the disturbed reaction of his Javanese friend
when a rather large toadstool grew up in the carpenter's house
in the space of a few days. The toadstool is not an important
symbol in Javanese life at all, but this particular one was "odd,"
"strange," "uncanny," and therefore it had to be explained. In
the broadest sense, the strange toadstool did have implications,
and critical ones for those who heard about it. "It threatened
their most general ability to understand the world, raised the
uncomfortable question of whether the beliefs which they held
about nature were workable, the standards of truth they used
valid." [14]

Religion, of course, directly interprets the ultimate questions
of existence, but the Ultimate has a way of impinging on our
everyday life a lot more frequently than we would like.

> What lies beyond a relatively fixed frontier of accredited
> knowledge looms as a constant background to the daily round
> of practical life. This unknown sets ordinary human experience
> in a permanent context of metaphysical concern and raises the

dim, back-of-the-mind suspicion that one may be adrift in an absurd world.[15]

The other two basic problems that religion attempts to cope with—moral evil and human suffering—are closely related, for all three problems have to do with things for which we cannot account through our ordinary common-sense explanations or our scientific explanations or our ideological or artistic ones.

> Thus the problem of evil, or perhaps one should say the problem *about* evil, is in essence the same sort of problem of or about bafflement and the problem of or about suffering. The strange opacity of certain empirical events, the dumb senselessness of intense or inexorable pain, and the enigmatic unaccountability of gross iniquity all raise the uncomfortable suspicion that perhaps the world, and hence man's life in the world, has no genuine order at all—no empirical regularity, no emotional form, no moral coherence. And the religious response to this suspicion is in each case the same: the formulation, by means of symbols, of an image of such a genuine order of the world which will account for, and even celebrate, the perceived ambiguities, puzzles, and paradoxes in human experience.[16]

Religion, then, deals with the "really real"—with that which is most ultimate because it is most baffling.

> From an analytic point of view, the essence of religious action is the imbuing with persuasive authority of a certain specific complex of symbols—symbols of the metaphysic that they formulate and of the style of life they recommend.[17]

But religion does more than describe the ultimate nature of reality. It also attempts to tell man how he must live in order that he might be at harmony with ultimate reality.

> It is a cluster of sacred symbols, woven into some sort of ordered whole, which makes up a religious system. For those who are committed to it, such a religious system seems to medi-

ate genuine knowledge, knowledge of the essential conditions in terms of which life must, of necessity, be lived.[18]

The approved style of life, the improved structure of reality are taken to be in fundamental concordance and congruence with one another.

> The demonstration of a meaningful relation between the values a people holds and the general order of existence within which it finds itself is an essential element in all religions, however those values or that order be conceived. Whatever else religion may be, it is in part an attempt (of an implicit and directly felt rather than explicit and consciously thought-about sort) to conserve the fund of general meanings in terms of which each individual interprets his experience and organizes his conduct.[19]

Religion is therefore the struggle for the real. It is rooted in the

> insufficiency . . . of common sense as a total orientation toward life; and it must also be viewed in terms of its formative impact upon common sense, the way in which, by questioning the unquestionable, it shapes our apprehension of the quotidian world of "what there is" and which, whatever different drummers we may or may not hear, we are all obliged to live.[20]

Religion, then, is a means of understanding ultimate reality. By answering the most basic questions that a man can ask, it provides him with an interpretation which will shape even the perspectives in which he views his daily life.

Common sense is not enough to explain life. The fact that life overflows the categories of practical reason is at the root of what Max Weber has called "the problem of meaning." It is most familiar in the West in the form of the problem of evil: " 'Why do the just suffer and the unjust prosper?' But it has many more dimensions, for the events through which we live are forever outrunning the power of our ordinary, everyday, moral, emotional, and intellectual concepts to construe them, leaving us, as a Javanese image has it, like a water buffalo listening to an orchestra." [21]

Geertz insists that even in primitive societies religious belief coexists with skepticism. "There is a great deal of skepticism . . . in traditional societies. The inevitable tension which remains between the deliverances of common sense and even the most compelling and comprehensive religion assures that, as does the widespread employment of religiously based power to less than elevated ends." [22]

If in the traditional societies skepticism persists, so even in the most modern societies, in Geertz's viewpoint, the religious perspective persists. At the heart of this perspective is

> not the theory that beyond the visible world there lies an invisible one (though most religious men have indeed held, with differing degrees of sophistication, to some such theory); not the doctrine that a divine presence broods over the world (though, in an extraordinary variety of forms, from animism to monotheism, that too has been a rather popular idea); not even the more diffident opinion that there are things in heaven and earth undreamt of in our philosophies. Rather, it is the conviction that the values one holds are grounded in the inherent structure of reality, that between the way one ought to live and the way things really are there is an unbreakable interconnection. What sacred symbols do for those to whom they are sacred is to formulate the image of the world's construction and to program for human conduct. . . .[23]

The sacred symbol, then, represents a conviction about the inherent structure of reality. It explains that reality to us and tells us how we ought to live so as to be at harmony with reality. Whether the symbols be a credal proposition, a religious organization, or liturgical ritual,

> [a people's] world-view is their picture of the way things in sheer actuality are, a concept of nature, of self, of society. It contains their most comprehensive ideas of order. Religious belief and ritual confront and mutually confirm one another; the ethos is made intellectually reasonable by being shown to represent a way of life implied by the actual state of affairs which the world-view describes. The world-view is made emotionally

acceptable by being presented as an image of an actual state of affairs of which such a way of life is an authentic expression.[24]

A religion is as good as its symbols. "The force of a religion in supporting social values rests then on the ability of its symbols to formulate a world-view in which those values as well as the forces opposing their realization are fundamental ingredients." [25] Man is a "symbolizing, conceptualizing, meaning-seeking animal," and religion is his attempt to symbolize the ultimate reality. A religion will be effective precisely to the extent that its symbols are effective.

The religious ritual is nothing more than the enactment in ceremony of a symbol or symbol system which provides one with an ultimate explanation. But it is a critically important ceremony.

> For it is in ritual—i.e., consecrated behavior—that somehow this conviction is generated that religious conceptions are veridical and that religious directives are sound. It is in some sort of ceremonial form—even if that form be hardly more than the recitation of a myth, the consultation of an oracle, or the decoration of a grave—that the moods and motivations which sacred symbols induce in men and the general conceptions of the order of existence which they formulate for men meet and reinforce one another. In a ritual, the world as lived and the world as imagined, fused under the agency of a single set of symbolic forms, turns out to be the same world. . . .[26]

Ethos and world view, then, are symbolically fused in religious ritual, a ritual which "engulfs the total person, transporting him . . . into another mode of existence." [27]

Religious belief is the "pale, remembered reflection of an experience in the midst of everyday life." Ritual, as we will see in a later chapter, does not merely allow man to understand the really real; it also brings him into contact with it.

In his book *Islam Observed*, Geertz turns to the basic question with which this book is concerned: How do men of religious sensibility react when the machinery of faith begins to wear out? What do they do when traditions falter?

Geertz attempts to answer these questions in a comparative study of Moroccan and Javanese societies under the impact of Westernization. The response in Morocco has been to establish a rigid line of demarcation between religion and the rest of life, particularly the Westernized dimensions of life, while in Java the reaction has been to absorb Western elements into a pliable, flexible, syncretistic version of Islam. In Morocco

> Devoutness takes the form of an almost deliberate segregation of what one learns from experience and what one receives from tradition, so that perplexity is kept at bay and doctrine kept intact by not confronting the map with the landscape it is supposed to illuminate. . . . In Indonesia it most frequently appears as a proliferation of abstractions so generalized, symbols so allusive, and doctrines so programmatic that they can be made to fit any form of experience at all. . . . But, formalism or intellectualism, it really comes down to about the same thing: holding religious views rather than being held by them.[28]

However, only a small proportion of both populations are directly affected by either formalism or intellectualism.

> All this is, however, still but a crumbling at the edges; the cores of both populations still cling to the classical symbols and find them compelling. Or anyway largely so; the mere awareness on the part of those for whom the inherited machinery of faith still works passably well (which is probably the most it has ever done) that it does not work nearly so well for a growing number of. others casts a certain shadow over the finality of their own perceptions. . . . A few untroubled traditionalists at one pole and even fewer radical secularists at the other aside, most Moroccans and Indonesians alternate between religiousness and what we might call religious-mindedness with such a variety of speeds and in such a variety of ways that it is very difficult in any particular case to tell where the one leaves off and the other begins. In this, as in so many things, they are, like most

of the peoples of the Third World, like indeed most of those of the First and Second, rather thoroughly mixed up.[29]

The change Geertz sees happening is a subtle one.

> This is not to say that everyone was highly religious or that everyone behaved in some fixed and stereotyped manner. It is merely to say that the conceptions, values, and sentiments which guided everyday behavior were, in a powerful and significant way, influenced by what were taken to be, by those who had them, revelations of the basic order of existence. Spiritual responsiveness varied then as it varies now, probably just as widely. There was a gap between social ideals and social practice as there is now, probably just as broad. What is different now is that even the spiritually responsive find revelations hard to come by, while the lives of even the unresponsive continue in large part to be based upon the assumption that they are not.[30]

Islam Observed closes on an enigmatic note with two pictures: one of a highly educated Moroccan on his first airplane trip away from home, bound for an American university "with the Koran gripped in one hand and a glass of scotch in the other." The second picture is that of a brilliant mathematics and physics student from the University of Indonesia explaining for hours a cabalistic scheme in which the truth of physics, mathematics, politics, art, and religion are indissolubly fused. He tells Professor Geertz that he spends all his free time working on the scheme because one cannot find one's way through modern life without a compass.

Geertz comments, "Indeed, one cannot; but of what materials is such a compass to be constructed?"

Both students are caught somehow or other in the tension between science and religion. "Even if they are not direct antithesis, there is a natural tension between the scientific and religious way of trying to render the world comprehensible. . . ."[31]

Geertz's point is clear but subtle. The very fact of the ability of scientific explanations for much of reality throws into question religious explanations which used to be required to make understandable that dimension of reality. In other words, when science reduces the area of bafflement, religion is no longer required for that area, or, at least, not nearly so much required. On the other hand, vast areas of bafflement remain, and some, of their very nature, will contiue to remain. But can the traditional religious symbols cope with a reduced area of competence? For most Moroccans and Javanese they have not been required to do so, for the tension between science and religion has been suppressed, or at least ignored. But the very fact that there exist in both societies men for whom the tension cannot be suppressed in itself has indirect impact on the old religious tradition. It survives and it suffices, but something of the spark has gone out of it.

I trust Professor Geertz will not mind my observing that, in some fashion, he seems almost as baffled as his two student friends, for he vigorously insists on the need for interpretability and for a system of ultimate interpretation, but no more than they is he able to suggest what alternatives are available when the old traditions seem to be weakened, at least for a handful of society.

I would suggest that the American agnostic, the Moroccan formalist, and the Javanese intellectualist all have come upon the three closely related religious issues which are the core of contemporary religious consciousness.

1. Religious symbols now must be interpreted. The very fact that science has reduced the area of bafflement and now explains satisfactorily the problems with which religion used to deal, requires that the symbols be translated in abstract and rational concepts, if only so that the border between religion and science can be more clearly defined and the unease which permeates the border region can be lessened. In other words, one must have some notion of where religion is on its own ground and not risk embarrassment by trying to demonstrate scientific competence. Or, as Nisbet points out—defending Durkheim's notion of the eternality of religion—there are at least three aspects of the human condition which require religious responses: the uncertainties of life, the alienation of the human mind, and the sense

of dependence that is found in all human beings (albeit in varying degree) as an inevitable consequence of being a social animal.[32] Try as we may, we will never be able to reduce all aspects of life, every moment in time, to the rational, calculated processes of preventive action.

> True, the nature of the uncertainties changes often in history. We no longer have to fear the predatory tiger or lion in the dark, but only a fool would say that these have not been replaced by other, equally death-dealing, entities and situations. We may build our automobiles to meet even the specifications of a Ralph Nader and our highways to the specifications of every safety engineer. Obviously, however, there are still possibilities of death or disability, no matter how carefully one chooses to drive himself. The possibilities of death or disaster for persons and societies can be reduced but never obviated totally. Hence the apprehension in most minds of the uncertainties of life, of the possibilities of bad luck, of malign circumstances.[33]

Religion, Nisbet concludes, as a sphere of control, "will narrow with man's expansion of knowledge of cosmos, society, and self."

> But the eternality of religion is rooted in the eternality of the sacred in human consciousness. . . . Note the ease with which those who abandon traditionally sacred norms or beliefs convert other norms—political, economic, scientific—from merely empirical or utilitarian significance to significance not the less sacred because no deities or supernatural spirits are involved.
> . . . the appeal of religion would not appear to have greatly lessened in twentieth-century industrial societies.[34]

But if religion is still required and if the symbols no longer mean precisely what they were thought to mean—which is to say, no longer apply to everything to which they once applied—then, clearly, an interpretation and reinterpretation of the symbols is of momentous importance. As Geertz himself said, out of what is the compass to be made?

2. One must choose. The grandparents of the Indonesian and the Moroccan students inherited but one religious system from their parents and did not have to face the question of competing alternatives. But Geertz's two Islamic intellectual friends must ask themselves whether scientism (by which I mean science as a religion—that is, an ultimate explanation of reality), Marxism, Christianity, American materialism (at least insofar as in distorted form it is perceived as an ultimate symbol system), secular nationalism, or even psychoanalysis can substitute for Islam as a comprehensive system. Even if they choose to remain Islamic, then they must choose for themselves which interpretation of the Islamic myths and symbols they are to accept, and to what extent they are going to attempt to integrate the dimensions, elements, and components of other meaning systems into their own versions of Islam.

In his book *The Invisible Religion,* Thomas Luckmann sees modern man as a "consumer of interpretive schemes." A man puts together an interpretive scheme of his own in which the official religion he chooses to subscribe to is combined with such major themes as "autonomy, self-expression, self-realization, mobility, ethos, sexuality, and familism." [35] Not only does man go shopping in the supermarketplace of meaning systems, but he also apparently selects the components for a high-fidelity stereo system.

Given the expansion of the number and kind of human relationships, new sets of values are required to enable one to cope with such relationships, surely—as Luckmann insists—in the private sphere of life and probably—despite Luckmann—in the public sphere, too. The old religions are caught in a peculiar sort of double tension. Science has restricted the areas of cosmological bafflement with which they were supposed to cope. The complexification of the social structure has widened the areas of social and interpersonal bafflement for which religion is expected to provide norms. Hence, new normative systems not directly religious in origin are co-opted into one personal religious system and take on a sacral or quasi-sacral character. The Javanese and Moroccan students must determine both how

Islamic myths can be contracted so they will not be in conflict with science and how they can be expanded so as to underpin commitment to, and norms for, a much broader social reality.

3. And they must do it to some considerable extent by themselves. Even if the scholarly leaders of a religious tradition have become sophisticated enough to reinterpret the myths by narrowing their cosmological and broadening their ethical purview, they no longer enjoy a unique position in the religious universe, nor do they have monopoly control over the marketplace in which contemporary man must shop. Furthermore, religious leaders have been slow to understand the nature of the interpretive problem they face and even slower to do anything about it. It also may be arguable that some religious traditions are more flexible in their capacity to reinterpret than others. Christianity, for example, was extraordinarily skillful at this task until well into the sixteenth century.

It is not merely the complexification of society, man's increased skills at abstract thought, and the enhancement of the physical energy and power available to the race that have made religious decision more of a choice than it was in the past. Professor Talcott Parsons argues that the world religions liberated man's religious decisions from the forces of nature and of the tribe; Christianity freed his religious conviction (in theory) from the dominance of the civil society; and Protestantism liberated him from the control of the church—at least, as far as his religious decisions are concerned. One may wish to argue with some of the details of Professor Parsons' broad strokes, but the outline of the picture he portrays seems accurate enough. Contemporary man is, of course, by no means free from the pressures of society, social class, ethnic groups, and religious background when it comes to making his own religious decision, but he is relatively more free than any of his predecessors have been. The moral *ideal* of freedom of conscience antedated the development of modern science and technology, though on balance science and technology have reinforced the possibility of free religious choice.

Again, let us be clear about the point we are making. Not every man makes his religious decision relatively alone. Most of us end up inheriting the interpretive scheme of our predecessors with only relatively slight personal modifications. Even those who do make a rather decisive and purposive choice do so within a context established by their cultural inheritance. Certainly, the alternatives from which they choose are, generally speaking, *given* by the culture. All we are asserting is that, relatively speaking, the individual in contemporary society not only enjoys more religious options but is much freer of communal constraint in exercising his options than were his ancestors.

On the other hand, if he is free of communal constraint he is also free of communal support. Freedom is a two-edged sword; while it enhances the personal control of the individual, it also increases his responsibility. If there has been an increase in the range of relatively free decisions in human life, it has to be considered a blessing. But it is not an unmixed blessing, or at least not a painless one. When options are made available to us, we must choose; when the constraints of the community which would direct us toward a choice are lessened, then we must choose by ourselves. Developing one's own interpretive scheme involved only minimal difficulty when one inherited an interpretive scheme from one's community and there were no options to choose from. One did not have to "search for meaning" because meaning was a given. Now, while the search for meaning can be exciting and challenging, it is not easy. The conventional wisdom is quite wrong when it says that ultimate meaning is no longer required by secular man. If it had argued, somewhat more modestly, that secular man—or at least man living in the contemporary world—has to go through the agony of elaborating his own meaning system it would have been much closer to the truth.

In contemporary religion, then, religious symbol systems must be interpreted. The religious agent is free to choose among a wide variety of possible meaning systems, and he exercises this terrible freedom to some considerable extent by himself. Geertz's two students are characteristic of the extremes of this religious problem. For most men, even in the highly "secularized" United States, the need for interpretation and for lonely decision-making is not so intense, though, as Geertz wisely notes, the very fact that some people in society clearly must make such choices raises the level of religious anxiety among many others in society.

But the necessity of interpretation and choice does not make men any less religious. If we define religion as a meaning system which need not be subjected to either interpretation or choice, then there can be no doubt that religion is less important to modern man than it was in the past. If, on the other hand, we argue that a meaning system which must be the object of relatively conscious and explicit choice is more important than one that is simply inherited, we would conclude that modern man is *more* religious than his predecessors precisely because now he must interpret and choose and his predecessors did not have to do either. I very much doubt that even the primitive is free from religious anxiety, but if the importance of a phenomenon is to be measured by the amount of tension, controversy, and anxiety it generates, then a good case could be made that religion is more important in the modern world than it has ever been before. Or, to put the matter somewhat differently, ultimate meaning is more on peoples' minds now than it was in the past.

However, the position assumed in the preceding paragraph is not essential for the basic theme of the book. It is sufficient to say that there is no *less* concern about ultimate interpretation today than in previous eras of history. I do not think that this point is debatable.

Nor can we accept the argument of the conventional wisdom that there is less "bafflement" than there was in past years. Some of the areas of "natural" bafflement have been reduced by the sciences. We understand thunder, lightning, storms, the movement of heavenly bodies, but a case could be made that even in physical science a good deal of bafflement remains. Few of us are qualified to understand either astrophysics or nuclear physics—much less the mathematical abstractions of theoretical physics.

These three disciplines reduce our bafflement only to the extent that we know there are some people in society who are not baffled by them. And as Monsieur Piccard remarked after his submarine journey in the Gulf Stream, "The more we learn about the mysteries of nature, the more unfathomable these mysteries seem to be; because the more we understand, the clearer it is to us how much we have yet to understand and how much we probably never will be able to understand."

But it is in the area beyond the physical sciences that the bafflement has become more intense. It is not merely that human relationships have become more complex and more puzzling, nor even that our psychologically sophisticated quest for self-fulfillment raises more difficult questions about self and fulfillment; it is, rather, that the more we understand about the depth and the height and the width of the human experience, the more puzzling and "baffling" both man and his experience seem to be. Indeed, one might even make a case that modern man is far more baffled than archaic man was, for archaic man could not scientifically explain the movement of the heavens or the origin of the weather, and modern man can. But for archaic man, the dimensions of human existence were relatively limited, the complexities of his life relatively few, and the mysteries of his relationships relatively uncomplex. He may have been baffled by the signs in the heavens, but he was less baffled by himself and his fellow man. We may understand more than he did about the heavens, but the mystery of man is far more convoluted for us than it was for him.

Both Peter Berger and Langdon Gilkey have addressed themselves to the question of the mystery of man. Peter Berger calls certain aspects of this mystery "rumors of angels" or "signs of the transcendent"; that is to say, hints toward an explanation of the mystery of man. The first such "rumor" is the "signal" of order.

A child wakes up in the night, perhaps from a bad dream, and finds himself surrounded by darkness, alone, beset by name-

less threats. At such a moment the contours of trusted reality
are blurred or invisible, and in the terror of incipient chaos the
child cries out for his mother. It is hardly an exaggeration to
say that, at this moment, the mother is being invoked as a high
priestess of protective order. It is she (and, in many cases, she
alone) who has the power to banish the chaos and to restore the
benign shape of the world. And, of course, any good mother
will do just that. She will take the child and cradle him in the
timeless gesture of the Magna Mater who became our Madonna.
She will turn on a lamp, perhaps, which will encircle the scene
with a warm glow of reassuring light. She will speak or sing
to the child, and the content of this communication will invari-
ably be the same—"Don't be afraid—everything is in order,
everything is all right." If all goes well, the child will be re-
assured, his trust in reality recovered, and in this trust he will
return to sleep.[36]

As Berger comments, if the natural is the only reality, then
the mother is lying to the child—lying out of love, but, in the
final analysis, lying all the same. The second signal comes from
play.

Some little girls are playing hopscotch in the park. They are
completely intent on their game, closed to the world outside it,
happy in their concentration. Time has stood still for them
—or, more accurately, it has been collapsed into the movements
of the game. The outside world has, for the duration of the
game, ceased to exist. And, by implication (since the little girls
may not be very conscious of this), pain and death, which are
the law of the world, have also ceased to exist. Even the adult
observer of this scene, who is perhaps all too conscious of pain
and death, is momentarily drawn into the beatific immunity.[37]

Is play merely Dionysian escapism by which we hide from
our fate until the lights go out, or is it a signal of something
else? It is not the purpose of the present volume to provide an
answer to the question but merely to note that the question represents a critical area of human "bafflement." Another signal is
man's blind, persistent hope.

In a world where man is surrounded by death on all sides, he continues to be a being who says "no!" to death—and through this "no!" is brought to faith in another world, the reality of which would validate his hope as something other than illusion. It is tempting to think here of a kind of Cartesian reduction, in which one finally arrives at a root fact of consciousness that says "no!" to death and "yes!" to hope. In any case, the argument from hope follows the logical direction of induction from what is empirically given. It starts from experience but takes seriously those implications or intentions within experience that transcend it—and takes them, once again, as signals of a transcendent reality.[38]

As Berger notes, religion vindicates the gestures in which hope and courage are embodied in human action. In other words, it provides some light for that very "baffling" behavior which we call hope.

One hears "a rumor of angels" in the phenomenon of moral outrage.

A somewhat different sort of reasoning is involved in what I will call the *argument from damnation*. This refers to experiences in which our sense of what is humanly permissible is so fundamentally outraged that the only adequate response to the offense as well as to the offender seems to be a curse of supernatural dimensions. I advisedly choose this negative form of reasoning, as against what may at first appear to be a more obvious argument from a positive sense of justice. The latter argument would, of course, lead into the territory of "natural law" theories, where I am reluctant to go at this point. As is well known, these theories have been particularly challenged by the relativizing insights of both the historian and the social scientist, and while I suspect that these challenges can be met, this is not the place to negotiate the question. The negative form of the argument makes the intrinsic intention of the human sense of justice stand out much more sharply as a signal of transcendence over and beyond socio-historical relativities.[39]

We will return to moral outrage later on in the book. Suffice it at the present time to say that one can scarcely justify outrage

from the conventional wisdom's perspective of positivist determinism. If there is something to be outraged about, it follows
that man must be free. And if man is free, then indeed we are
very baffled because we must ask the question: why are we free?
A final signal of the transcendent is the comic.

> *The comic reflects the imprisonment of the human spirit in the
> world.* This is why, as has been pointed out over and over since
> classical antiquity, comedy and tragedy are at root closely re-
> lated. Both are commentaries on man's finitude—if one wants
> to put it in existentialist terms, on his condition of "thrown-ness."
> If this is so, then the comic is an objective dimension of man's
> reality, not just a subjective or psychological reaction to that
> reality.[40]

Berger observes that Don Quixote is a prototypical comic
figure of the Western world, a comic figure who points to both
the pathos and the mystery of the human condition. Berger
quotes with approval the words of Enid Welsford:

> To those who do not repudiate the religious insight of the race,
> the human spirit is uneasy in this world because it is at home
> elsewhere, and escape from the prison house is possible not only
> in fancy but in fact. The theist believes in possible beatitude,
> because he disbelieves in the dignified isolation of humanity.
> To him, therefore, romantic comedy is serious literature because
> it is a foretaste of the truth: the Fool is wiser than the Hu-
> manist; and the clownage is less frivolous than the deification
> of humanity.[41]

It is not my purpose in this chapter, or indeed in this volume,
to argue that there is a transcendent which is signaled by Berger's signs—or that there are angels whose rumor we are hearing.
I merely wish to note that Berger's "rumor-mongering" does, indeed, indicate that even though the scientific bafflement may have
declined, bafflement over the human condition continues as
strong as ever—and stronger, because now it is more explicit.
Perhaps the most astute and penetrating analysis of the sur-

vival of ultimacy in contemporary society is that of the theologian Langdon Gilkey, in his *Naming the Whirlwind*. Gilkey attempts to analyze what he calls the "secular experience" to show that at its very core there is a "context of ultimacy" which is at least a negative hierophany from the beginnings of a positive one. In direct response to the Bonhoeffer dictum that man has come of age, Gilkey says that

> secular experience contradicts secular self-understanding in the precise sense that the anxieties, the joys, and the tone of ordinary life reflect the context or framework of ultimacy. Such a context is specifically denied by a secular understanding proud that man has come of age in a cosmos essentially irrelevant to his being, his meanings, and his passage. But as did ancient man, modern man continues to live in this context of ultimacy. Thus he finds his life blessed at the most basic level by aspects of the given which establish his reality, found his values, make possible his meanings, and give him courage to face both the future and death. What is sacred in and to his existence comes actually not from his autonomy but from beyond himself as the source and ground of his autonomy. Conversely, what worries him most is not, we have suggested, so much the "problems" which his intelligence and technology can solve, but the continuing "mysteries" which reflect the transcendent content of his life: fate, meaninglessness, the unpredictable future, and death. Thus the fundamental traits of man's religious existence are as characteristic of modern secular life as they were of any life in the past; again it is the sacred that establishes and makes possible and of value the profane, and it is the sacred dimension that continually threatens all that man has built. To leave these supremely significant areas of our existence unsymbolized, unpondered, and so uncomprehended, is to leave secular life impoverished with regard to its real values, and vulnerable with regard to its real fears. Religious discourse is essential if secular life is to achieve a creative worldliness.[42]

Secular man, to the extent that he exists, is sure that he has come of age and has no religious problems, and yet, the gnawing fact of death refuses to let him escape from his own contingency; it insistently raises ultimate issues.

Modern secular culture, sure on the surface that it has come
of age and has no remaining religious problems, spends a good
deal of its resources to hide the reality of death from its awareness—all totally unsuccessful. The Void without the divine eternity is ever with us, and an awareness of this Void is one of
the characteristic features of the world's life.[43]

It is this very sense of our own mortality, our own finitude
which makes us desperately search for something that will protect us from the Void and give some permanency to our efforts,

in the Void of mortality which nothing finite can overcome. And
in the awareness of this Void, and the anxiety that is consequent
upon it, the loss of eternity appears in secular experience. For
with that loss we seek desperately to make our own mortal works
and powers eternal, and that search penetrates into and influences
almost every one of our ordinary secular attitudes and activities.
The search here is for what will last, a temporal embodiment, so
to speak, for some eternity transcendent to mere passage that
has been lost, and an assurance about a directed structure of
time in which both we and what we value will not vanish away
into nothingness.[44]

But not only do we experience the Ultimate directly through
our perception of an unconditioned Void which resolutely pur-
sues our life, it is also experienced indirectly in our responses
to the Void.

A "hierophany" and so an experience of an unconditioned dimension of existence is not at all absent from ordinary life, as the
philosophies of secularism maintain. This dimension or framework of ultimacy appears *directly* in the awareness of an unconditioned Void, and a dim but powerful awareness of this negative context of ultimacy is the source of our common traits
of fanaticism, frantic striving, meaninglessness and boredom, and
terror at death and the future—an awareness that is thematized
in our puzzled and often painful personal questions about life's
meaning, and more formally in the literature that explores this
range of ultimate questions. It is experienced *indirectly* in the
joyful wonder, the creative meanings, and the resolute courage

of life despite its obvious contingency, relativity and temporal character; and this awareness of the power and meaning of life is thematized in o.te way or another in every positive philosophy of man, secular or otherwise, and in all of his religions. The human experience of being in the world and in time appears, therefore, to involve at its deepest levels more than what we usually call the world or temporality. It seems open to another, an infinite dimension; perhaps in terms of the dim awareness of anxiety and an unconditioned Void that is encountered in feeling, perhaps in terms of formulated questions about an ultimate security, meaning, and permanence in existence; perhaps in terms of a positive apprehension of the power and meaning of our existence which enables us to live with serenity and courage. This dimension at this level of our analysis is still undefined and unclear, though its character, as we have seen, is to us of the utmost significance, in fact of ultimate concern. For it appears as a Void that raises but may not answer all our ultimate questions about life, and produces in dim awareness the anxiety our ordinary life reveals; or it may appear as that ultimate mystery whose presence produces our existence and shapes its meaning, the "Holy Nothingness" which is the beginning from which we come, the inscrutable fate that rules over our meanings, and the dark end to which we go.[45]

Gilkey advances a number of other manifestations of the Ultimate. Like Berger, he sees the shadow of the Ultimate in man's sense of morality.

The presence of the sacred and ultimate as condemnation—God's absence as creative love and his presence as wrath, to use Luther's language, is deeply felt in secular experience, especially at the moment. It is one of the most universal of human experiences: we all know inside culpability and fault, and outside injustice, oppression, and conflict. And we know their results: guilt, isolation, alienation, and broken community, each immensely destructive privately and publicly. Consequently, a new kind of search for the ultimate on which we depend appears: not this time for an ultimate security or meaning in existence, nor even for a standard by which to live. Rather, it is outwardly a search for an authentic world or social order, a kingdom manifest in history and so for a historical ground for hope. Inwardly, it is a search for the ability to accept ourselves, to feel solid and real and creative again, for the power to become what we wish to be, and above all, for the capacity of reconciliation, to reestablish community, to love, and to hope for a better world.[46]

It is also present in feelings of guilt and the quest for cleansing from guilt.

> For modern life is as much qualified and shaped by the search for personal reintegration and innocence, and for the healing of our broken communities, as has been that of any other age. What else explains the almost universal response to the healing arts of psychoanalysis; our frantic moral claims of innocence in almost all aspects of our communal existence; and our continual flight into racial and political communities which, on the one hand, absorb and subvert our hostilities and at the same time give to them a cleansing moral justification? The need for *religious* justification and reconciliation is surely not explicitly felt among us; but much of our lives and our wealth is spent in the search for psychological, moral, and social forms of the same necessary blessings.[47]

Gilkey, as we have noted, is a theologian, and his analysis of the ultimacy lurking in the secular experience is a "prolegomenon" to the developing of a positive theological response to the question of ultimacy. We are not concerned in this volume with the merit of such a response but only with Gilkey's analysis of the secular condition. When man experiences guilt, reconciliation, moral judgment, the inevitability of death, and the joyous, constructive response of his personality to the challenge of the Void, he is moving in an area which Geertz would describe as one of "bafflement." The conventional wisdom would persuade us that either man is not baffled by these experiences or that now he has come of age and understands the scientific and psychological conditions of bafflement and consequently may dismiss it as irrelevant. We are not denying that some men do, but we are questioning whether this is a new event in human history and whether it represents evolutionary progress.

This volume is essentially a study in the sociology of religion. It is rooted in the general insights of Max Weber and Émile Durkheim, the former contending that man is a meaning-seeking animal and the latter, a community-building animal. In this chapter we have taken the Weberian position, particularly as it is mediated through the thinking of Clifford Geertz. Our adversaries are those proponents of the conventional wisdom who argue that man does not need ultimate meaning, that he can survive in the midst of existential bafflement, or, alternately, that existential bafflement has been eliminated by scientific progress. I have relied on Peter Berger and Langdon Gilkey, not as men who established the fact of the transcendent, but simply as men who point out the persistence of bafflement even in a supposedly scientific and rational world. The core of my argument is Geertz's point that without meaning we are incomplete and unfinished animals, and that man without culture and without meaning is not man. Indeed, the essence of his argument is, "becoming human is becoming individual, and we become individual under the guidance of cultural patterns, historically created systems of meaning in terms of which we give form, order, point and direction to our lives." [48] Life has no direction at all unless it has some ultimate direction. Approximate direction in the midst of an ultimate existential drift produces an overriding sense of "bafflement," which some men may be able to tolerate but which most men reject. Man will no longer need a "faith" only when he has evolved beyond the experience of bafflement.*

---

* It should be carefully noted that at this point I am only arguing for the need of an ultimate interpretive scheme. I am not arguing that such a scheme must involve a "transcendental reference," much less that it need be based on a traditional religious scheme or institutionalized in a traditional church.

4. Myth and Man

IN THE PREVIOUS CHAPTER we argued that religion is an interpretive scheme which provides man with a map that enables him to chart his course in the areas of bafflement he encounters in the course of his life. Such a culture system or interpretive scheme is conveyed in a collection of "symbols." On a priori grounds there is no reason why the symbols cannot take on any form which man chooses to give them. I suppose it is possible to state one's interpretive scheme in mathematical or symbolic-logical form. The great theological works of the Western world, such as St. Thomas Aquinas' *Summa Theologica* or Calvin's *Institutes of the Christian Religion,* are certainly very abstract series of propositions. However, the most common kind of symbol used to convey religious meaning is the myth. In this chapter I propose to address myself to the question of whether myth is necessary for religion.

Even though most men who have been on the earth have relied on myths to express their religious viewpoints, one could argue that man's increased skill with abstract thought has eliminated the need for mythology in his religious interpretations. Indeed, a very considerable number of theologians have devoted their efforts for the last several decades to demythologizing religion; they have tried to take the "intellectual" or "rational" contents out of the symbols in which they have been encapsulated. Such an enterprise has been justified by the argument that modern man, living in a scientific and technological world, is no longer able to accept mythology.

It is difficult for those of us educated in what is reported to be a science-permeated educational system to cope with the concept of myths. We recollect from our grammar school and high school history courses that myths were rather bizarre tales told by the Greeks or Egyptians about their strange gods and goddesses before man became scientific. The tales seemed immensely complicated and generally very unedifying. What is more important, they were obviously untrue and hence did not have to be taken very seriously, for only those things that were true—those things which were literal and scientific—had to be believed. Therefore, when someone suggests that the myths were very serious and contained important truths we find ourselves pushed almost unwillingly into an unreal world. We want to ask whether our ancient ancestors did or did not "really believe" these myths. Did they think they were "true" or "not true"? To be told that archaic man did believe they were true but did not think they were true in the way we think scientific propositions are true simply befuddles us. When someone argues, as I propose to do in this chapter, that there is strong reason to question whether man's mythopoetic proclivities have at all vanished from the earth, we are profoundly shocked. We are convinced that we have left myth far behind.

A myth is simply a symbolic story, one that is frequently told by being enacted in a ritual. Professor Alan Watts describes a myth as "a complex of stories—some no doubt fact, and some fantasy—which for various reasons human beings regard as demonstrations of the inner meaning of the universe and of human life." [1] According to Watts, "The meaning is divined rather than defined, implicit rather than explicit, suggested rather than stated." [2] He adds, "the language of myth and poetry is integrative, for the language of image is organic language." [3]

In a companion volume, Professor Charles Long argues: "myth . . . points to the definite manner in which the world is available for man. The word and content of myth are revelations

of power." [4] Myth integrates man's total life experience and interprets it for him; myths go both higher and lower than scientific
propositions.

> A great deal of our modern cultural life presupposes the equa-
> tion of literalness = truth. To some degree this is dictated by
> the scientific–technological character of our culture, but we
> would find it difficult to believe that anyone in our culture lives
> entirely in a world of literal meanings. There are human experi-
> ences on the personal and cultural levels which can only be
> expressed in symbolic forms. These meanings are in many cases
> the most profound meanings in our personal and cultural lives.
> They are profound because they symbolize the specificity of our
> human situation—they make clear to us how the world exists
> for us and point up the resources and tensions which are present
> in our situation.[5]

Although one is not willing to have a dichotomy between the
mythic and the scientific,

> The presence of the type of thought which we call scientific is
> too pervasive in our contemporary life to justify such an alterna-
> tive. We do not, however, interpret this to mean that the mythic
> as a structure of human awareness is no longer operative in our
> age. Rather, it presents to us the problem of dealing with the
> fundamental relatedness of the mythic and the scientific. One
> mode cannot replace the other; the generalizing method of sci-
> entific thought cannot do justice to the life of man as he ex-
> periences it, and the mythic mode of apprehension cannot remain
> so specific and concrete that it becomes esoteric or subjective.[6]

Mircea Eliade, the greatest of the students of what used to be
called comparative religion and is now called history of religion,
observes,

> What we may call *symbolic thought* makes it possible for man
> to move freely from one level of reality to another. Indeed, "to
> move freely" is an understatement: symbols . . . identify, assimi-
> late, and unify diverse levels and realities that are to all appear-
> ances incompatible.[7]

Eliade sees the myth as integrating man not only with the rest of the universe but also with himself and argues that such integration makes possible a "wholeness" in human life that is impossible for man who attempts to suppress his mythopoetic inclinations.

> Man no longer feels himself to be an "air-tight" fragment, but a living cosmos open to all the other living cosmoses by which he is surrounded. The experiences of the world at large are no longer something outside him and therefore ultimately "foreign" and "objective"; they do not alienate him from himself but, on the contrary, lead him towards himself, and reveal to him his own existence and his own destiny. The cosmic myths and the whole world of ritual thus appear as existential experiences to primitive man: he does not lose himself, he does not forget his own existence when he fulfills a myth or takes part in a ritual; quite the reverse; he finds himself and comes to understand himself, because those myths and rituals express cosmic realities which ultimately he is aware of as realities in his own being. To primitive man, every level of reality is so completely open to him that the emotion he felt at merely *seeing* anything as magnificent as the starry sky would have been as strong as the most "intimist" personal experience felt by a modern. For, thanks chiefly to his symbols, the *real existence* of primitive man was not the broken and alienated existence lived by civilized man today.[8]

Eliade argues that the myth is a paradigm, a primordial event which took place in "real" time. What has happened since the myth is simply a reflection of that myth. The gods *ordered* the universe. Man's reenactment of the myth is his participation in and reflection of that act of ordering.

> The myth relates a sacred history, that is, a primordial event that took place at the beginning of time, *ab initio*. But to relate a sacred history is equivalent to revealing a mystery. For the persons of the myth are not human beings; they are gods or culture heroes, and for this reason their *gesta* constitute mysteries; man could not know their acts if they were not revealed to him.

The myth, then, is the history of what took place *in illo tempore*, the recital of what the gods or the semidivine beings did at the beginning of time. To tell a myth is to proclaim what happened *ab origine*. Once told, that is, revealed, the myth becomes apodictic truth; it establishes a truth that is absolute. "It is so because it is said that it is so," the Netsilik Eskimos declare to justify the validity of their sacred history and religious traditions. The myth proclaims the appearance of a new cosmic tradition or of a primordial event. Hence it is always the recital of a creation; it tells how something was accomplished, began to *be*. It is for this reason that myth is bound up with ontology; it speaks only of *realities*, of what *really* happened, of what was fully manifested.[9]

The myth, then, brings mankind into contact with the *real*. It enables him to transcend the phenomenal world of confusion and threatening chaos in which he lives and break through to the ordering by which chaos was first defeated and continues to be restrained.

This faithful repetition of divine models has a twofold result: (1) by imitating the gods, man remains in the sacred, hence in reality; (2) by the continuous reactualization of paradigmatic divine gestures, the world is sanctified. Man's religious behavior contributes to maintaining the sanctity of the world.[10]

Henri Frankfort in *Before Philosophy* insists that,

The imagery of myth is therefore by no means allegory. It is nothing less than a carefully chosen cloak for abstract thought. The imagery is inseparable from the thought. It represents the form in which the experience has become conscious.

He goes on to say:

Myth is a form of poetry which transcends poetry in that it proclaims a truth; a form of reasoning which transcends reasoning in that it wants to bring about the truth it proclaims; a form of action, of ritual behavior, which does not find its fulfillment in the act but must proclaim and elaborate a poetic form of truth.[11]

In other words, myth is truth told not abstractly, but concretely. The myth-maker may be a poet but he is not a superstitious fool; he has chosen to grapple with reality with a story rather than a schematic proposition. Frankfort explains the difference between how the Babylonians would react to a rainstorm and the way we would react.

> We would explain, for instance, that certain atmospheric changes broke a drought and brought about rain. The Babylonians observed the same facts but experienced them as the intervention of the gigantic bird Imdugud which came to their rescue. It covered the sky with the black storm clouds of its wings and devoured the Bull of Heaven, whose hot breath had scorched the crops.
>
> In telling such a myth, the ancients did not intend to provide entertainment. Neither did they seek, in a detached way and without ulterior motives, for intelligible explanations of the the natural phenomena. They were recounting events in which they were involved to the extent of their very existence. They experienced, directly, a conflict of powers, one hostile to the harvest upon which they depended, the other frightening but beneficial: the thunderstorm reprieved them in the nick of time by defeating and utterly destroying the drought. The images had already become traditional at the time when we meet them in art and literature, but originally they must have been seen in the revelation which the experience entailed. They are products of imagination, but they are not mere fantasy. It is essential that true myth be distinguished from legend, saga, fable, and fairy tale. All these may retain elements of the myth. And it may also happen that a baroque or frivolous imagination elaborates myths until they become mere stories. But true myth presents its images and its imaginary actors, not with the playfulness of fantasy, but with a compelling authority. It perpetuates the revelation of a 'Thou.' [12]

Frankfort, like most contemporary scholars, rejects the notion that primitive man was somehow prelogical. The ancients were as aware as we are of the linkage between cause and effect, but:

> Our view of causality, then, would not satisfy primitive man, because of the impersonal character of its explanations. It would not satisfy him, moreover, because of its generality. We understand phenomena, not by what makes them peculiar, but by what makes them manifestations of general law. But a general law cannot do justice to the individual character of each event. And the individual character of the event is precisely what early man experiences most strongly.[13]

Ancient man's way of telling the truth was to become emotionally and poetically involved in it. Frankfort calls the myths "emotional thought" and points out that there is some loss when man loses his capacity for this sort of thought.

> The basic distinction of modern thought is that between *subjective* and *objective*. On this distinction scientific thought has based a critical and analytical procedure by which it progressively reduces the individual phenomena to typical events subject to universal laws. Thus it creates an increasingly wide gulf between our perception of the phenomena and the conceptions by which we make them comprehensible. We see the sun rise and set, but we think of the earth as moving round the sun. We see colours, but we describe them as wave-lengths. We dream of a dead relative, but we think of that distinct vision as a product of our own subconscious minds. Even if we individually are unable to prove these almost unbelievable scientific views to be true, we accept them, because we know that they can be proved to possess a greater degree of objectivity than our sense-impressions. In the immediacy of primitive experience, however, there is no room for such a critical resolution of perceptions. Primitive man cannot withdraw from the presence of the phenomena, because they reveal themselves to him in the manner we have described. Hence the distinction between subjective and objective knowledge is meaningless to him.[14]

Man the myth-maker is trying to come to terms with the problem that man the scientist has tried—perhaps unsuccessfully—to déclare insoluble, for ancient man was puzzled by the greatest mystery of all: the problem of human existence. In Paul Ricoeur's words:

> Still more fundamentally, the myth tries to get at the enigma of human existence, namely, the discordance between the fundamental reality—state of innocence, status of a creature, essential being—and the actual modality of man, as defiled, sinful, guilty. The myth accounts for this transition by means of a narration. But it is a narration precisely because there is no deduction, no logical transition, between the fundamental reality of man and his present existence, between his ontological status as a being created good and destined for happiness and his existential or historical status, experienced under the sign of alienation. Thus the myth has an ontological bearing: it points to the relation—that is to say, both the leap and the passage, the cut and the suture—between the essential being of man and his historical existence.[15]

Claude Lévi-Strauss speaks of savage thought as a system of concepts imbedded in image, but he contends that the savage mind is logical in the same sense and the same fashion as modern man's, and that messages by which primitive man tried to describe reality in some ways anticipate the findings of modern science.

> In treating the sensible properties of the animal and plant kingdoms as if they were the elements of a message, and in discovering "signatures"—and so signs—in them, men have made mistakes of identification: the meaningful element was not always the one they supposed. But, without perfected instruments which would have permitted them to place it where it most often is—namely, at the microscopic level—they already discerned "as through a glass darkly" principles of interpretation whose heuristic value and accordance with reality have been revealed to us only through very recent inventions: telecommunications, computers and electron microscopes.
>
> Above all, during the period of their transmission, when they have an objective existence outside the consciousness of transmitters and receivers, messages display properties which

they have in common with the physical world. Hence, despite their mistakes with regard to physical phenomena (which were not absolute but relative to the level where they grasped them) and even though they interpreted them as if they were messages, men were nevertheless able to arrive at some of their properties. For a theory of information to be able to be evolved it was undoubtedly essential to have discovered that the universe of information is part of an aspect of the natural world. But the validity of the passage from the laws of nature to those of information once demonstrated, implies the validity of the reverse passage—that which for millenia [*sic*] has allowed men to approach the laws of nature by way of information.[16]

Archaic science and modern science operate in different fashions:

The physical world is approached from opposite ends in the two cases: one is supremely concrete, the other supremely abstract; one proceeds from the angle of sensible qualities and the other from that of formal properties. But the idea that, theoretically at least and on condition no abrupt changes in perspective occurred, these two courses were destined to meet, explains why both, independently of each other in time and space, should have led to two distinct though equally positive sciences: one which flowered in the neolithic period, whose theory of the sensible order provided the basis of the arts of civilization (agriculture, animal husbandry, pottery, weaving, conservation and preparation of food, etc.) and which continues to provide for our basic needs by these means; and another which places itself from the start at the level of intelligibility, and of which contemporary science is the fruit.[17]

Lévi-Strauss sees more than just basic compatibility between mythological thought and scientific thought. He sees in our own time a convergence and a combination of the two as the contemporary sciences seek more and more to understand the qualitative. As he says in the concluding paragraph of *The Savage Mind:*

We have had to wait until the middle of this century for the crossing of long separated paths: that which arrives at the physical world by the detour of communication, and that which as we have recently come to know, arrives at the world of communication by the detour of the physical. The entire process of human knowledge thus assumes the character of a closed system. And we therefore remain faithful to the inspiration of the savage mind when we recognize that, by an encounter it alone could have foreseen, the scientific spirit in its most modern form will have contributed to legitimize the principles of savage thought and to re-establish it in its rightful place.[18]

Perhaps Lévi-Strauss is being a bit premature. There are very considerable numbers of physical and social scientists who are not yet willing to admit the place of the mythopoetic in any comprehensive system of human knowledge. One assumes that Lévi-Strauss is not so much describing a present situation as making a prediction of what seems to be an inevitable development in the not-too-distant future.

The myth, then, is a comprehensive view of reality; it explains it, interprets it, provides the ritual by which man may maintain his contact with it, and even conveys certain very concrete notions about how reality is to be used to facilitate mankind's life and comfort. To fall back on Clifford Geertz's model, myth attempts to integrate all of the different cultural systems: religion, ideology, science, art, and common sense. The men who created the myths and lived by them were not superstitious, foolish savages. They were not our predecessors in the evolutionary process. Biologically such a statement is a truism—Cro-Magnon man and contemporary man are virtually the same biologically. Intellectually, their style is different from ours—or at least from ours when we engage in abstract, objective science. But science as practiced by men like Claude Lévi-Strauss and their colleagues seems to be in the process of discovering that mythopoesis as thought and expression may be indispensable in any comprehensive and adequate system of human knowledge.

The myths attempted to wrestle with man's existential situation, if not to solve the insoluble then at least to produce some order and meaning in it, to reduce the amount of bafflement to manageable proportions. It is not the purpose of the present chapter to describe in any great detail either the variety or the unity of human mythology. Indeed, it would seem that all myths in the final analysis attempt to cope with the same problem: the mystery of man in the world. But a brief outline of the different divisions that scholars have elaborated of human mythologies will give some indication of the kinds of problems the myth-maker faced.

Paul Ricoeur sees the myth-maker struggling with the question of good and evil in the world and trying to explain it through various theories of creation. There are four different solutions to the problem. The first, most typical of the nature religions, locates evil and good in the very act of creation itself. The god or the demigod (such as the Babylonian Marduk) establishes some sort of order out of chaos, but the conflict between order and chaos endures, since chaos is simply restrained and not eliminated. Reality existing before the intervention of the creator is therefore a complex of good and evil.

The second modality of creation myths Ricoeur calls the "tragic." It was typical of much pre-Socratic Greek thought. Reality and the gods who dominated it were at least capricious if not evil. The gods are jealous of man and cannot endure any greatness besides their own. Any attempt on man's part to rise beyond his state will result in instantaneous angry punishment from the gods. One escapes from the basic irrationality of existence either through the calm, resigned, wise, and gentle style of the Apollonian or through the orgiastic, ecstatic, "turned-on" style of the Dionysian. But while there is some vague hint that someday the gods might be converted and the tragic burden might be lifted from man, there is little hope in either the Dionysian or the Apollonian response to the tragic myth.

The third set of creation mythologies, which Ricoeur calls "Adamic," sees creation as basically good. Evil comes into the world through man's fault, but God, somehow or other, triumphs over evil with his own power of goodness. In this version of reality, creation is *not* an ordering of preexisting chaos but a production *ex nihilo*. Hebrews and Christians, incidentally, are not the only ones to have a creation myth *ex nihilo*. Charles Long cites a Polynesian creation myth which, while not as elaborate as Genesis, is, nonetheless, strikingly similar.

> He existed, Taaroa was his name,
> In the immensity (space)
> There was no earth, there was no sky.
> There was no sea, there was no man.
> Above, Taaroa calls.
> Existing alone, he became the universe.
> Taaroa is the origin, the rocks,
> Taaroa is the sands,
> It is thus that he is named.
> Taaroa is the light;
> Taaroa is within;
> Taaroa is the germ.
> Taaroa is beneath;
> Taaroa is firm;
> Taaroa is wise.
> He created the land of Hawaii,
> Hawaii the great and sacred,
> As a body or shell for Taaroa. . . .[19]

Finally, Ricoeur describes the myth of the exiled soul which is saved through knowledge, a myth contained in the Orphic mysteries of ancient Greece and rationalized in the great Greek philosophers, particularly Plato. The soul is in exile, imprisoned in the body; only by knowledge can it break free of the body and liberate itself. The soul is goodness, the body is evil. God comes from the soul, evil from the body; evil is conquered by the triumph of the soul over the body through knowledge.

In each of the four mythologies of creation there is some room for salvation. In the dualistic world of the nature religions one is saved through ritual which keeps one in contact with the ordering power against the forces of chaos. In the tragic myths one achieves some sort of salvation by coming to terms with the tragedy either ecstatically or stoically. In the Platonic myth sal-

vation comes through knowledge which triumphs over the im-
prisoning forces of the body. Finally, in the Adamic myth salvation comes through the intervention of God in history and man's
allying himself with God's intervening power. Ricoeur attempts
to show how the Adamic myth integrates the other three into its
vision of reality. But this effort, however persuasive or unper-
suasive it may be, is beyond the scope of the present volume.

Charles Long uses a somewhat different typology of creation
myths: (1) Emergence myths by which order and human life
emerge slowly from some primal mass (as in the Navaho creation
story in which mother earth gives birth to creation). (2) World-
parent myths in which intercourse between male and female
deities produces the created world. Here the well-known Babylonian epic is the classic example. (3) Creations from chaos and
from the cosmic egg in which the primal mass produces the cosmic egg that hatches created reality. (4) Creations from nothing
—of which the Adamic myth is the one we know best. (5) The
earth-diver symbolism in which a divine being (usually an animal) dives into the water to bring up the first particles of earth.
The particles of earth are the germs from which the entire universe grows.

It will be readily seen that while Long's division of creation
myths is different from Ricoeur's, the difference is not very great,
for his categories 1, 2, 3, and 5 are all varieties of Ricoeur's ordering of chaos, and both the tragic and Platonic myths—developments of Greek creative genius—are, in the final analysis, merely
highly developed aspects of the ordering-of-chaos myths.

But whether one sees creation emerging from an egg, or developing from particles that a diver has rescued from the depths,
or as parts of the body of a slain monster, or as the result of
intercourse between deities, or from a simple divine fiat, the
creation myths are all attempts to explain the human condition,
both its factuality and its strange blend of good and evil. These
are the two ultimate issues with which the myth-maker wrestled.
And while one suspects that his answers were not perfectly satisfactory to either him or his colleagues, it cannot be claimed

that modern science has produced any more adequate answers.

Another way of viewing the myths is provided by Professor Alan Watts. He sees myths as an attempt to transcend duality in a search for unity. Mythological language

> expresses a point of view in which the dark side of things has its place, or, rather, in which the light and the dark are transcended through being seen in terms of a dramatic unity. . . . The "problem of duality" arises only when the abstract is confused with the concrete, when it is thought that there are as clearly distinguishable entities in the natural universe. As we have seen, factual language, in which categories of this kind belong, is never more than strictly limited symbolism for what is happening in nature. The image, poetic or mythic, is closer than linguistic categories to events themselves, or to what I would rather call natural patterning. We pay for the exactitude of factual language with the price of being able to speak from only one point of view at a time. But the image is many-sided and many-dimensioned, and yet at the same time imprecise; here again, it is like nature itself.[20]

In rational thought, according to Watts, we think by ignoring; that is, we attend to one term of the relationship and neglect the other. But in mythology we recognize "the two-sidedness of the one." Myth, on the other hand, tries to combine the two sides of the one, seeing light in dark, good in evil, order in disorder, and some sort of higher unity. The myth attempts to get at the whole picture.

> The import of what has been said thus far is that, however immersed in the pursuit of success, pleasure, survival, and the good life, man retains in the back of his mind an apprehension of the figure/ground structure of all his perceptions. This apprehension expresses itself in mythic and poetic images rather than factual statement. And this "back" of the mind refers alike to what is back in time, as primitive intuition, to what is repressed to emerge only in the symbolism of "the unconscious," and to what is "recovered" in mystical wisdom by deep insight. The apprehension is simultaneously holy, or esoteric, and obscene, or un-

mentionable, because it subverts in one way or another the conscious ideals of the social order, intent, as they are, on achieving
the victory of light over darkness. The higher subversion is the
way of the monk or ascetic who sets himself apart from the life
of the world. The lower subversion is the way of the libertine
who defies the order of the world.[21]

Watts sees four different mythological attempts to cope with
the problem of duality. (1) In Chinese and Indian myths the
principle of polarity and of the inner unity of opposites is explicitly recognized (for example, in the famous Ying/Yang mythology). (2) In the "two brothers" myths from the Middle East
the conflict is seen between two equal brothers, one of whom
stands for evil, the other for good. They are separated, and yet,
since they are brothers, they are still basically united. (3) What
Watts calls "ultimate dualism" is represented especially by Christianity, in which the disappearance of the inner unity between
good and evil is, in Watts's words, "extreme" and "absolute." (4)
In the "dismemberment remembered" myths the separation of
polar opposites—accomplished in the creation of the world by
the cutting up of some primordial being—leads to the duality of
the world (heaven and earth, male and female, etc.) and then is
seen slowly being transcended by the human ideal—the "androg-
ynous sage," or "divine-man," whose "consciousness transcends
the opposites and who, therefore, knows himself to be one with
the cosmos." [22]

It will be readily seen that Watts is merely viewing mythological activity from a somewhat different perspective than
Ricoeur and Long, though such a view is justified by the fact that
myth-makers themselves approach the problems from different
perspectives. Man is faced with the problem of how things came
to be, how they are a complex of good and evil, how both unity
and diversity seem characteristic of the created condition. The
myth-maker makes up "stories" based in part on the physical and
social realities around him and in part on the operations of his
own unconscious in order that through these "stories" he may

achieve some "understanding," both cognitive and affective, of what reality is all about.

Myths may also be viewed from the perspective of their attempt to answer the questions about the human struggle. Joseph Campbell in his *The Hero with a Thousand Faces* [23] sees many of the myths organized to tell the story of "the adventure of the hero" which follows a clearly described pattern: "A separation from the world, a penetration to some source of power, and the life-enhancing return." The hero with the call to adventure crosses the threshold of the unknown, perhaps receiving the help of the gods, spends a long period in darkness, contends with forces of evil, achieves union with the woman figure, or conquest or peace with the father figure, and then crosses the threshold of return to come back, sometimes very reluctantly, to the everyday world, that he may live his ordinary life, now in a transformed and transmuted fashion. The hero may be a warrior, a lover, a king, or a redeemer, or a saint, but he symbolizes man's struggle against the adversities of life, a struggle in which he sometimes triumphs, and sometimes even the myth is destroyed. The departure of the hero, his initiation into the world of the depths, his journey through that world, and his eventual return—frequently by passing through waters—is an attempt on the part of the myth-maker to wrestle with the problem of death and life and the paradoxical unity between the two, a paradox expressed by the nineteenth-century poet Francis Thompson:

> 'Til skies be fugitives,
> 'Til time, the hidden root of change up-dries,
> Our death and birth, inseparable upon earth
> For they are twain, yet one,
> And death is birth.

The sacred rituals, and particularly the ritual by which one is initiated into the sacred mysteries, are seen as paradigmatic reenactments of the journey of the hero. That the initiation ceremony frequently involves some sort of passage through water is to be understood as a reenactment of the hero's passage from this world to the other world through the deep waters, and also his return from the other world to this world through the waters.

In a frequently maddening and always remarkable book Giorgio de Santillana argues that most of the myths developed since 3000 or 4000 B.C. were essentially cosmological myths; that is to say, myths designed to explain the three different kinds of motion perceived in the sky: the daily change from day to night, the yearly march of the sun between the two equinoxes, and the "great year"—the 26,000-year cycle of "precession," which is the apparent rotation of the heavens caused by the circular motion of the earth's axis. The precession phenomenon, which means that every 2000 years or so a new constellation will precede the sun into the sky on the day of the spring equinox, accounts for history being divided into ages. The ages were given names of the signs of the zodiac. The end of an old age and the beginning of a new one seems a time of great disaster. As described in Santillana's book, *Hamlet's Mill*,[24] the rotating circle of the heavens is thought of as having jumped out of its socket and vast torrents of water poured through the hole. One age is drowned and another age comes into being. Cosmological mythology both records and accounts for these dramatic events in heaven. Santillana suggests, too, that the Hamlet myth seems to be almost universal among archaic people. He traces it from the Near East to Ireland, to Iceland, to Scandinavia, and, finally, to Shakespeare's England. He also suggests that the myth of the flood, which is equally widespread, records not a flood on earth but a flood in heaven on the occasion of a change from one age to another.*

Life and death, good and evil, unity and diversity, these are the existential characteristics of the human situation to which the myth-maker addresses himself. They are issues which cannot be answered merely on the rational plane because they so permeate

---

* Incidentally, according to Santillana's calculations, we are still in the Age of the Fish and will remain there for several more centuries before the Age of Aquarius actually dawns.

the whole of man's experience and so challenge and threaten the whole of his being, that he must respond to them with a totality of selfhood. It is only with major effort that he is able to ignore his emotions and his poetic and artistic insights when he is faced with these critical issues. Modern man with his heightened competencies in abstract thought is able to restrain his emotions, at least while engaged in the exercise of scientific thought. But whether this exercise ought to become normative for the human condition, whether man ought to become so scientific as to repress all mythopoetic responses to the enigmas of reality seems to be problematic. Indeed, as we shall see later in the chapter, it is dubious whether man *can* repress his mythopoetic inclination save for those brief interludes of time when he is engaged in objective science.

In the vast repertoire of mythologies the ultimate reality appears in many different fashions. The most primordial is apparently the "Sky God," the single all-powerful deity of pastoral peoples, who resides in the heavens and dominates all. Secondly, there appear the multitudinous gods of the fertility religions. Finally, we encounter the aloof creator-god of the world religions (who, at least in the Christian and Jewish traditions, ceases to be aloof and enters the "game" on man's own ground).

As Mircea Eliade points out, we have no archeological records of the people who knew only the Sky God. He is always found existing—usually very far in the background—in a situation populated by the multitudinous deities of the fertility cults of the agricultural society. Any attempt to see an evolutionary process running either from primitive animism to Judeo-Christian monotheism or from primitive monotheism through polytheism and back to monotheism is based on a priori models and not on reading of the data. But what can be said is that man's image of God is conditioned by the circumstances in which he finds himself. Simple pastoral and food-gathering peoples need only one deity, though they may fear many evil spirits. More elaborately organized pastoral people with large flocks and agricultural societies, both depending for their existence on the reproductive processes of plants and animals, will evolve a fertility religion within which many different deities will flourish (though the Sky God may lurk in the background). As man begins to develop his capacities for abstract thought and his ability to universalize, he will begin to fashion an image of God which transcends the boundary of the tribe or city in which he lives—a God who becomes quite distinct from the biological and social processes on which the tribe or the city depend.

God's attitude toward man in the myths will also vary. In some of the nature religions he emerges as a crusty and cantankerous monarch, jealous of his prerogatives and punctilious in his insistence on ritual. The rites must be carried out perfectly. Any deviation, however unconscious or undeliberate, will be punished. God must be placated (or the gods must be placated). In other manifestations of fertility religion the god is more absentminded than angry. He has every intention of helping man if he can remember to do so. The rituals are then performed not so much to placate the god as to remind him of man's dependence on him.* Yet another divine attitude is found in the tragic tradition in which the gods are seen as implacably bent on keeping man in his place, and man becomes a powerless plaything subject to the whims of the gods. Then there is the deistic god who set the whole operation of the universe in motion but then apparently lost interest in the project to busy himself about other things. He may be the Sky God of the nomadic tribe, the Sun God of Egypt, Aristotle's Prime Mover, or the Enlightenment deists' Grand Architect. Whatever he is called, he really couldn't care less about what man does.

The final image of the deity is the Jewish and Christian one in which God is a jealous lover seen as intervening in history in pursuit of man with whom he has for some reason become emotionally involved, whether he be Hosea's husband pursuing a faithless wife or Francis Thompson's Hound of Heaven, or

---

* Both the cantankerous god and the absentminded god have survived in the poetry of the world religions. Thus, in the Hebrew psalms God is both pleaded with and shouted at.

Paddy Chayefsky's Angel telling Gideon that he's really not sure what he sees in man. The Jewish and Christian God is, from one point of view, altogether too much involved with man's plight.

There is, of course, a great deal of diversity in the mythologies of the world. The scholars who have lovingly collected the myths have frequently found striking patterns of similarity. There are two basic approaches to explaining both the similarity and the diversity of human mythologies. The first explanation relies heavily on the writings of Freud and of C. G. Jung. The latter's theory of the "collective unconscious" emphasizes the psychological or, in the case of Jung's disciple Joseph Campbell, the biological unity of the human species. Men's myths are similar because man has the same psychological and biological needs, the same kind of unconscious processes no matter what the situation is in which he finds himself. As Campbell says,

> Mythology is not invented rationally; mythology cannot be rationally understood. Theological interpreters render it ridiculous. Literary criticism reduces it to metaphor. A new and very promising approach is opened, however, when it is viewed in the light of biological psychology as a function of the human nervous system, precisely homologous to the innate and learned sign stimuli that release and direct the energies of nature—of which our brain itself is but the most amazing flower.[25]

On the other hand, many anthropologists, particularly the disciples of Émile Durkheim, stress the diversity of the human experience and the different social and geographic circumstances in which man finds himself. Campbell quotes with obvious disapproval A. R. Radcliffe-Brown speaking of the Andaman Islanders:

> A society depends for its existence on the presence in the minds of its members of a certain system of sentiments by which the conduct of the individual is regulated in conformity with the needs of the society. Every feature of the social system itself and every event or object that in any way affects the well-being or the cohesion of the society becomes an object of this system

of sentiments. *In human society the sentiments in question are not innate but are developed in the individual by the action of the society upon him* [italics mine]. The ceremonial customs of a society are a means by which the sentiments in question are given collective expression on appropriate occasions. The ceremonial (i.e., collective) expression of any sentiment serves both to maintain it at the requisite degree of intensity in the mind of the individual and to transmit it from one generation to another. Without such expression the sentiments involved could not exist.[26]

Campbell comments:

It will be readily seen that in such a view the ceremonials and mythologies of the different societies are in no sense manifestations of psychologically grounded "elementary ideas," common to the human race, but of interests locally conditioned; and the fundamental contrast of the two approaches is surely clear.[27]

It may be something, perhaps, of a tempest in a teapot. In his more recent *The Flight of the Wild Gander* Campbell makes it quite clear that external circumstances do affect the way man's primary biological and psychological responses shape his mythology.

Roheim has indicated the problem of man-growing-up, no matter where—defense against libidinal quantities with which the immature ego is not prepared to deal; and he has analyzed the curious "symbiotic mode of mastering reality," which is the very fashioner, the master builder, of all human societies. "It is the nature of our species," he writes, "to master reality on a libidinal basis, and we create a society and environment in which this and only this is possible." "The psyche as we know it, is formed by the introjection of primary objects (superego) and the first contact with environment (ego). Society itself is knitted together by projection of these primary introjected objects or concepts followed by a series of subsequent introjections and projections." This tight-knitting of defensive fantasy and external reality is what builds the second womb, the marsupial pouch that we call society. Hence, though man's environment greatly varies in the corners of the planet, there is a marvelous monotony about his ritual forms. Local styles of the century, nation, race, or social class obviously differ; yet what James Joyce calls the "grave and constant in human sufferings," remains truly constant and grave. It arrests the mind, everywhere, in the rituals of birth, adolescence, marriage, death, installation, and initiation, uniting it with the mysteries of eternal recurrence and of man's psychosomatic maturation. The individual grows up, not only as a member of a certain social group, but as a human being.[28]

Alan Watts, while accepting the importance of "Jung's point that the mythic image, the archetype, whether submerged in the collective unconscious or the social matrix or both, is a powerful and indispensable organizer of action and experience," [29] is still not persuaded that Jung gives sufficient importance either to the natural world or to human society.

For Jung, the external world seems to be a somewhat indifferent screen which receives our psychic projections. He is overcareful to avoid the pathetic fallacy. For my part, I believe that these images—mythic, poetic, and artistic—reveal the outer world as well as the inner. For it is only when translated into the somewhat specialized and limited instrument of factual language that the outer world appears to be this prosaic assembly of "nobody here but just us objects." To survey and control the earth we must reduce its formations to the formal abstractions of geometry, and translate it into the flat and dry symbolism of maps. But, as Korzybski so often repeated, the map is not the territory.[30]

Mircea Eliade sees the patterns of similarity in mythologies resulting from a similarity in the "existential situations" in which man finds himself. The situations which involve similarities are social relationships (particularly male and female, parent and child), physical environment (storms, sun, moon, stars, water, drought), and similarities of human experience (birth, growth, maturity, old age, death). In other words, any attempt to separate the biological, psychological, and sociological dimensions of the human condition is bound to be self-defeating. There were vast diversities in archaic peoples and vast diversities in their myths, but as human beings living in some kind of society and somewhere on the planet earth, wrestling with the same kinds of problems of goodness and evil, life and death, unity and diversity, they, not at all surprisingly, came up with mythologies that have a great deal in common one with the other.

It is worthwhile to look in some detail at Eliade's description of the role of myth in the life of an agricultural community.[31] The village was considered to be a place of order, the place whose huts and walls excluded the chaos in the world outside. By putting order into the fields in which the crops grew, the villagers continued the work of creation, of pushing back the forces of chaos. The place of worship or the central pole of the village represented the center of the universe, that point in which the really real came into contact with the everyday. It is as though the ordering principle flowed through the pole to the place of worship, through the villagers in their rituals, which reenacted the paradigmatic ordering of the universe, and then through their efforts in the fields to continue and expand the ordering. Similarly, the routines of time in the village—morning and night; spring, summer, fall, and winter; planting, cultivating, and harvesting—were seen as linking the villagers through their time-regulated rituals to the sacred time—the time when the paradigmatic action of imposing order on chaos took place. The village in its activities, then, was linked through their ritual to the sacred time in space of the really real, and the individual villager found meaning for ultimate reality, for his own life, and for his activities in the fields. In addition, the rituals provided him with the very practical, concrete information of when and how to plant, cultivate, and harvest his crops. Science, art, history, metaphysics, politics, and theology were all contained in one highly poetic and emotionally charged narrative.

Can man do without myth? It ought to be clear by now that I do not think so and neither do the authors that I have quoted. While Campbell's rhetoric has grown more obscure with the passage of years (though even his earliest books are not terribly clear), it nevertheless seems that he is arguing that man is now in a state where for at least a time he does not need or will not have myths.

> The scientific method has released us, intellectually, from the absolutes of the mythological ages; the divine authority of the religiously founded state has been completely dissolved, at least in the Occident; and the power-driven machine is progressively releasing human energy from the onerous physical tasks that were formerly rationalized as valuable moral disciplines: thus released, these energies constitute what Jung has termed a quantum of disposable libido—now flowing from the corporeal to the spiritual task. And this spiritual task can now be only that which I have here termed the task of art.[32]

Unlike Lévi-Strauss, whom we quoted earlier, Campbell does not see science tending toward some sort of integration with the mythological.

> Within the time of our lives, it is highly improbable that any solid rock will be found to which Prometheus can again be durably shackled, or against which those who are not titans will be able to lean with confidence. The creative researches and wonderful daring of our scientists today partake far more of the lion spirit of shamanism than of the piety of priest and peasant. They have shed all fear of the bounding serpent king. And if we are to match their courage, and thus participate joyfully in their world without meaning, we must allow our own spirits to become, like theirs, wild ganders, and fly in timeless, spaceless flight—like the body of the Virgin Mary—not into any fixed heaven beyond the firmament (for there is no heaven out there), but to that seat of experience, simultaneously without and within, where Prometheus and Zeus, I and Father, the meaninglessness of the sense of existence and the meaninglessness of the meanings of the world, are one.[33]

And he concludes *The Flight of the Wild Gander* with an angry, mythological statement of his own.

"Man is condemned," as Sartre says, "to be free." However, not all, even today, are of that supine sort that must have their life values given them, cried at them from the pulpits and other mass media of the day. For there is, in fact, in quiet places, a great deal of deep spiritual quest and finding now in progress in this world, outside the sanctified social centers, beyond their purview and control: in small groups, here and there, and more often, more typically (as anyone who looks about may learn), by ones and twos, they are entering the forest at those points which they themselves have chosen, where they see it to be most dark, and there is no beaten way or path.[34]

All of which, of course, is very fine, or perhaps not so very fine, depending on one's viewpoint. But if we accept Campbell's basic assumption that myth-making is rooted in man's biological processes, and if we further accept the obvious fact that the biological processes have not changed since the Ice Age, it seems rather unusual to argue that man is now able to get along without myths, at least any more than he was then. He makes his myths in different sets of circumstances, perhaps; they may take different shapes, but make them he still does.

Eliade is prepared to concede that some men are so scientific that they are able to dispense with myths, but he takes a much less benign and agnostic view of these men than does Campbell. Modern, nonreligious man may refuse transcendence; he may regard himself solely as the subject of agents of history; he may accept no model for humanity outside that which he can validate himself; he may feel that he can only be free when he desacralizes himself and his world, that he can only be truly free when he has "killed the last god." But, Eliade comments,

Do what he will, he is an inheritor. He cannot utterly abolish his past, since he is himself the product of his past. He forms himself by a series of denials and refusals, but he continues to be haunted by the realities that he has refused and denied. To acquire a world of his own, he has desacralized the world in which his ancestors lived; but to do so he has been obliged to adopt the opposite of an earlier type of behavior, and that behavior is still emotionally present to him, in one form or another, ready to be reactualized in his deepest being.[35]

From Eliade's viewpoint, then, nonreligious man is a comparatively rare phenomenon, and even those who claim that they have dispensed with mythologies are, in fact, deeply involved in mythological attitudes and behaviors that betray not only their pasts but their present existential religious situation.

> A whole volume could well be written on the myths of modern man, on the mythologies camouflaged in the plays that he enjoys, in the books that he reads. The cinema, that "dream factory," takes over and employs countless mythical motifs—the fight between hero and monster, initiatory combats and ordeals, paradigmatic figures and images (the maiden, the hero, the paradisal landscape, hell, and so on). Even reading includes a mythological function, not only because it replaces the recitation of myths in archaic societies and the oral literature that still lives in the rural communities of Europe, but particularly because, through reading, the modern man succeeds in obtaining an "escape from time" comparable to the "emergence from time" effected by myths. Whether modern man "kills" time with a detective story or enters such a foreign temporal universe as is represented by any novel, reading projects him out of his personal duration and incorporates him into other rhythms, makes him live in another "history." [36]

Furthermore, the greatest of secular religions, Marxism, is in Eliade's frame of reference thoroughly and pervasively mythological.

> Marx takes over and continues one of the great eschatological myths of the Asiatico-Mediterranean world—the redeeming role of the Just (the "chosen," the "anointed," the "innocent," the "messenger"; in our day, the proletariat), whose sufferings are destined to change the ontological status of the world. In fact, Marx's classless society and the consequent disappearance of historical tensions find their closest precedent in the myth of the Golden Age that many traditions put at the beginning and the end of history. Marx enriched this venerable myth by a whole

Judaeo-Christian messianic ideology: on the one hand, the prophetic role and soteriological function that he attributes to the
proletariat; on the other, the final battle between Good and
Evil, which is easily comparable to the apocalyptic battle between Christ and Antichrist, followed by the total victory of
the former. It is even significant that Marx takes over for his
own purposes the Judaeo-Christian eschatological hope of *an
absolute end to history;* in this he differs from other historicistic
philosophers (Croce and Ortega y Gasset, for example), for
whom the tensions of history are consubstantial with the human
condition and therefore can never be completely done away
with.[37]

One might add that Professor Eliade wrote that paragraph
long before the incredible mythologizing of Chairman Mao in
Red China. Mao has, in fact, become the Marduk of the contemporary Chinese.

So Eliade would view the modern man who claims to be free
from myth as a tragic and incomplete human being. Indeed, he
goes so far as to suggest that in attempting to leave behind the
mythological, man has experienced another "fall."

From one point of view it could almost be said that in the case
of those moderns who proclaim that they are nonreligious, religion and mythology are "eclipsed" in the darkness of their unconscious—which means too that in such men the possibility
of reintegrating a religious vision of life lies at a great depth.
Or, from the Christian point of view, it could also be said that
nonreligion is equivalent to a new "fall" of man—in other
words, that nonreligious man has lost the capacity to live religion consciously, and hence to understand and assume it; but
that, in his deepest being, he still retains a memory of it, as,
after the first "fall," his ancestor, the primordial man, retained
intelligence enough to enable him to rediscover the traces of
God that are visible in the world. After the first "fall," the religious sense descended to the level of the "divided consciousness"; now, after the second, it has fallen even further, into the
depths of the unconscious; it has been "forgotten." [38]

Paul Ricoeur, taking a somewhat more positive viewpoint

than Eliade, sees our age as a time when, while to some extent
the sacred and the signs of the sacred have been forgotten, the
sacred can be understood as never before because of the possibility of making the substance and the content of myths and symbols more *explicit*.

> It is in the age when our language has become more precise,
> more univocal, more technical, in a word, more suited to those
> integral formalizations which are called precisely symbolic logic,
> it is in this very age of discourse that we want to recharge our
> language, that we want to start again from the fullness of
> language.
>
> That also is a gift of our "modernity," for we moderns are
> the heirs of philology, of exegesis, of the phenomenology of
> religion, of the psychoanalysis of language. The same epoch
> holds in reserve both the possibility of emptying language by
> radically formalizing it and the possibility of filling it anew by
> reminding itself of the fullest meanings, the most pregnant ones,
> the ones which are most bound by the presence of the sacred
> to man.[39]

We see, then, some kind of convergence between the thinking
of Ricoeur and Lévi-Strauss. If small segments within the
population for a time rejected the subjective value of myths in
order to make them an object for scientific examination, the time
has come now when many scientists and philosophers see that
the mythopoetic cannot be excluded from an adequate system
of human knowledge; and, indeed, it is necessary as a complement to scientific knowledge. Man can still find meaning in
myths, though now, unlike his predecessors, he is conscious of
the search for meaning and must *interpret* the myths.

> Does that mean that we could go back to a primitive naiveté?
> Not at all. In every way, something has been lost, irremediably
> lost: immediacy of belief. But if we can no longer live the great
> symbolisms of the sacred in accordance with the original belief
> in them, we can, we modern men, aim at a second naiveté in
> and through criticism. In short, it is by *interpreting* that we
> can *hear* again. Thus it is in hermeneutics that the symbol's gift

of meaning and the endeavor to understand by deciphering are knotted together.[40]

Ricoeur concludes with the contention that modern criticism must "demythologize"; that is to say, it must separate the historical and the pseudohistorical in the myth, but it must not then go on to "demythicize," or, in other words, cast myths onto the trash heap of history. On the contrary, it must then begin to investigate the myth as a primordial sign of the sacred.

> We see, then, with what prudence one can speak of "demytholo-gization"; it is legitimate to speak of "demythologizing" if de-mythologizing is distinguished carefully from "demythicizing." All criticism "demythologizes" insofar as it is criticism; that is to say, it always adds to the separation of the historical (according to the rules of the critical method) and the pseudohistorical. What criticism continually endeavors to exorcize is the *logos* of the *mythos* (for example, the representation of the universe as a series of places, one above the other, with the earth in the middle, the heavens above, and hell below). As an advance post of "modernity," criticism cannot help being a "demythologiza-tion"; that is an irreversible gain of truthfulness, of intellectual honesty, and therefore of objectivity. But it is precisely because it accelerates the movement of the symbol, as a primordial sign of the sacred; it is thus that it participates in the revivification of philosophy through contact with symbols; it is one of the ways of rejuvenating philosophy. This paradox, in accordance with which "demythologization" is also a recharging of thought with the aid of symbols, is only a corollary of what we have called the circle of believing and understanding in hermeneutics.[41]

In *The Flight of the Wild Gander,* Campbell argues (again speaking mythologically, one suspects) that in 1492 the mandala broke—that mysterious and fascinating circular symbol of reality which, in Campbell's words, "had been fashioned six thousand years before, in the period of the Halaf and Samarra bowls." [42] Perhaps; though one can wander through the National Opinion Research Center almost five centuries after Columbus sailed and see on the doors of reputable social scientists—or at least their reputable research assistants—mandala posters. One is confident that similar posters exist in both student dormitories and faculty apartments around the university campuses. Maybe, just maybe, the mandala wasn't broken after all.

On the dust jacket of Lawrence Kubie's book, *Neurotic Distortion of the Creative Process*, there appears, oddly enough, a mandala symbol.[43] Kubie sees three levels of human "mentation": the conscious, the unconscious, and the preconscious. On the conscious level we deal with communicable ideas. On the unconscious, we deal with our own internal struggles, and in the preconscious, we deal "with swift condensations of multiple allegorical and emotional import, both direct and indirect." [44] The preconscious is the world of symbols and, one suspects, the world where myth is born.

> These approximate less closely the limited one-to-one relationships of the fully matured language of conscious symbolic functions, but retain a broader overlapping base of multiple meanings. This enables them to use the symbolic process in a more allegorical and figurative fashion. In the adult who is not hamstrung by conscious or unconscious fear and guilt, preconscious processes make free use of analogy and allegory, superimposing dissimilar ingredients into new perceptual and conceptual patterns, thus reshuffling experience to achieve that fantastic degree of condensation without which creativity in any field of activity would be impossible. In the preconscious use of imagery and allegory many experiences are condensed into a single hieroglyph, which expresses in one symbol far more than one can say slowly and precisely, word by word, on the fully conscious level. This is why preconscious mentation is the Seven-league Boot of intuitive creative functions. This is how and why preconscious condensations are used in poetry, humor, the dream, and the symptom.[45]

It is interesting to note that it is in the preconscious that Kubie sees creativity working and that he argues that a healthy, functioning preconscious can be inhibited either by the tumultuous anxieties in the unconscious or by the rigid repressions of the conscious. A psychologically healthy man cannot help having a creative preconscious. A psychologically healthy man cannot help but respond to reality in a symbolic way. In Kubie's view of things, the man who can deal with reality only on the rational, abstract, conceptual level of consciousness is a man who is emotionally unhealthy. Or, to use somewhat stronger terms than Kubie uses, the question is not whether man can do without myths but whether he can possibly prevent himself from making them.

We can say that at the very minimum there is strong reason to doubt that man is capable or ever will be capable of dispensing with myths. The clergyman or divinity school student who proudly announces that he has passed beyond mythological religion may think that he is in the avant-garde of the evolutionary process; the first of a new breed of scientific clergymen. In fact, if one accepts Mircea Eliade's viewpoint, he is now, if not a once-fallen, a twice-fallen creature. If one agrees with Alan Watts and Lévi-Strauss, he is also misunderstanding completely the direction in which modern science is most likely to go. Finally, if one accepts Lawrence Kubie on the preconscious, he is also frustrating the most creative dimensions of his personality and, according to Paul Ricoeur, missing the whole point of the myth as a primordial sign of the sacred.

But this clergyman or student of ours is completely unaware of how busy he is in creating new myths of his own. For example, he is likely to deplore the possibility of a return to the "McCarthy era" (by which he means Joseph and not Eugene), but he does not mean, one suspects, the strict historical facts of the McCarthy era. The late junior senator from Wisconsin was not a pleasant man, and the years of which he is a mythological symbol were uncomfortable years, but in mythology Senator McCarthy has become a far more horrendous demon than he was in fact. Far fewer people suffered because of him than the mythology would have us believe. There was unpleasantness and difficulty in American academia; there was not in any sense a reign of terror (to fall back on yet another mythology). But this is not to say that the McCarthy myth is untrue, for it represents the fact of the alienation of the American intellectual; an alienation which is in part imaginary, in part self-imposed, but also in part an accurate description of the anti-intellectualism of American society. The intellectual may have far higher prestige than he is willing to admit to himself, and yet he is still the object of ambivalence, the negative pole of which is suspicion and distrust. The McCarthy mythology does not merely convey the fact of that ambivalence but prescribes an approved reaction to it and even a set of ritualistic incantations that the academic is supposed to go through to prevent the return of the demon.

I am not being sardonic, at least not completely so, but I will be persuaded that *Homo academicus* is completely demythologized when I see that he has given up the myths of his own creation, of which the McCarthy myth is but one. If *Homo academicus* can be content with dry, precise, documented, rationalistic statements about what he means when he uses mythology of the "establishment," then I will concede that he is demythologized. In the meantime, it is perfectly all right with me if he goes on cheering J. William Fulbright as he slays the monsters and the dragons. I'll cheer for him, and for the Kennedys, and Martin Luther King, and Franklin Roosevelt, too, and all the other great mythological heroes of our time. One of the big advantages of the modern world is that you can become a saint much more quickly than you could in archaic ages.

W. Lloyd Warner, in his famous account of the religion of "Yankee City," describes how the two great "religious" feast days in Yankee City—Memorial Day and the Fourth of July—commemorate the great religious myths around which the American republic is organized. One is the myth of liberation and freedom with its strong Exodus coloration, with George Washington as its Moses figure. Another is the myth of the Civil War with its Good Friday–Easter Sunday dimension of suffering, death, and resurrection, with Abraham Lincoln as the Christ figure. It does not matter to the citizens of Yankee City that many of the facts of the Revolutionary War and the Civil War are omitted and that

others are completely transformed in the "mythological narration." It does not matter that the "father of our country" was at
times a rather dull and stodgy fellow, nor that the Great Eman-
cipator was a rude, crude, sometimes vulgar, and always very
clever politician. The myths are rooted in some kind of factuality
but are not an attempt to give a factually accurate description of
what happened. They are, rather, a symbolic interpretation of
the meaning of American society.*

Robert Bellah, in his careful study "Civil Religion in America,"
shows how the inaugural addresses of our presidents rely heavily
on two mythological descriptions of American society—the new
Canaan and the new Rome.[46] We are a republic put together in
imitation of the sober, responsible civic virtues of ancient Rome,
but also a new Promised Land offering freedom from slavery and
oppression to those who come to it. It may be argued that both
comparisons are monstrously inaccurate on all kinds of historical
grounds, but the point is they were not intended to be accurate.
They were intended to be interpretations which would symbolize

---

* In the final chapter we will address ourselves once again to the
question of factuality in myth, but it is worth noting that no myth is
concerned about strict historic truth. It is not trying to tell strict history;
it is, rather, trying to capture in a concrete and vivid way an interpretation of history which gives meaning and purpose to the lives of those for
whom the history is important. Thus, even shortly after an event occurred, its symbolic purpose as a description of "the way things really
are" is far more important to both the teller and the hearer than are the
factual historical details. I was recently told by a liberal from New York
that "everyone knows that Judge Hoffman is one of the worst men who
ever bought a judgeship from Richard Daley." I responded rather mildly
that Judge Hoffman had been appointed by a Republican President,
Dwight D. Eisenhower, before Richard Daley was mayor of Chicago. My
friend was completely untroubled by this minor historical inaccuracy, for
the events of the conspiracy trial had now taken on for him mythological
value. They symbolized "the way things really are," in Chicago and the
nation, and historical details were unimportant. Is his myth thereby
"false"? As scientific rational history it has at least one false statement,
but he was not attempting scientific, rational history. He was telling a
story which symbolized and summarized for him in a concrete and emotionally powerful way what the political reality "really is." The myth may
be an inadequate interpretation of reality but it does not purport to be a
scientific description of reality, and it will never be refuted merely by its
opponents listing historical or scientific inaccuracies.

in a poetic or quasi-poetic fashion the golden visions of American society. Bellah quite correctly points out that if American society is to be criticized it ought not to be criticized on the grounds that it lacks noble and dignified mythological values; it ought to be criticized on its failure to live up to those values.

A classic example of how the conventional wisdom, caught as it is in its own simpleminded evolutionary perspective, approaches the question of myth is cited in John F. Hayward's article in *New Theology* where he quotes anthropologist David Bidney:

> My conclusion is that while in times of crisis the "noble fiction" may have its immediate, pragmatic utility in promoting social faith and solidarity, faith in reason and in the ability of democratic man to govern himself rationally requires a minimum of reliance upon myth. . . . Myth must be taken seriously precisely in order that it may be gradually superseded in the interests of the advancement of truth and the growth of human intelligence. Normative, critical, and scientific thought provides the only self-correcting means of combatting the diffusion of myth, but it may do so only on condition that we retain a firm and uncompromising faith in the integrity of reason and in the transcultural validity of the scientific enterprise.[47]

Bidney, like all speakers of conventional wisdom on mythology, would modestly argue that his position is the "scientific" one, but Hayward responds by pointing out that Bidney's position cannot be justified by empirical science and in fact overlooks a vast amount of empirical scientific findings.

> It may be objected that any world view or system of values which remains within the human sphere should hardly be called transcendent, especially in view of the fact that it maintains a modest reserve toward cosmic. belief or universal speculation. Nonetheless, although it appears to be more modest than its predecessors, it is actually less so. It says that man is the true and sole author of his own destiny. Further, it exalts not man in general but rational, conscious, deliberate, scientific man; and it relegates to positions of lesser importance and authority all

the other faces and facets of man which we have to acknowledge within man's brief history. The devotees of scientific rationalism put their faith ultimately in man's conscious self rather than his unconscious self, in his decisive behavior rather than his unpremeditated behavior, in his reason rather than his instinct, in his observational and analytical skills rather than his artistic and synthetic skills. Finally, and perhaps most important of all, basic trust is lodged in a presupposed harmony of the brotherhood of all rational men. Such a model thus transcends a huge weight of counterevidence and a huge volume of despair, cynicism, and radical doubt in the minds of all who do not share the faith. Of all the transcendence models of our time, one of the least logical, least empirical, least credible is that of autonomous, scientific man providing successfully, over the passage of time, for his own well-being.[48]

Langdon Gilkey continues the same line of thought in his book *Religion and the Scientific Future.* He first contends that we meet "an ultimacy, an aspect or trace of the unconditioned; a whiff, if you will, of the sacred as the source and ground of this most human, rational and secular of activities." He points out that although it is argued that the scientist

used the real as exhaustively defined by the contingent and the relative, and man's hopes as based exclusively on his own autonomous powers . . . [and] that secularity . . . is the rejection of a meaningful dimension of ultimacy or of transcendence either in experience or in the language that meaningfully thematizes our experience.[49]

In fact, the history of science shows us that in actual practice science is based on creative leaps of imaginative vision and that

Knowing is thus through and through a *human* act, an act of daring, commitment, and risk, a reaching for what can never be incontrovertibly demonstrated, but which the rational consciousness finds itself compelled on its own self-accredited grounds to acknowledge and then to assert. Ironically, because it is a *rational* act and so autonomous, dependent on no external, necessitating authority but only on the self-validation of the rational consciousness, cognition is also an intensely *existential* or *willed* act, dependent on a self-affirmation of the self as knower, and of the truth so known as true—an affirmation that nothing else but the rational consciousness itself can finally establish.[50]

Books such as Michael Polanyi's *Personal Knowledge,*[51] Thomas Kuhn's *The Structure of Scientific Revolution,*[52] and Stephen Toulmin's *Foresight and Understanding* [53] make it quite clear that our culture has wrongly separated passion and commitment from objectivity. Quite the contrary,

it is a commitment in the sense that it is a personal act of acceptance and affirmation of an ultimate in one's life, of the good of knowing for its own sake, and thus of knowing according to a set of undemonstrable but commonly shared standards and aims, and it involves a quite undemonstrable belief in the continuing rationality of experience.[54]

Ultimacy, then, according to Gilkey, appears in the midst of the inquiries of the scientific community because of

affirmation that knowing is possible and in the shared *commitment* of this community to know, their personally held belief in the reality of order, and their passion for scientific integrity, their disdain for anything but the beauty, order, and simplicity of scientific explanation, and their refusal to affirm anything but what is veridically based on the evidence alone.[55]

But more than just the ultimate is found in science and in the secular world. Myths are there, too, and myths in the strict sense according to which Gilkey defines them.

Myths to us, then, are not just ancient and thus untrue fables; rather, they signify a certain perennial mode of language, whose elements are multivalent symbols, whose referent is in some strange way the transcendent or the sacred, and whose meanings concern the ultimate or existential issues of actual life and the questions of human and historical destiny.[56]

While these myths tend to be sociohistorical rather than cosmo-logical or ontological, they all "explicate a vision of the ultimate nature of reality . . . and seek to understand man's nature, obli-gations, and destiny in the light of the total cosmic vision." [57] Whether it be evolution or Marxism or scientism, all of them "deal with universal structures and patterns of things . . . pro-viding 'meaning' in life in that they are explanatory of its evils and reassuring about its prospects . . . [and] imply within their scope models and norms for individual existence, for social and political decision, and for the patterns of education, social life characteristic of the cultures which live by them." [58]

The last of these three myths—scientism—is perhaps the one most successful in the liberal and academic Western intellectual world. Gilkey calls this myth "gnostic."

> It is no surprise, therefore, but surely ironic in a naturalistic culture uncertain there is anything other than matter, that these secular and so naturalistic myths are generally *gnostic* in form: the sacred is precisely not matter but spirit, manifesting itself in and through the given of natural or historical process. Each form of modern anthropocentric myth—asserting that man be-comes *man* and can control his life and destiny if he is educated, liberal, analyzed, scientific, and "expert," etc.—assumes that for man at last to understand, to know about, or to be aware of something—for him to have a sacral gnosis—is for him to be able in a quite new way to control that object of knowledge, to direct it, and to use it teleologically; that knowledge and aware-ness can turn whatever has been a blindly determining force *on* and *in* man. Or, in the language of modern life sciences, that a blind "natural" evolution can become a purposive and benevo-lent "culture" evolution; or, in classical language, that knowl-edge gained by science and applied technologically as know-how will provide at least human self-fulfillment or *arete*.[59]

This anthropocentric myth—the myth of the new scientific man—is, in fact, a much more sophisticated form of ancient dualism.

In the topology of the myths of humanity generally, therefore, modern anthropocentric myths are dualistic accounts of destiny in which "evil" is a result of the chaos of the unorganized and so unintelligible given; but it is a "given" which the intelligence and good will of the trained, the self-aware, or the critically intelligent man may, like Indra or Zeus of old, subdue into order through a sacral gnosis and autonomous freedom.[60]

Gilkey quotes Dr. Glenn Seaborg in a classic statement of the myth of scientific man:

> man could, if he tried, solve all of today's agonizing problems —war, hunger, the population explosion, water shortages, pollution. "Man may well have reached that point in history, that stage in his development . . . where he has not only been made master of his fate, but where his technology and morality have come face to face." . . . Science has given mankind an opportunity "to control and direct our future, our creative evolution. . . . I believe we can be masters of our fate." [61]

In the final chapter of this book, where we discuss the problem of technology, we will return to Gilkey's criticism of the myth of scientific man. At the present time, it is only necessary to point out that it is indeed a myth, a story—with a future-oriented scenario—which purports to describe ultimate reality, to establish norms for human behavior and to reassure man about his life and his prospects, and, like all myths, it is in no sense verifiable by empirical evidence. When Dr. Seaborg says he "*believes*," he is expressing exactly what he is engaged in: an act of faith.

Herbert Richardson, in his book *Toward an American Theology*, discusses an attempt by the conventional wisdom to counterattack the position of the scholars being relied upon in this book.

> The proponents of a demythologizing theory of intellectual evolution reply to these sociological and historical findings as follows: The empirical studies of Lenski, Angell, Frankfort, and others do describe the *present* state of society—for ancient myth

and ritual possess tremendous residual power which enables
them to persist in spite of the new forces that work against
them. But how, these critics ask, can we conclude from these
empirical descriptions of the present-day function of myth that
mythical thinking will continue to play the same vital role in
the society of tomorrow? The world is historical; therefore it
is always changing. So how can descriptions of yesterday and
today be a basis for a prediction about the future? [62]

Richardson replies by in effect accusing demythologizers of
begging the question. "Sociological studies of different modern
societies together with historical studies of many different past
civilizations show that myth persists and plays the same social
function even in cultures that are radically different. This constitutes a legitimate basis for predicting that a future society
will also be integrated by myths and religion." [63]

Richardson then goes on to describe another counterattack of
the demythologizers, namely, that if "sociology contradicts the
program of demythologizing, then sociology is not scientific but
ideological!" [64]

In the following passage Richardson quotes Professor Harvey
Cox's response to a criticism that I leveled at his book *Secular
City*.

> He [Cox] asserts that those sociologists whose studies lead them
> to conclude that urban society is "made up of symmetrically
> stable components of religious and profane" hold to a "kind of
> homeostatic theory, very common in contemporary sociology,
> but certainly not beyond criticism. The critics of homeostatic
> theory say that although it makes sense of systems and stability
> in a society, it has trouble dealing with authentic change and
> newness. Some of its critics would even maintain that homeostatic
> social theory betrays a conservative ideological bias. It can be
> used to rationalize stability and *status quo*, to oppose change." [65]

It is the same Professor Cox who but a few years later would
observe in an interview for *Psychology Today* that religion's real
trouble is that it is not nonrational enough.

It's my conviction that conventional religion has declined not because of the advance of science or the spread of education or any of the reasons normally advanced for secularization. The reason is simple but hard to see because it is embedded in our local environment: the tight, bureaucratic and instrumental society—the only model we've known since the industrial revolution—renders us incapable of experiencing the nonrational dimensions of existence. The absurd, the inspiring, the uncanny, the awesome, the terrifying, the ecstatic—none of these fits into a production and efficiency-oriented society. They waste time, aren't dependable. When they appear we try to ban them by force or some brand-name therapy. Having systematically stunted the Dionysian side of the whole human, we assume that man is naturally just a reliable, plane-catching Apollonian.[66]

But Cox goes even further in the interview. The same man who in 1966 was accusing me of a "conservative ideological bias" because I argued for the persistence of myth now tells us (speaking of Émile Durkheim):

Oh, he took on very early the sociologists who wanted to get rid of religion. Religion is not a carry-over from the age of superstition, he pointed out, because religious symbols are essential. They unify the social group. Maybe the best behavior definition of religion is simply that it's the highest order of symbol system—the one by which other symbol systems and metaphors and myths and values of a culture are ultimately legitimatized. The clammy inanities of present church liturgy have no power to bring us together.[67]

Professor Cox, of course, is well within his rights to change his mind, though some observers would be excused for feeling some reservations about a commentator who so dramatically and completely changes his mind without even pausing to acknowledge the change. To criticize the churches in the early 1960's for being too mythical and in the later 1960's for not being mythical enough would, in a lesser man, be a contradiction and not merely a change.

Even though one carefully defines the meaning of the word

"myth," it is almost inevitable that when one speaks of it one's listeners will ask, "But are the myths true?" So steeped are we in positivism, so completely have our mythopoetic instincts been repressed by positivist education, that we simply don't seem to be able to grasp the point that of course the myths are true, not so much as videotape "instant replay" history, but rather as stories that purport to interpret the *meaning* that underlies the events of history. One suspects that in the final analysis only someone who has the capacity for enjoying, and perhaps even producing, poetry can grasp the reality of myths. Those of us who lack these talents must still face the fact that, in most situations, man has used interpretive stories to convey his view of what the universe is all about. Nor is there any reason to believe that, when all is said and done, contemporary man is very much different, even though he may have less intuitive understanding of both the nature and the message of myth. He who thinks that his work is done when he has established that myths are historically inaccurate according to the canons of modern scientific history simply fails to understand what religion is all about.

5. Religion and Community

IN THE PAST two or three years there has been a remarkable development of "communes." There are communes in Cambridge, Massachusetts, in the Big Sur, in New York City, in the South Shore district of Chicago, in New Mexico and Arizona, along the banks of the Colorado River, on the side of Mt. Shasta, and, of course, in Berkeley, California. Some of the communes are interested in rock music, others in Orthodox Jewish dietary laws. Some are radical New Left communes, others are communes of Jesuit seminarians. Some are extraordinarily idealistic, others are demonic, if not diabolic. Some are "into" drugs, others "into" uninhibited free sex. Some specialize in group dynamics, others in astrology, others in witchcraft. Some are interested in educational reform, others in destroying the Establishment, and still others in creating a new separatist society. Some expect the imminent end of the world, others are completely celibate, and still others vegetarian, or specialists in the mysticism of the Orient. Most aspire to some sort of participatory democracy, though practically all of them get deeply involved in interpersonal conflicts among their members. Some last only a few weeks or only a few days, others have lasted for years. Almost all in some way or another are in revolt against "the established society," and almost all in one way or another, explicitly or implicitly, are concerned with the religious and the sacred.

These communes are not filled with that sort of person who traditional sociology says should join such groups. They are not the uneducated, the poor, the socially rejected, or the failures. They are, quite the contrary, made up for the most part of the sons and daughters of the well-to-do, graduates of or at least students from the best colleges and universities in the land. By traditional standards they are not the off-scouring of society, but rather its elite. They are the ones that the conventional wisdom of pop sociology and the official models of "scientific" sociology would have considered the least likely to engage in religious or tribal experience. While to some extent their alienation may be explained by the disaster of the Vietnam war, the communal movement is too wide, too deep, and too steeped in its own frequently quasi-mystical ideology to be merely a reaction to the war.

The conventional wisdom is unequipped to explain the communal movement. It may mutter something about the alienation of the sons and daughters of the rich or a "counterculture" set up against a technological society. The conventional wisdom is simply at a loss to explain the profound religious atmosphere of most of the communes. However, if the communitarian development is viewed from the perspective being presented in this book, it is considerably less surprising; for in the perspective we have elaborated thus far, religion is assumed to have survived as one of the basic and primordial activities of the human organism, and the emergence of small religious communities, particularly in times of stress and crisis, is almost as old as religion itself.

There are two major traditions of the sociology of religion. The first, following Max Weber, stresses the meaning function of religion, while the second, following Émile Durkheim, stresses religion as community (and, conversely, community as religion). In the previous two chapters we have, following Clifford Geertz, who is by his own admission more of a Weberian than a Durkheimian, taken essentially Weber's perspective. But the two perspectives do not necessarily exclude one another. Indeed, as Professor Thomas Luckmann has shown in his *Invisible Religion*, they complement and reinforce one another. To understand the survival of religion as community and community as religion, therefore, we must turn to Durkheim and his school. For him religion has its source in man's perception of a power outside himself, both exercising constraint on him and providing him with reinforcement and support. This "power" is in fact the power of society. Religion, then, is society's consciousness of itself, a consciousness which is particularly manifest in what Durkheim calls the *représentations collectifs;* that is to say, those ritual actions in which the whole of a human community assemble to ratify, celebrate, and reinforce their unity. It is in the "collective effervescence" of such religious rituals that religion is born. In *The Elementary Forms of the Religious Life,* Durkheim defines religion as follows:

> The really religious beliefs are always common to a determined group, which makes profession of adhering to them and of practicing the rites connected with them. They are not merely received individually by all the members of this group; they are something belonging to the group, and they make its unity. The individuals which compose it feel themselves united to each other by the simple fact that they think in the same way in regard to the sacred and its relations with the profane world, and by the fact that they translate these common ideas into common practices, in what is called a Church. In all history, we do not find a single religion without a Church.[1]

Durkheim's analysis, done almost three-quarters of a century ago, was based on a study of the primitive tribes of Australia. A good deal of ink has been spilled on the subject since then, questioning both the accuracy of Durkheim's assumptions about the Australian society and the validity of the theoretical deductions he makes from these observations. It is not appropriate at this point for us to enter too deeply into the debate. It is sufficient to say that most analysts at the present time would not accept completely Durkheim's identification of religion with the collective consciousness of society, although practically everyone would acknowledge a deep debt to him for pointing out the profoundly social dimension of religion.

Durkheim's students and disciples have devoted considerable effort to analyzing the social "functions" of religion; that is to say, the role religion plays in holding a society together, enabling both the group and the individual to cope with the ordinary problems of everyday life as well as the extraordinary crises which befall both individual and community. The Anglo-Polish anthropologist Bronislaw Malinowski, for example, has carefully analyzed the role of religious ritual in reintegrating the human social group when it is faced with the ultimate problem of death.

> The death of a man or woman in a primitive group, con- sisting of a limited number of individuals, is an event of no mean importance. The nearest relatives and friends are dis- turbed to the depth of their emotional life. A small community bereft of a member, especially if he be important, is severely mutilated. The whole event breaks the normal course of life and shakes the moral foundations of society. The strong tendency . . . to give way to fear and horror, to abandon the corpse, to run away from the village, to destroy all the belongings of the dead one—all these impulses exist, and if given way to would be ex- tremely dangerous, disintegrating the group, destroying the ma- terial foundations of primitive culture. Death in a primitive society is, therefore, much more than the removal of a member. By setting in motion one part of the deep forces of the instinct of self-preservation, it threatens the very cohesion and solidarity of the group, and upon this depends the organization of that society, its tradition, and finally the whole culture. For if primitive man yielded always to the disintegrating impulses of his reaction to death, the continuity of tradition and the existence of material civilization would be made impossible.
>
> . . . religion, by sacralizing and thus standardizing the other set of impulses, bestows on man the gift of mental integrity. Exactly the same function it fulfills also with regard to the whole group. The ceremonial of death which ties the survivors to the body and rivets them to the place of death, the beliefs in the existence of the spirit, in its beneficent influences or malevolent intentions, in the duties of a series of commemorative or sacrificial ceremonies—in all this religion counteracts the

centrifugal forces of fear, dismay, demoralization, and provides the most powerful means of reintegration of the group's shaken solidarity and of the reestablishment of its morale.

In short, religion here assures the victory of tradition and culture over the mere negative response of thwarted instinct.[2]

More recent authors, however, such as Robert K. Merton, have pointed out that religion is at best ambivalent as a social integrator. At times it can hold society together, at other times it can tear it apart. Millenarian movements, for example, within a society can be utterly destructive of the social fabric. In the society where there are different religions, religious conflict can be dysfunctional for social unity. Once one gets beyond the relatively small human community, religion, while it still remains preeminently a social form of behavior, is not necessarily just social cement. Nevertheless, the integrative function of religion remains important, even in contemporary American society. Will Herberg, whose book *Protestant, Catholic, Jew* is a classic analysis of religion in the United States, points out with considerable persuasiveness how the overarching religion of "Americanism"— with its Protestant, Catholic, and Jewish components—provides a social consensus which is at the root of American unity, while at the same time the various components that make up this consensus provide for the members of the society a "self-definition," a "social location," in contrast with other groups within the larger society. Religion simultaneously integrates a pluralistic society and provides differentiation in location for individual members of this society. Religion, in Herberg's phrase, provides in the United States an answer to the question, "What are you?" According to Herberg, we will most likely answer by saying that we are a Protestant, or that we are a Catholic, or that we are a Jew.

It seems to me that a realistic appraisal of the values, ideas, and behavior of the American people leads to the conclusion that Americans, by and large, do have their "common religion" and that that "religion" is the system familiarly known as the Ameri-

can Way of Life. It is the American Way of Life that supplies
American society with an "overarching sense of unity" amid
conflict. It is the American Way of Life about which Americans
are admittedly and unashamedly "intolerant." It is the American
Way of Life that provides the framework in terms of which
the crucial values of American existence are couched. By every
realistic criterion the American Way of Life is the operative
faith of the American people.[3]

Nor is this American Way of Life religion merely a common
denominator which takes the least objectionable parts from all
the denominations and combines them. Rather, it is a religion in
itself.

It should be clear that what is being designated under the
American Way of Life is not the so-called "common denominator"
religion; it is not a synthetic system composed of beliefs to be
found in all or in a group of religions. It is an organic structure
of ideas, values, and beliefs that constitutes a faith common to
Americans and genuinely operative in their lives, a faith that
markedly influences, and is influenced by, the "official" religions
of American society. Sociologically, anthropologically, if one
please, it is the characteristic American religion, undergirding
American life and overreaching American society despite all in-
dubitable differences of region, section, culture and class.[4]

This American Way of Life religion pulled together in one
set of beliefs those qualities which Americans would claim are
basic to the political and social greatness of their republic:

If the American Way of Life had to be defined in one word,
"democracy" would undoubtedly be the word, but democracy
in a peculiarly American sense. On its political side it means
the Constitution; on its economic side, "free enterprise"; on its
social side, an equalitarianism which is not only compatible with
but indeed actually implies vigorous economic competition and
high mobility. Spiritually, the American Way of Life is best expressed in a certain kind of "idealism" which has come to be
recognized as characteristically American. It is a faith that has
its symbols and its rituals, its holidays and its liturgy, its saints

and its sancta; and it is a faith that every American, to the degree that he is an American, knows and understands.[5]

It is hard to quarrel with Herberg's astute observations. Like all official religions, in Herberg's view, the American Way of Life religion is designed to provide faith in the society of which the believer is a part and also to strengthen the society in confrontation with its enemies:

> In a more directly political sense, this religiosity very easily comes to serve as a spiritual reinforcement of national self-righteousness and a spiritual authentication of national self-will. Americans possess a passionate awareness of their power and of the justice of the cause in which it is employed. The temptation is therefore particularly strong to identify the American cause with the cause of God, and to convert our immense and undeniable moral superiority over Communist tyranny into pretensions to unqualified wisdom and virtue. In these circumstances, it would seem to be the office of prophetic religion to raise a word of warning against inordinate national pride and self-righteousness as bound to lead to moral confusion, political irresponsibility, and the darkening of counsel. But the contemporary religious mood is very far indeed from such prophetic transcendence. Aside from occasional pronouncements by a few theologians or theologically-minded clergymen, religion in America seems to possess little capacity for rising above the relativities and ambiguities of the national consciousness and bringing to bear the judgment of God upon the nation and its ways. The identification of religion with the national purpose is almost inevitable in a situation in which religion is so frequently felt to be a way of American "belonging." In its crudest form, this identification of religion with national purpose generates a kind of national messianism which sees it as the vocation of America to bring the American Way of Life, compounded almost equally of democracy and free enterprise, to every corner of the globe; in more mitigated versions, it sees God as the champion of America, endorsing American purposes, and sustaining American might. "The God of judgment has died." [6]

One can subscribe to the general accuracy of Herberg's analysis without having to accept the strongly pejorative tone of the analysis. For what we propose to argue in this chapter is that religion is necessarily a social activity and always has been; that it provides a man with a community to belong to and always has. Herberg and others like him who insist that the Jewish and Christian religions are prophetic religions which stir men out of their complacency instead of reassuring them in it will have to acknowledge, I very much fear, that a religion can do this only when it has first provided a man with a social ground on which to stand and with a communal center out of which to operate.

Let us first be clear about what we mean by community.

> By community I mean something that goes far beyond mere local community. The word, as we find it in much nineteenth- and twentieth-century thought encompasses all forms of relationship which are characterized by a high degree of personal intimacy, emotional depth, moral commitment, social cohesion, and continuity in time. Community is founded on man conceived in his wholeness rather than in one or another of the roles, taken separately, that he may hold in a social order. It draws its psychological strength from levels of motivation deeper than those of mere volition or interest, and it achieves its fulfillment in a submergence of individual will that is not possible in unions of mere convenience or rational assent. Community is a fusion of feeling and thought, of tradition and commitment, of membership and volition. It may be found in, or be given symbolic expression by, locality, religion, nation, race, occupation, or crusade. Its archetype, both historically and symbolically, is the family, and in almost every type of genuine community the nomenclature of family is prominent. Fundamental to the strength of the bond of community is the real or imagined antithesis formed in the same social setting by the noncommunal relations of competition or conflict, utility or contractual assent. These, by their relative impersonality and anonymity, highlight the close personal ties of community.[7]

Religion, we propose to argue, is learned and exercised within a community and is also a "natural" focus for man around which man organizes his communities. We are most likely to join in intimate relationships with those who share the same interpretive schemes, culture systems, and mythologies that we do.

Professor Thomas Luckmann provides us with the tools to continue the analysis. In his view, religion emerges precisely in the instant that the individual in the midst of the social processes experiences himself as distinct from and over against others. The depth of experience, he contends, "considered in isolation is restricted to mere actuality and is void of meaning." [8] Meaning comes only from interpretive acts. "The meaning of experience depends, strictly speaking, on one's 'stopping and thinking.' . . . The interpretive scheme is necessarily distinct from ongoing experience." [9]

One acquires meaning only when one is engaged consciously and explicitly in social interaction, only when "participation involves interpretation." Man transcends his biological nature and becomes fully human when he interprets. He interprets only when involvement with others requires interpretation. It is precisely the experience of others as his partners in interaction that demands of man that he begin to evolve a meaning system. As Luckmann sums up the process:

> Detachment from immediate experience originates in the confrontation with fellow men in the face-to-face situation. It leads to the individuation of consciousness and permits the construction of interpretive schemes, ultimately, of systems of meaning. Detachment from immediate experience finds its complement in the integration of past, present and future into a socially defined, morally relevant biography. This integration develops in continuous social relations and leads to the formation of conscience. The individuation of the two complementary aspects of Self occurs in social processes. The organism—in isolation nothing but a separate pole of "meaningless" subjective processes—becomes a Self by embarking with others upon the construction of an "objective" and moral universe of meaning. Thereby the organism transcends its biological nature.[10]

But of course one does not acquire an interpretive scheme *ex nihilo*. We do not at some point in our life sit down and say in effect, "My God, there are others around here. What in the world do they mean? As a matter of fact, what in the world do *I* mean?" And then go on to evolve in splendid isolation an interpretation to explain the astonishing phenomenon of others to ourself. We tend, rather, to inherit our culture systems as part of a society, a nation, a religious group, an ethnic group, and a social class. We fashion our interpretive scheme as part of the process of growing up, in other words, through the socialization experience.

> Empirically, human organisms do not construct "objective" and moral universes of meaning from scratch—they are born into them. This means that human organisms normally transcend their biological nature by internalizing a historically given universe of meaning, rather than by constructing universes of meaning. This implies, further, that a human organism does not confront other human organisms; it confronts Selves. While we so far described the formal structure only of the social processes in which a Self emerges, we must now add that these processes are always filled with "content." To put it differently, the human organism becomes a Self in concrete processes of socialization. These processes exhibit the formal structure previously described *and* mediate, empirically, a historical social order. We suggested before that the transcendence of biological nature by human organisms is a fundamentally religious process. We may now continue by saying that socialization, as the concrete process in which such transcendence is achieved, is fundamentally religious. It rests on the universal anthropological condition of religion, individuation of consciousness and conscience in social processes, and is actualized in the internalization of the configuration of meaning underlying a historical social order. We shall call this configuration of meaning a world view.[11]

This interpretive scheme or world view, then, antedates our arrival on the scene, but is integrated into our personalities in the most intimate maturational processes. We learn the world view rather as we learn the language, and this explains why it is so difficult to change or transcend it; also, in fact, why religion is so persistent in human society. It is one of the first things men learn, and, equally, one of the first things they pass on to their children. Religious fixity is rooted in the socialization process, particularly insofar as the socialization process provides ultimate meaning for others and for Self. We cannot, in Luckmann's view of things, transcend our biological natures without acquiring some sort of religious perspective.

> We may say, in sum, that the historical priority of a world view provides the empirical basis for the "successful" transcendence of biological nature by human organisms, detaching the latter from their immediate life context and integrating them, as persons, into the context of a tradition of meaning. We may conclude, therefore, that the world view, as an "objective" and historical social reality, performs an essentially religious function and define it as an *elementary social form of religion*. This social form is universal in human society.[12]

There are disadvantages, of course, in absorbing the world view the way we absorb our language. But as Luckmann makes clear there are also advantages. We do not, as it were, start from scratch. Even those youths who believe they are going to rebuild society *ab ovo* are, in fact, doing so in terms of an interpretive scheme which is very much part of the Western tradition that produced them.

> Instead of constructing a rudimentary system of meaning the individual draws upon a reservoir of significance. The world view, as the result of universe-constructing activities of successive generations, is immeasurably richer and more differentiated than the interpretive schemes that could be developed from scratch by individuals. Its stability, as a socially objectivated reality, is immeasurably greater than that of individual streams of consciousness. The world view, as a transcendent moral universe, has an obligatory character that could not be approximated in the immediate context of social relations.[13]

I remember being on a panel with a very courteous college student discussing the problems of student life. He was courteous but obviously with an effort, because it was clear that beneath the veneer of politeness there burned radical passions. Finally, he burst forth, "I don't see how you can expect young people to accept anything from the past. There are yellow men being murdered in Vietnam, and there are black men being oppressed in the streets of the city. That is the world that your past has produced. Why should we accept it at all?"

The question is so common—and the conventional wisdom on which it is based so pervasive—that no one in the room seemed to be particularly surprised; and I suppose that no one in the room understood what I was talking about when I replied that there were two important moral assumptions that the young man was making:

1. Thou shalt not make aggressive warfare on weaker peoples.
2. Thou shalt not oppress men because they have different-colored skins.

I observed that neither of these two moral propositions was self-evident; that indeed in most societies they would be categorically rejected, and that young men my colleague's age in other societies would have thought it highest virtue to engage in aggressive warfare against weaker people and to oppress those whose skin color was different. The only reason this young man quite properly (at least in my frame of reference) accepted those two moral propositions as self-evident was that he stood on the shoulders of predecessors who had developed such ethical principles over several thousand years, a development which was arduous and which, be it confessed, may not be irreversible. His predecessors may not have provided the young man with many models for implementing such moral propositions, but they at least provided him with the propositions, and that was no small feat. Whether he and his peers will be able to broaden those propositions and develop better models to implement them is a question which only the history books of the future will be able to answer definitively. For the young man and his peers to assume that they will succeed because of some inherent moral superiority which their youth bestows upon them is self-deception of the most childish sort.

We acquire our interpretive schemes, therefore, in a process which is social in two ways. An interpretive scheme is required by the fact that we become conscious of interacting with others; and it is provided by the others with whom we interact: our family, our friends, those who inhabit our immediate environment, and, standing behind them, those who formulated the cultural system which we inherit.

But more must be said than that. Our religion is not merely acquired as the result of a social process. It also serves as the basis for continued social processes. In most societies that the world has known, interaction occurred only with those who shared one's interpretive scheme. Others were simply not available—in all likelihood not available physically, but even if they were, not available psychologically. As a pastor in the west of Ireland once remarked to me, "Sure, I'm all for the ecumenical movement. The only trouble is, in my country there's no one to 'ecumen' with."

However, in corporate industrial society we do interact, particularly in our more gesellschaft relationships, with those whose world view is more or less different from our own. The proponents of the conventional wisdom allege that such interaction weakens man's religious commitment, "secularizes" him, and leads to religious crisis and decline. Such assertions, however, are based more on a priori notions about the social evolutionary process and about how things *ought* to be than any empirical data on how things really are. Several years ago Harold Walenski published two articles in *The American Sociological Review* which purported to show that those most involved in the corporate structures were also most likely to marry outside their own religious denomination. Without raising any questions as to which way the direction of causality in such situations might go, one simply is forced to comment that Professor Walenski's differences were only a couple of percentage points, based on tiny numbers of respondents (as I remember, seven in one cell), and generally not very convincing even to himself. If this is the best data that can be advanced in support of the notion that religious conviction is no longer important as a norm for choosing one's intimate role opposites (and I am unaware of any more convincing data), then it must be said that the conventional wisdom is extremely weak in empirical support.

Indeed, recent data collected in the National Opinion Research Center merely confirms the importance of religion in the choice of one's spouse.

Most research done on religious intermarriage lumps all Protestant denominations together, if only because it requires very large samples to make possible the distribution of Protestants into the various denominations. The evidence in these studies seems to indicate that Jews are the least likely to marry members of other faiths, Catholics most likely, and Protestants somewhere in between. However, the release of the tabulations of the 1957 Current Population Survey of Religion enables us to determine rates of religious intermarriage for a number of the Protestant denominations. The first row in table 1 provides the rather striking information that approximately four-fifths of the members of each of the four Protestant denominations are married to people whose present religious affiliation is the same as their own. Not only are Protestants married to other Protestants, as previous studies have shown, but they are married to Protestants who share the same denominational affiliation. And the ratio of mixed marriages *does not vary much across denominational lines.*

The 1957 census data contained information for the whole population. If there had been some decline in homogeneity of denominational affiliation, one would expect to find evidence of it among the young and the better educated. Furthermore, one would expect that the data gathered after 1957 would show such a change.

In 1968, eleven years after the national census of religion, NORC collected data on original and present religious denominations of both the respondent and spouse, as part of its ongoing study of June 1961 college graduates. The second row in table 1 shows the proportions of the major denominations who are presently married to spouses who share the same religious affiliation.

TABLE 1

DENOMINATIONAL INTERMARRIAGE (Per cent)

Denominational Intermarriage	Catholic	Baptist	Lutheran	Methodist	Presby-terian	Jewish
Proportion of U.S. population married to member of same denomination in 1957	88	83	81	81	81	94
Proportion of 1961 alumni married to member of same denomination in 1968	86	84	83	86	78	97
Number of cases	(1,130)	(355)	(354)	(712)	(402)	(353)
Proportion of alumni in which marriage took place between two people whose original denomination was the same and who currently belong to that denomination	75	35	34	30	15	94
Proportion of alumni whose original denomination has remained unchanged and whose spouse has converted to that denomination	11	14	22	16	15	2

There is virtually no difference between the endogamy ratios for young college alumni in 1968 and the general population in 1957. The tendency to seek denominational homogeneity in marriage does not seem to have weakened in the slightest.

The first two rows in the table represent data indicating present denominational affiliation of both respondent and spouse, but they do not tell us whether the denominational homogeneity in marriage has been attained by marrying within one's own denomination, or by substantial conversions at the time of marriage (or at least in relation to the marriage). However, the third row in table 1 shows the proportion of respondents who married a spouse whose original religious denomination was the same as their own, with both now practicing that religion. It becomes clear that denominational homogeneity is maintained by Catholics and Jews through the process of marrying within one's own denominational boundaries, whereas it is maintained by other religious groups largely through considerable shifting of denominational affiliations. For Catholics and Jews it is important that one marry within one's own denomination (and far more important for Jews than for Catholics). When Catholics marry into other denominations, the non-Catholic is likely to convert. Protestants may marry across denominational lines, but then denominational change occurs in order to maintain religious homogeneity in the family environment.

It also appears from the fourth row in table 1 that those of Lutheran background are able to attract a considerable proportion of their non-Lutheran spouses to join their own Lutheran denomination; thus one-fifth of the Lutherans have married people who have converted to Lutheranism, but none of the other three major Protestant denominations seem to have any special relative strength in the game of denominational musical chairs that is required to maintain the family religious homogeneity.

We do not know, of course, whether the patterns of denominational change to maintain homogeneity observed in the college population is the same as the pattern in the more general population, since the 1957 census did not provide information about original denominational affiliation. However, further research on the subject is clearly indicated.

In summary, then, one may say that America is still very much a denominational society to the extent that denominational homogeneity in marriage exists for at least three-quarters of the major religious denominations.[14]

Thus, when it comes to choosing one's marriage partner one obviously is very likely to choose one's "own kind of people." But it is not merely a marriage partner that comes from one's own religious denomination; 75 per cent of the Catholics and 75 per cent of the Protestants in another NORC sample reported that their three best friends were of the same religion as they. The practice of law, medicine, and dentistry in our large cities still tends to be organized very much along denominational lines. Neighborhoods within cities tend to have heavy proportions of members of one or the other of the three major religious groups. Voting patterns differ greatly among the three principal groups (and among the many smaller denominations, too, for that matter). While the United States is not as much a denominational society as Holland, or Canada, or the north of Ireland, it is still a nation in which, insofar as it is possible, people would rather like to choose their interaction partners from within their own denominational membership. Indeed, in one well-to-do suburban community I studied, the local country club, neatly divided in half between Protestant and Catholic, implicitly and perhaps unconsciously preserved religious segregation even on the golf links where Catholics chose other Catholics over Protestants as golf partners by a ratio of seven to one (and, of course, Protestants chose other Protestants by the same ratio).

The purveyor of the conventional wisdom who believes that in an enlightened society religion would be unimportant laments such diversity. What he forgets, of course, is that society is structured not by everyone being like everyone else but rather by people finding community in the midst of diversity, or even as Lévi-Strauss has pointed out in his study of the primitive totems, by being able to integrate commonality and diversity. Religious pluralism provides richness, structure, and strength for a society, although it may lead to conflict and violence (as in the north of Ireland). Such a result is not inevitable, but rather comes from historical and social situations which could turn a source of strength into a source of violent conflict. Men choose to identify with their religion, as Will Herberg has wisely pointed out, because they must identify with something, and religion is one of the most intimate and personal things they have. A religious collectivity is a "natural" for human solidarity.

It is generally assumed in pop sociology that the number of community-like relationships available to modern man is considerably less than what was available to his ancestors. We are told that ours is an impersonal, or a dehumanized, or even a "mass" society. The nostalgia for the old village commune is powerful, particularly for the romantic social critics who, generally speaking, would be happier in any country but our own, any society but our own, and in any time but our own—or at least who think they would be. However, the research tradition discussed in Chapter 2 makes this contention somewhat dubious. The number of gemeinschaft relationships probably has not declined since our peasant grandparents left their villages in Europe. It is altogether possible that the quality of these relationships has improved. On balance, one would be inclined to suspect that the quality of the relationship between husband and wife is better than it was in the village commune. In addition, there is a good deal more room for creativity, spontaneity, privacy, and individuality in the gemeinschaft relationships of family and friendship group now than there was one hundred and fifty years ago —or at least a persuasive case could be made for such an improvement.

If we abandon a priori theories and look at the historical facts we will see that amid the severe personal and social dislocations of the immigration process, our parents, grandparents, and great-grandparents strove mightily to keep alive as best they could the gemeinschaft relationships of their villages. One moved to a neighborhood in New York, or Chicago, or Boston where one's friends from the old village had moved. In the time immediately after the Second World War, blocks on the East Side of Manhattan could readily be labeled with the name of the Sicilian or Neapolitan village from which its inhabitants had come. The ethnic groups were for the most part products not of the Old World but of the New. In the Old World society we were Neapolitans, or Sicilians, or Florentines, or Kerry men, or Cork men, or Mayo men, or Galicians, or Bohemians, or Croats, or Trondheimers. We became Czechoslovaks, Yugoslavs, Irish, Italians, Norwegians only when such ethnic groups became obvious means of social support and political power in the New World.

The difference between the folk society and the urban society is not so much that gemeinschaft has gone away, but rather that substantial segments of human life must be spent in the world where only a part of the human personality can be involved and where one is to be respected and approved not because of who one is but because of what one does. The achievement-oriented gesellschaft society does not replace gemeinschaft relationships for most of us but simply adds a new level of relationships which did not previously exist.

Even in the world of achievement and production gemeinschaft operates in two fashions: (1) We seek to break down formal, impersonal, official organizational charts to establish informal, casual friendship groups where we can relate to our colleagues as human beings and not merely as occupants of occupational roles. (2) We also seek out our own kind, unconsciously perhaps, but none the less effectively. It is no accident, for example (though neither is it a conspiracy), that in one major airline seven of the nine company lawyers are Irish Catholics. Nor is it merely the result of legitimate self-defense against a hostile gentile society that many Jews choose to go into business with one another. Finally, the survival of the Philadelphia aristocracy described by E. Digby Baltzell and the Bostonian society described by Cleveland Amory is not exclusively or even principally the result of conscious snobbery on the part of the Wasp elite. We associate with our own kind, even in the world of business, profession, and finance, whenever it is feasible to do so. No one should be surprised, for example, that during the few brief years we had an Irish President he surrounded himself with an "Irish Mafia." Surely John Kennedy was not likely to discriminate in favor of the Irish, but it is also quite clear that he felt more at ease with politicians who were "his kind of people."

Whence, then, the manic "quest for community" which is manifested in so many different ways in contemporary society, be it the homogeneous suburb, the hippie commune, or the nude marathon group? I would contend that there are basic causes for the quest for community, and the most powerful is the fact that there is inevitable stress and strain between gemeinschaft relationships and gesellschaft relationships. The strain which is most immediately obvious, for example, is the tension the business executive feels between the demands of the corporate life and the demands of his wife and children. Make no mistake about it, the world of business, profession, or the research center is an exciting, stimulating world. It lacks the depth, the warmth, and the intimacy of family and friendship group, though in some sets of circumstances one is only too happy to be free from the rigorous demands of intimacy. But it also has more excitement, more sense of accomplishment and achievement, more challenge to the instrumental dimensions of the personality than does the gemeinschaft world. On the other hand, while it is not as impersonal and dehumanized as some social critics and novelists would have us believe, it is organized in such a way that the person can easily be thought of and come to think of himself as a collection of highly specific skills and not a full human being.

The quest for community, then, can mean a number of different but related things:

1. Man is seeking more intimacy in the midst of the gesellschaft society.*

* In my book *The Friendship Game* (Garden City, N.Y.: Doubleday, 1970), I have argued that it is likely that gesellschaft will only be able to operate effectively when there is more intimate community inside its structures.

2. Man is seeking for some way to harmonize the demands of his gemeinschaft life and his gesellschaft life—his private and his public life.

3. Man is seeking some sort of relief from the incredible strain and tension the public sphere imposes upon him.

4. Man (or, more likely, young man) is attempting to escape entirely from the gesellschaft life and limit his relationships to gemeinschaft ones.

5. Man is seeking intimacy in community simply because he has become aware that it is something to be sought and because he has been equipped with a set of intellectual categories and a vocabulary which enable him to facilitate such a search.

Once something becomes possible, man is rather inclined to do it. He seeks intimacy in community because Sigmund Freud and a host of psychologists after him have pointed out that this is both possible and desirable. As a matter of fact, the sort of personal intimacy which is both supportive and pervasive and at the same time free and open-ended, which very considerable numbers of people are seeking (most notably in the communes), is something quite new in human history. Many of the enthusiastic young communitarians could find plenty of community in the old neighborhoods in which their grandparents still live; but the community of the ethnic neighborhood, while relatively free as compared to the old peasant village, still imposes considerable restrictions on privacy and spontaneity. The difference between the commune and the old neighborhood is that the commune attempts to combine the intimacy of community with the freedom of personal, contracted commitment. The communes are an attempt to reestablish the tribe by a free contract; or, to be true to my own ethnic tradition, they are an attempt to reestablish the clan, no longer on the strength of bonds of blood and tradition, but solely on the bonds of personal commitment. It is an admirable effort. How successful it will be, particularly in these initial experimental manifestations, remains to be seen.

But it is not surprising that religion becomes an important part of such communitarian ventures, whether they be in the new one-class suburbs or among the youthful communes. Almost any intimate community man has ever known has been structured around a set of convictions about the nature of reality. In some of the utopian communities of nineteenth-century America, such as New Harmony or Brook Farm, these convictions were not explicitly religious; nevertheless, they very quickly took on religious and sacred value. To have intimate community without a shared world view is, humanly speaking, just about impossible. If one wants to rationalize or justify one's departure from the ordinary norms of human interaction—as do the new communitarians—then one must certainly appeal to some higher and more or less sacred interpretive scheme to justify one's deviation.

Herbert Gans, discussing the relationship between religion and community in Levittown, observes:

> The role of the community comes through clearly in the reasons Jews and Protestants give for increasing worship. Among the former, the search for friends, the need to have the children educated in Jewish ways, and the adult desire to be part of the Jewish subcommunity were mentioned in equal numbers. As one respondent summarized it, "To be honest, it's partly social. There is a moral responsibility to make a good synagogue and to have a Sunday school for the children, but it's also for affairs and activities." "Belonging" was the most important to former city dwellers, and in the words of one, "In New York, [religious observance] was only for the very old and the very religious. Here you get an identity and you flock to your own kind." While most Jews would eventually have joined a synagogue to educate their children, living among non-Jews hurried the process and produced an unintended effect of the move to Levittown. That the search is for ethnic cohesion rather than religiosity is brought out by the fact that none of the Jews with Christian spouses reported increased synagogue attendance.[15]

Gans's mistake, however, is in assuming that one can distinguish between "getting an identity" and "flocking to your own kind" and religion. The two, we are arguing in this chapter, are inseparable. That peculiar kind of snobbery characteristic of so many American commentators on religion that believes religion is serious only when it is isolated from all community involvement and relationship is simply at variance with everything we know about the history, psychology, and sociology of religion. As Clifford Geertz comments:

> This is not because religion is a disguised extension of common sense, . . . but because, like art, science, ideology, law, or history, it springs from a perception of the insufficiency of common-sense notions to do the very task to which they are dedicated: making sense out of experience. . . .[16]

Also:

> The notion that the demand for religious conformity can produce hypocrites but not believers is simply wrong. It is difficult to say whether more men have achieved faith because it was expected of them than have achieved it because they were internally driven toward it; and perhaps, as both factors are always involved to some degree, the question is pointless. But it would not do to adopt too much of an inner-compulsion view on the matter.[17]

The Protestants in Levittown also associate religion and community.

> Protestants stressed even more that "it's for the children's sake," and "to be a part of the community." They do not see the community as a group of fellow religionists, however, but as a place in which to settle down. One pointed out, "We are active in the community, so we should be active in the church too." A former tenant explained his failure to go to church before he moved to Levittown by saying, "Apartment living is not conducive to churchgoing; you are withdrawn into yourself, you don't do as many things." In fact, former apartment-dwelling Protestants in both samples increased their church attendance more than row house or single-family home occupants, and former city dwellers more than suburbanites. Among Phila-

delphia Protestants, but no others, higher church attendance was also associated with increased visiting, suggesting that the church helped integrate them into social life—or vice versa. Purely social motives for church attendance were rare, however, only 20 percent of Protestant friendships being made in church, as compared to 42 percent among Jews. My hunch is that Protestants who felt themselves part of the community were more active religiously and socially, whereas those left out of it were less active.[18]

While we agree with Gans's analysis, we once again must register dissent with the slightly pejorative implication. With Geertz we would comment that it is simply not true to say that religion which is associated with and reinforced by social pressures is not authentic religion. It is the only kind of religion that man has ever known. Religion, as we have stressed repeatedly in this chapter, is social behavior. It is learned socially, it is practiced socially, and it is one of the principal foci around which men organize their social collectivities.

There is a good deal of contempt in elite American society for middle-class religion, indeed, for the whole middle class. In a later chapter we will discuss this contempt as it is displayed by the clergy who are appointed, allegedly, to minister to that middle class. Studies exist to show the connection between religiousness and prejudice or anti-Semitism—although these studies conveniently overlook Gordon Allport's important distinction between intrinsic and extrinsic religiousness.* Other studies exist which show how frightened middle-class parishioners are when their homes and neighborhoods are threatened by members of other religious, ethnic, or racial groups.

One is tempted to ask the critics—themselves generally free from the threats of changing neighborhoods—what in the world

---

* The former is a religious orientation of the personality which opens one up in a pervasive way toward one's fellow men. The latter is a "closing in" kind of religiousness which serves to cope with neurotic personal insecurities. Those who are intrinsically religious are less prejudiced than anyone else, though the social researchers who are busy trying to demonstrate that middle-class religion is the same as prejudice and bigotry conveniently ignore (or are unaware of) Allport's distinction.

they would expect from people who find their homes and neighborhoods threatened. A grave injustice has been done for centuries to American blacks, but it is rather foolish to expect lower-
middle-class and middle-middle-class families cheerfully to pay
the price required for redressing this wrong, particularly when
the elite groups of society who insist that the wrong be redressed
are not themselves required to pay any price at all.

It is not my intention to defend bigotry, but I do propose to
defend any group of people from blanket indictments of bigotry,
whether they be black or white, red or brown, old or young, rich
or poor. Undoubtedly, there is bigotry in middle-class neighborhoods and middle-class congregations strongly identified with
middle-class religion; but not all members of middle-class congregations are bigots, and not all fears about threats to one's
home and neighborhood can simply be described as bigotry. Nor
is all religion that is intimately connected with home, family, and
neighborhood community to be written off as narrow and "unauthentic culture" despite all the snobbery in divinity school
faculties. The lower and middle classes may not know all the
theological distinctions, they may not subscribe to the *Christian
Century*, they may not have read the latest radical theology
books, but their devotion ought not to be dismissed out of hand
as worthless, or old-fashioned, or a manifestation of some earlier
phase of the evolutionary process. As difficult as it is for members
of the elite contemporary society to believe, there are many men
and women in American society who view their homes as an
extension of their own personality, and the neighborhood in both
its geographic and social dimensions as an extension of home
and family. Such vigorous loyalty to community is apparently to
be applauded when it is manifested by blacks or by young people
on the banks of the Colorado River but denounced when it is
manifested by the majority of middle Americans.

Nor is it at all surprising, given the fact that religion shapes
one's primordial world view and one's basic values, that religion
is called upon to reinforce and sacralize the intimate local community of which one is a part. Given the things we have said

about religion thus far, it would be astonishing if religion was not deeply involved with local community and personal identity in that community.

I am not saying that the clergy should cease to denounce bigotry, much less that they should cease to strive to achieve a just life for minority groups in American society; but I am arguing that, if they expect to be persuasive with their congregations, it will do no good to denounce them as unredeemed bigots, or to confuse bigotry with the investment of one's selfhood in home, family, neighborhood, and local religion. In Jewish and Christian traditions, at any rate, the local parish presumably ought to be a base for operations beyond its own boundaries. It is not likely to become so, not even for a small number of its members, unless the clergy are willing to put aside that proposition of the conventional wisdom which holds that gemeinschaft religion, tied to family and land, is an evolutionary anomaly. Those religious leaders, young or old, who are willing to try to understand the religious postures of their parishioners sympathetically and from the inside are the only ones who are likely to be able to lead the members of the religious community to perform effectively beyond the community limits. Unquestionably, many middle-class parishioners are benighted, but not because they are still involved in a religious style similar to that which marked our ancestors in the Paleolithic caves in southern France. Such a style seems to be part of the human condition wherever it is manifest: be it in the caves, the monastic communities of the desert, the Indian tribes of the Great Plains, among the friars of the Middle Ages; or in the communes of the Big Sur, the marathon sessions of Esalen, and the middle-class suburbs that ring our great metropolises. Man seeks community with his own kind, with those who share his own values and his own interpretation of the ultimate meaning of life. With this "band of brothers" he can organize space and time. Like the inhabitants of Eliade's peasant village, together they can strive to keep the forces of chaos outside the village, and occasionally even push them further back into the wilderness.

6. Religion and the Sacred

SOME YOUNG FRIENDS of mine who are deeply involved in the rock-music culture tell me about a recent addition to the countless small rock groups that entertain great dreams of some-day making it to the top just as the Beatles did. Each group must have some sort of gimmick to differentiate itself from other such groups—a sort of latter-day equivalent of the Beatles' long hair. The particular group about which my friends tell me is called The Coven; it purports to be composed of four warlocks (for the uninitiated, male witches). The members of The Coven live in an apartment of which all the walls are painted red. They go through the historically approved rituals of witchcraft and even claim the "power." However great their "power" is, they don't really seem to have made it to the big time quite yet, and they assure their devoted band of followers that, while they can indeed use the "power" for good or evil, they are very careful to use it only to help people and not hurt them. Perhaps this is why they haven't caught up yet with The Rolling Stones.

A young nun I know telephoned me one morning to say that she had had a horrendous experience. She confessed that in this age of Roman Catholic enlightenment she no longer took seri-ously the "myths" about devils or angels, but one of her students (a girl in her late teens) had descended upon the convent the previous night with a terrifying tale about being a witch. She rather enjoyed being a witch it turned out, because the ritual was

dramatic and "swinging," unlike the rather staid ritual of the
Roman Catholic Mass. She also enjoyed the "power" that being
a witch brought her. Nonetheless, she was terrified of the thought
that if she should die, her pact with the devil would send her
off to hell instantaneously. The young nun, who had given up
much of her belief in the supernatural, found herself in an awk-
ward position, particularly since her former student was quite
serious. She *really* believed in her malevolent powers and her
alliance with the Prince of Darkness.

Witchcraft is a big thing. One can walk into serious book-
stores and find whole shelves of books devoted to it, some very
ancient and others very new, some very serious and others quite
obviously potboilers. We can read, for example, from the British
scholar Margaret Murray that witchcraft is a survival of the
Celtic pre-Christian nature religions that flourished at one time
in the British Isles and which continued as the unofficial and
underground religion all through the Christian era. We are told
by Dr. Murray that even some of the most distinguished kings of
England and such lesser famous figures as the Black Prince were
in fact priests of the "old religion."

That there are some elements of Celtic religions in the contemporary witchcraft manuals may very well be true. Certainly
one need not suppose that all nature-religion symbols and practices were eliminated by Christianity. But it does seem more
likely that witchcraft as we now know it was composed in the
late Middle Ages and the Renaissance from a vast variety of different oriental and Western sources. However, despite what
theories one holds about the origins of witchcraft, there isn't
much doubt that for a small and apparently growing group of
people in the United States and Great Britain it has become a
religion—one that purports to bring them into intimate contact
with nature and to give them a share of nature's great "power."
The "old religion" is not made any less attractive by the assertion
that sex and the human body are "natural." In many covens,
therefore, everyone but the head witch or priest participates in

the ceremony in the nude, and the ritual initiations into the various levels of witchcraft include sexual gestures, which seem to be more homosexual than heterosexual; however, it is argued by some of the defenders of this new "old religion" that sexual gestures are ritualistic and symbolic and have nothing to do with physical orgasm.

I certainly would not want to argue that the apparent resurgence of witchcraft demonstrates that the sacred is still with us and not in decline. My only point is that the conventional wisdom is in no position to cope with the renewed interest in bizarre and esoteric forms of the sacred, whereas the model I am supporting would take it for granted that, if industrialized society attempts to ignore the sacred in substantial segments of men's lives, and if the churches listen to those divinity school professors who believe that contemporary man no longer needs or wants the sacred, then it is going to spring up in all sorts of odd and unexpected places. When professors of physics begin to argue seriously in favor of astrology, something is clearly very wrong with conventional wisdom.

The sacred is the intrusion of the transcendental—real or imagined—in our ordinary life. In perhaps the most famous book on the sacred, *Das Heilige,* Rudolph Otto describes our experience of the sacred as resulting from the contact with the "numinous," the "wholly other" (*ganz andere*). The "other" is perceived as not only *tremendum,* that is to say, awe-inspiring, but also *fascinans,* seductively fascinating. Faced with a reality whose majesty emanates an overwhelming superiority of power and at the same time reveals a perfect fullness of being, man finds himself simultaneously frightened and attracted. Something quite different from his usual experience has intruded itself into his life.

For Mircea Eliade the sacred is a hierophany, that is to say, an act by which "something sacred shows itself to us." It is not so much that we have sought out the sacred as that it seeks us out, or that we perchance stumble upon it.

From the most elementary hierophany—e.g., manifestation of the sacred in some ordinary object, a stone or a tree—to the supreme hierophany (which, for a Christian, is the incarnation of God in Jesus Christ) there is no solution of continuity. In each case we are confronted by the same mysterious act—the manifestation of something of a wholly different order, a reality that does not belong to our world, in objects that are an integral part of our natural "profane" world.[1]

But the sacred in Eliade's perspective is not merely the intrusion of a reality quite nonhomogeneous with our ordinary experience; it is an intrusion which precisely gives order to our ordinary experience. As he says of the relationship between sacred space and profane space:

It must be said at once that the religious experience of the nonhomogeneity of space is a primordial experience, homologizable to a founding of the world. It is not a matter of theoretical speculation, but of a primary religious experience that precedes all reflection on the world. For it is the break effected in space that allows the world to be constituted, because it reveals the fixed point, the central axis for all future orientation. When the sacred manifests itself in any hierophany, there is not only a break in the homogeneity of space; there is also revelation of an absolute reality, opposed to the nonreality of the vast surrounding expanse. The manifestation of the sacred ontologically founds the world. In the homogeneous and infinite expanse, in which no point of reference is possible and hence no *orientation* can be established, the hierophany reveals an absolute fixed point, a center.[2]

Scholars who have studied religious experience have collected a large number of accounts of dramatic hierophany. William James, in his classic work *The Varieties of Religious Experience*, cites the following story:

I remember the night, and almost the very spot on the hilltop, where my soul opened out, as it were, into the Infinite, and there was a rushing together of the two worlds, the inner and the outer. It was deep calling unto deep—the deep that my own struggle had opened up within being answered by the unfathomable deep without, reaching beyond the stars. I stood alone with Him who had made me, and all the beauty of the world, and love, and sorrow, and even temptation. I did not seek Him, but felt the perfect unison of my spirit with His. The ordinary sense of things around me faded. For the moment nothing but an ineffable joy and exaltation remained. It is impossible fully to describe the experience. It was like the effect of some great orchestra when all the separate notes have melted into one swelling harmony that leaves the listener conscious of nothing save that his soul is being wafted upwards, and almost bursting with its own emotion. The perfect stillness of the night was thrilled by a more solemn silence. The darkness held a presence that was all the more felt because it was not seen. I could not any more have doubted that *He* was there than that I was. Indeed, I felt myself to be, if possible, the less real of the two.[3]

And F. C. Happold, in his book *Mysticism,* quotes from the account of Dr. R. M. Bucke.

Like a flash there is presented to his consciousness a conception (a vision) of the meaning and drift of the universe. He does not come to believe merely; but he sees and knows that the cosmos, which to the self-conscious mind seems made up of dead matter, is in fact far otherwise—is in truth a living presence. He sees that the life which is in man is eternal . . . that the foundation principle of the world is what we call love. . . . Especially does he obtain such a conception of *the whole*—as makes the old attempts mentally to grasp the universe and its meaning petty and ridiculous.[4]

In both these stories, and they are typical of many, many others, the abstract descriptions of Otto and Eliade are dramatically confirmed. In the ecstatic experience one is simultaneously terrified and fascinated, but one also discovers the center, an ordering point around which the rest of one's life can be organized.

My colleague Professor Philip Ennis, in an interesting article on the sociology of ecstasy, shows that such distinguished scholars as Mannheim, Weber, and Freud all recognized the ecstatic experience.

> Mannheim: "It is that achieving from time to time a certain distance from his own situation and from the world [that] is one of the fundamental traits of man as a truly human being"; Weber: ". . . a state of possession, not action, and the individual is *not* a tool but a *vessel* of the divine"; and Freud: "A peculiar feeling . . . of something limitless, unbounded, something 'oceanic' . . ."—having all described the ecstatic experience even though admitting that they did not fully understand it.[5]

Ennis then goes on to describe the ecstatic experience by somewhat humorously suggesting that one could construct an ecstasy machine.

> In principle it is quite easy to make an ecstatic machine. You build, in an empty lot, a high circular fence with a small door. Inside the fence, there is either a deep well that goes down to nowhere or a high ladder that goes up to nowhere. The direction is a matter of taste. Then you let people in a few at a time—you can't let everyone in because someone has to watch the store. Before you let them down into the well or up onto the ladder, you tie a rope around their waist to make sure you can get them back. Since the capacity for ecstasy varies among individuals, as does their height and weight, people can climb down or up as far as they like to find their level of ecstatic satisfaction.
> This, in essence, is the architectural mode of the cathedral, the theatre, the lover's couch and the bottle. For separately and in various combinations, the institutions of religion, the arts, of love, and finally alcohol and other drugs have all been charged at one point or another in history with the mission of being the vehicle of legitimate ecstatic transcendence.[6]

Thus, there are many phenomena that can occur in a man's life that will take him out of himself by giving him the feeling

of release from the bonds of matter and mortality and of being
in touch with the *real*. By no means are all such experiences
religious. There does seem, however, to be a tendency to equate
many of them with religion; for example, the frequent use of
religious terms describing the effect of hallucinogenic drugs. Nor
do all forms of the sacred need to be so dramatically ecstatic.
Clifford Geertz's story of the Javanese toadstool (see Chapter 3,
p. 62) shows that the "other" can intervene in much less dramatic
ways.[7]

The totally "other," then, can stir man outside himself so that
he feels he is in direct contact with the real, or it can manifest
itself in an inexplicable and uninterpretive and apparently un-
interpretable way, though even in the latter instance, one suspects
that the awareness of something "strange" happening is disturbing enough to impel some kind of explanation. Geertz's Javanese,
for example, were sufficiently jolted out of the routine of their
everyday life that, until they found an explanation for the toadstool, it was difficult for them to return to work.

Edward Shils makes explicit what is implicit in Eliade and
Geertz:

> The sacred seems to be part of the condition. Ritual is a stereo-
> typed, symbolically concentrated expression of beliefs and senti-
> ments regarding ultimate things. It is a way of renewing contact
> with ultimate things, of bringing more vividly to the mind
> through symbolic performances certain centrally important proc-
> esses and norms. . . . the importance of ritual in any large
> society lies in its expression of an intended commitment to the
> serious element of existence, to the vital powers and norms
> which it is thought should guide the understanding and conduct
> of life. . . . As long as the category of the "serious" remains in
> human life, there will be a profound impulse to acknowledge
> and express an appreciation of the "seriousness" which puts the
> individual into contact with words and actions of symbolic
> import.[8]

Shils, perhaps going further than most sociologists would,
argues that the sense of the serious is man's religious impulse,

and is "given in the constitution of man in the same way that
cognitive powers are given or locomotive powers are given."
Shils asserts that this sense of the serious is unevenly distributed
and unevenly cultivated; some people have it almost all the time,
others have it intermittently, and a few are "utterly opaque to
the serious."

Shils leaves no doubt as to what he expects the future to be:

> To satisfy this universal need for contact with sacred values,
> for many persons the inheritance of religious beliefs with which
> our dominant rituals are associated will probably continue to
> serve. They have already shown much greater tenacity than
> nineteenth-century positivists and utilitarians assumed. The need
> for order, and for meaning in order, are too fundamental in
> man for the human race as a whole to allow itself to be bereft
> of the rich and elaborate scheme of metaphorical interpretation
> of existence which is made available by the great world religions.
> The spread of education and of scientific knowledge, as well
> as the improved level of material well-being, will not eradicate
> them unless those who have these religions in their charge lose
> their self-confidence because of the distrust the highly educated
> hold toward the inherited metaphors.
>
> The significance of authority is not going to diminish either,
> nor will the vicissitudes which endanger human life and which
> infringe on the foundations of morally meaningful order. As long
> as the biological organism of man passes through stages resem-
> bling those now known to us, there will be transitions from one
> stage to the next; each successive stage will require some sort
> of consecration to mark its seriousness. Nor will the spirits em-
> bodied in nuclear weapons ever allow themselves to be put
> back into Pandora's box. Mankind will never be able to forget
> the fact that the means for its very large-scale and almost in-
> stantaneous destruction exist and continue to exist. And with this
> will be attendant a sense of need to reaffirm the moral standards
> through which mankind might be protected from this monstrous
> danger.
>
> There will be a need for ritual because there is a need to
> reaffirm contact with the stratum of the "serious" in human ex-
> istence. But the question is whether a new type of ritual which
> expresses the same persistent preoccupations in a new symbolic

idiom will emerge. It is possible that the need for ritual will exist in varying degrees of intensity but that an acceptable ritual will not come into existence and become newly traditionalized, because, on the one hand, the system of beliefs that engendered the inherited ritual is no longer acceptable, and, on the other, the new beliefs about the "serious" will not find a widely acknowledged idiom or a custodianship intellectually, morally, and aesthetically capable of precipitating a new ritual.[9]

The caveman painted the walls of his cave and molded figurines of fertility goddesses in order that he might maintain contact with the basic forces that underpinned his own existence and the survival of his tribe in the life processes of the universe. His successors, who inscribed the mandalas on pottery or later built the observatory at Stonehenge, also believed that their activities were bringing them into contact with the really real, the awe-inspiring, the fascinating, and the ordering. Sometimes there was ecstasy in their activity, sometimes boredom, sometimes belief, sometimes skepticism. Some members of the tribe were much more interested in religious behavior than others, but some sort of contact with the real, with the totally other, was still considered necessary by most archaic men. In the modern world the absolute number of numinous objects may have declined, but as long as man has retained his capacity to be surprised by the strange and unexpected, to be frightened by the destructive, to be awed by the beautiful, and to be puzzled by the ultimate, he will experience a strong urge to establish and maintain contact with the really real. Some men may be able to exclude the sacred from their lives and even think that they represent the progressive features of mankind for being able to do so. How progressive they really are or how successful their attempts to dispense with the sacred will, however, be problematic.

Secular man, to the extent that he exists, may say that he no longer needs to experience the sacred, that he can maintain contact with himself, his community, and his world by purely rationalistic and scientific means. It is, then, not so surprising that witchcraft should be flourishing, that Buffy Sainte-Marie sings,

"God is alive, Magic is afoot," or that Donovan's stories about the
origins of the gods and the lost continent of Atlantis should be
so popular with young people. The sacred seems to be playing
the same function in the life of the new mystics that it traditionally has. It provides meaning and contact with the really real.
Furthermore, it provides the basis around which a community
can be constructed. The communes, rock music (particularly as
presented by such groups as the Jefferson Airplane, The Doors,
and The Grateful Dead), hallucinogenic drugs, the *I Ching*,
tarot cards, astrology, witchcraft, the Meher Baba cult, etc.,
are an attempt to reassert meaningful community in ecstasy in
a rationalistic hyperorganized world which had assumed, in keeping with the tenets of the conventional wisdom, that man could
dispense with all these elements.

The new—or resurgent old—religious forms of the youthful
counterculture attract great attention for a number of different
reasons. The mass media are fascinated by youth and in this
respect merely reflect the rest of American society. The secular
campus is the last place we would have expected superstition to
rear its head once again. The new religious forms among the
young are bizarre and outlandish—frequently, one suspects, deliberately so—but I do not propose to argue merely from the
resurgence of the exotically religious on the college campus that
the sacred is still with us. As in so many other respects, the
young frequently do little more than caricature that which exists
in the rest of society. Astrology was big business long before
students discovered it. A Dell paperback, for example, which
instructs one how to cast one's own horoscope has sold a million
copies a year for more than a decade. Pentecostalism may be the
most vital religious movement in the country. Faith healing is
big business, as the career of Oral Roberts shows so well.
Eschatological cults and sects were flourishing in the country
before the hippies moved to the Big Sur, and the private revelation "business" flourishes in the Roman Catholic church despite
the modernization of the Second Vatican Council. The Cardinal
Archbishop of St. Louis venerates the "Fatima Virgin," and the

Catholic Pentecostals "lay on hands" and "expel the devil." *
The conventional wisdom would write off such behavior as a
residue of the superstitious past, but it will also have to provide
a similar explanation for the ritual observance, less dramatic and
spectacular, be it admitted, of most Americans. Church attendance, baptism, marriage, funeral, confirmation—these are all part
and parcel of the American culture, however industrialized,
rationalized and secularized that culture has become. The purveyor of the conventional wisdom dismisses this as part of the
"private sphere" of life, as though it were something unimportant
to man and as though the pervasive attempt to maintain at least
intermittent contact with the numinous in the private sphere is
something that requires no scholarly explanation. The neosacred
manifestations on campus are but the tip—though a highly spectacular tip—of the iceberg.

We do not have at the present time any "hard" statistical
data on campus superstition. One wonders in passing why the
various agencies concerned with mental health have not been
interested in studying such phenomena; perhaps because the
conventional wisdom persuades the review boards of such agencies that the phenomena will soon go away. There can be no
doubt that part of the counterculture is a reaction to the Vietnam
war, nor can there be any doubt that some of its bizarre and
exotic nature is guerrilla theater—a put-on of adult society. I
asked one young man why in the age of the IBM 360 he used the
I Ching to make decisions. He responded by saying, "The 360
has immense power over me. It can determine whether I get
into graduate school, whether I'm drafted, whether I'm sent to
Vietnam, what kind of job I get; but it does not care at all
about me. I would like to think there is a power in the world
that is stronger than the 360 on which it and I depend and which
does care for me. I would also like to think that the *I Ching*
may be one way for me to come into contact with that power.

* Perhaps I should have advised the young nun mentioned at the
beginning of the chapter that she should have sent her witch to a Pente-
costal meeting.

Science really hasn't told us what life is all about. It was natural that we took it seriously for a century or so. It gave us all kinds of interesting new playthings, but now we realize that there are many problems it can't solve, and so we turn to other faiths to see if they can help us solve the problems." Yet another student observed, "I could die in my room at this university and it would be several days before anybody knew or cared whether I was dead; but if I belong to a religious community, all the other members of the community care, and we all believe that Someone else cares too."

Anyone who has dealt recently with college students realizes that such comments are typical and that the refusal of other students who may not be "into the sacred thing" to criticize it is also typical. The new sacred on campus may go away and it may not. What one thinks will happen depends, I suppose, on one's ideological or theoretical presuppositions. The neosacred ought to be carefully studied despite such presuppositions. But one cannot help observing that it has been a hell of a shock to the conventional wisdom; so much of a shock, in fact, that some of those who less than a decade ago were criticizing the churches for not being secular enough are now criticizing them for not being "turned on" enough, for not being as "sacred" as young people want them to be. It is an interesting paradox: when young people on the college campuses want the bizarrely sacred it becomes praiseworthy, when middle-aged people in middle-class suburbs want the somewhat more sedately sacred it must be condemned as unauthentic. Certainly to those of us who accept the perspective of Eliade, Geertz, Shils, and the other authors I have cited in this volume, it will seem that both the suburban Sunday congregation and the college witchcraft coven are looking for the same thing—some kind of contact with the "totally other."

An increasing number of theological commentators are beginning to recognize that something is going on in American culture. David L. Miller in his *Gods and Games* sees this as a turning toward a new frontier of play.

Thus in saying that play may be the root metaphor of an emergent mythology, we are implying that in America today we are forgetting the old frontier philosophy in which the emphasis was upon doing-centered activism. We may be witnessing a mythological revolution, turning toward a new frontier in which leisure, meditation, and contemplation are potentially dominant. Instead of work being our model for both work and play, play may be the model for both our games of leisure and our games of vocation. Play may be the mythology of a new frontier.[10]

This new culture is celebrated not cerebrated: "body seeing, body knowing: seeing with the whole body, with the wholeness of the body." [11] The new prophet is Norman O. Brown, who argues that man must be polymorphously perverse, that is, open to a wide variety of sensual feelings. Sam Keen concludes that if man loses his capacity for wonder—by which I take it he means his capacity to be in contact with the numinous—he ceases to be man.

Our judgment must be that the basic attitudes a person adopts toward the world are a more significant indication of his psychological and spiritual health than the specific symbols he uses to express these attitudes. Whether we continue to talk about God is not so important as whether we retain the sense of wonder which keeps us aware that ours is a holy place. Whether the language that gives us our primary orientation to what we consider the ultimate context of human existence is political, mythological, poetic, philosophical, or theological is not so important as the manner in which the language functions. Any contextual language must be judged by its ability to nurture those attitudes which are essential to authentic life: openness, availability, epistemological humility in the face of the mystery of being, and the ability to admire and be grateful. If we are not to fall into theological, ethical, or political idolatry, we must bear in mind that all symbols, concepts, theories, and myths are inadequate and crude efforts to domesticate a reality that eludes explanation. And if we must live in the anxiety of our vision and our gratitude, it is well to remember the words of Dag Hammarskjöld: "God does not die on the day when we cease to believe in a personal deity, but we die on the day when our lives cease to be illumined by the steady radiance, renewed daily, of a wonder, the source of which is beyond all reason." [12]

Robert E. Neale in his *In Praise of Play* [13] says that the worker—that is to say, the man who is so deeply involved in his career or profession that he cannot pull back from it—is incapable of worship and of religion; that only the "player," that is, the man who is open to experiencing reality through his affective and emotive faculties as well as his cognitive, is the man who can become religious. Only he who is nonserious (at least in the Western puritanical sense) can be ecstatic.

Orr and Nichelson in their book *The Radical Suburb* [14] contend that an "expressive" man—that is, the suburbanite whose life is organized around a quest for ever more expansive experience—is a true radical who is remaking the culture in American society.

And Professor Harvey Cox, perhaps doing penance for the strident secularism of *The Secular City,* has really become turned on; *Newsweek's* account of his celebration of Easter shows just how turned on.

By the Jewish calendar, it was Passover; by the Orthodox calendar, it was Easter. And by the reckoning of Harvard Divinity School Prof. Harvey Cox, this congruence of holy days last week was just the right time to test his theology of fantasy, festivity and celebration. "Theology has to do more than think," says Cox. "It needs a laboratory to help us find out how to relate our thoughts to concrete action."

Shortly after midnight, hundreds of students, hippies, straights, blacks, whites, artists and clergymen converged on "The Boston Tea Party," a discotheque in a converted warehouse huddled between Fenway Park and the Massachusetts Turnpike, to participate in Cox's liturgical experiment. To loosen up, some congregants painted wall posters, others scribbled graffiti: "Free Bobby Seale" and "The Third Rail Lives." A projector flashed images of Vietnam atrocities in an updated version of the Stations of the Cross. White-clad dancers from the Harvard

Divinity School mimed agony, while harsh background music boomed a dissonant Passion of Christ.

By 3 A.M., chains of dancers formed, swaying and lifting each other aloft. The crowd swelled to 1500 and a rock band called The Apocrypha played "I Can't Get No Satisfaction." Then Cox entered, dressed in white satin vestments trimmed in pink embroidery, followed by five other clerics costumed variously in Byzantine and psychedelic robes. The Baptist minister stepped forward to an altar laden with fruit, bread and wine to read the Gospel account of Christ's resurrection. And when he finished, the silence was suddenly burst by the deafening crash of Handel's "Hallelujah" chorus.

Using the highly politicized liturgy of the Berkeley Free Church, Cox intoned the "Kyrie Eleison" (Lord, have mercy), to which the crowd responded: "Right on!" Bread and wine were passed around and the congregants reacted by feeding each other. Bright balloons wafted to the low warehouse ceiling and incense sweetened the air. At 5:45, someone pointed to the patch of morning visible through the skylight and the entire crowd rushed outside, chanting, "Sun, sun, sun." "This isn't religion," complained an Irish cop assigned to enforce state laws against Sunday dances. "This is goddamned chaos." [15]

Newsweek quotes Cox as saying, "Anyone who doesn't see a great hunger for a spiritual revival these days is blind." And *Newsweek*'s witty religion editor adds the comment that Cox sounds something like his fellow Baptist Billy Graham.

In an article in *Playboy,* Professor Cox even suggests that what the resurrection of Jesus really symbolizes is Jesus' awakening to sexual desire—a notion which I am sure delighted both the editors and the readers of *Playboy.*

Play, celebration, experience, the senses, ecstasy, the non-rational—if not the irrational—these are elements of the new Dionysian culture which the so-called theologians of play see awakening in American society. The present writer has ambiguous and ambivalent feelings about the theologians of play. Such a dramatic shift in the theological fashion comes as a bit of a shock to one whose Roman Catholic background led him to believe that theologians ought to be concerned about preserving and interpreting the wisdom of the past rather than being in the avant-garde of the wisdom of the future. On the other hand, to discover that man is sense as well as reason, that he is sacred as well as secular, that religion appeals, if it appeals at all, to the whole man, and that ecstasy or at least the possibility of ecstasy is inherent in religious behavior is, or so it seems to me, to forsake the conventional wisdom for the traditional wisdom and to rediscover religious truths which were perfectly obvious to those who built the Gothic cathedrals or wrote the Reformation hymns. Professor Cox's pilgrimage from *The Secular City* to *The Feast of Fools* is, be it noted, a pilgrimage to a medieval feast; and if his liturgies sound like a strange combination of a Solemn High Mass of pre-Vatican II Catholicism and the Coptic liturgy of Africa, it may only be the result of the fact that when an American Baptist discovers liturgy for the first time he will respond to it as does a young person to a new toy.

Yet I have two very distinct problems with the theologians of play. The first is that I very much doubt that what they have uncovered is, to use Peter Berger's word, "resacralization." The only group in society which has notably been resacralized is the young—with whom the theologians, as do most other academics, strongly identify (for reasons best worked out between them and their psychiatrists). I contend, rather, that theologians have merely rediscovered a sacralization that has always existed, but which for ideological reasons they did not choose either to respect or to recognize. The eruption of the sacred on campus is merely one manifestation, though admittedly a fascinating one, of the quest for religious or mystical or ecstatic experience that has been part of the human condition for a long time. It may have disappeared from the secular university campus, but it never disappeared from the human condition. The theologians have recovered what their congregations always knew.

Second, in their swing from the Apollonian to the Dionysian the play theologians seem not to have been able to break out of the tragic world view of which both Apollo and Dionysus are components. For the sacred, as historians like Eliade and anthropologists like Geertz point out, is intimately linked with man's world view. An experience of the sacred orders the world because it not only provides a channel for man to come into contact with the really real, the numinous; it also enables him to share in the work of ordering a created reality. Religious moods have an "aura of unique factuality" precisely because these symbols attempt to deal with the ultimate nature of reality. The theologians of play exhort us, "Celebrate!" but they are rather less than clear about the nature of the world view which should lead to celebration. In other words, is the celebration in the play theology a Dionysian escape from reality's ultimate tragic nature or a Jewish and Christian response showing gratitude to a reality that is seen as ultimately benign? From denying that a world view was possible, fashionable theologians have moved to a position where they enthusiastically embrace the sacred without pausing to consider whether one need have a world view, an interpretive scheme, a culture system that underpins an involvement in the sacred. But then it is very difficult to remain a fashionable theologian, and some things are bound to be overlooked.

Man's experience of the sacred, then, is the response of his total personality to the really real, insofar as that really real is perceived as underpinning his meaning system. But this is to put the matter too disjunctively. Since his meaning system deals in some fashion with the totally other, with power that is both tremendous and fascinating, the meaning system itself *is* sacred and generates (if only intermittently for most men) an experience of the sacred—an experience which for a few is powerful and pervasive, and which for most others is both awe-inspiring and reassuring in critical occasions in their lives. I am not suggesting that for all men their meaning system generates an experience of the numinous, but I am saying that there is a strain in one's interpretive scheme toward an experience of the numinous; a strain which can be resisted in whole or in part, but a strain which is there just the same. By the very fact that we attempt to explain a reality which is beyond our everyday life and which underpins that life to give it meaning, we are venturing into an area dealing with something extraordinary, unusual, and powerful. We can keep our interpretive scheme so implicit that we need not worry about the numinous, or we can make it quite explicit and contend that it is absolutely no different from the common sense that regulates our everyday life. We can even persuade ourselves that knowledge and experience which transcend the essentially cognitive domain of common sense is a residue of the past. But for most men the ultimate interpretive scheme has meant something that transcends the everyday and goes beyond the limits of the cognitive, involving both mystical and orgiastic forms of ecstasy, frequently in strange combinations. The purveyors of the conventional wisdom would argue that "modern" man's capacity to eliminate both the mystical and the orgiastic atmosphere from his interpretive scheme is a sign of great progress. Professor Cox once seemed to agree, but now, apparently, he has changed his mind. My own position is that the orgiastic, the mystical, the contemplative, the boringly ritualistic, the intermittent ecstasy (at key times in life), and even the repression of the sacred are response patterns to the numinous that are as old as man's religion. The changes that occur, and there is no doubt that one change is occurring presently among the academic elite, are changes that affect only small proportions of the population, though these changes may be highly visible.

Professor Cox and his colleagues, frequently equipped with quotes from Joseph Campbell and other scholars, lament the fact that the symbols of the sacred available in the contemporary world have lost much of their force and their ability to "turn men on," by which, I take it, they mean their ability to bring men into contact with the numinous and the transcendent. I will not disagree with such a judgment, but I simply would observe that it is a judgment which is not new to our time. Indeed, the great religious reformers in ages past have all lamented the fact that symbols seemed to have lost their driving power, their ability to command conviction and commitment. Martin Luther was not the first Protestant, and one suspects that Harvey Cox will not be the last.

There is, of course, a difference in modern man's apprehension of sacred symbols. In an era when man has developed to a remarkable extent his passion for abstract thought and rationalistic organization, verbal or ritual symbols must be interpreted. Even the numinous must be explained after it has been experienced, though all the explanations in the world will not induce a hierophany. The final question which the defenders of the conventional wisdom could ask me is whether I am willing to accept the contention that a smaller proportion of men is predisposed toward numinous experience now than was in the past. My answer is that I don't know and neither do they. The assumption that the capacity for the numinous has declined is an a priori assumption based on a model of an evolutionary process that cannot be substantiated by any sort of convincing historical data. As Shils remarked in a passage cited earlier, some men have always had a more highly developed capacity for (and need of) the sacred than others. The little we know about archaic cultures and the projections we can make on the basis of the primitive cultures that anthropologists study today enable us to assume that not all primitive men were mystics and not all archaic men ecstatics. Clearly, our knowledge of historical societies justifies us in saying that the man with a highly developed sense of the numinous was a relative rarity in such societies—as he is a relative rarity today—and that those who have "ordinary" sensitivities to the numinous do not seem appreciably less numerous than they were in Greece, or Rome, or medieval or Renaissance Europe. But in the final analysis, if the question is unanswerable, it is also irrelevant. It may very well be that a sense of the sacred grows or expands as social conditions change, but that does not mean that there has been a steady evolutionary decline in man's capacity for the sacred. Even if the current campus superstitions are a passing phenomenon, even if the students' quest for meaning in ecstasy is merely a put-on of the square "Establishment" responsible for the Vietnam war, one would still have to say that in our highly rationalistic, technological, and scientific society the capacity for the sacred has managed to survive and even to come back to haunt some of those who but a few years ago celebrated its demise.

7. Religion and Sex

WRITING IN THE April 25, 1970, issue of *The Saturday Review,* marriage counselor Herbert A. Otto makes the following observation in his article "Has Monogamy Failed?"

> Never before in the history of Western civilization has the institution of marriage been under the searching scrutiny it is today. Never before have so many people questioned the cultural and theological heritage of monogamy—and set out in search of alternatives. The American family of the 1970s is entering an unprecedented era of change and transition, with a massive reappraisal of the family and its functioning in the offing.

Later on in the article Otto says, "There is no question that sex-role and parental rigidities are in the process of diminishing and new dimensions of flexibility are making their appearance in marriage and the family."

All this is patent nonsense. Otto is speaking of a tiny segment of American society. All the available data on the attitudes toward marriage and family in the general population indicate a remarkable permanency and persistence in attitude rather than dramatic changes of attitudes. If there was a sexual revolution at all in the United States it probably occurred in the 1920's and not in the 1970's. As we shall see in the concluding chapter, even the fabled generation gap is highly dubious. Robert Nisbet's comment cited in an earlier chapter, that while it may change in its manifestations, monogamy—like Ol' Man River—just keeps rolling along, is a far more accurate summation of the present situation than Otto's flamboyant rhetoric. Indeed, if anything, much of the sexual experimentation reported among young people on college campuses (be it noted, a minority of young people) is directed toward a far more serious form of monogamy than existed in the past. Most of those young people who have lived together before marriage are doing so not because they consider monogamous marriage less important but, rather, more important; so important, in fact, that one must determine compatibilty before one enters upon the enormous commitment of a monogamous marriage.

Otto's argument is based on the time-honored sociological fallacy of "the good old days." Just as the conventional wisdom about religion assumes that there was a time when men were more religious than they are today, with equal gratuitousness the conventional wisdom on marriage assumes that there was a time when chastity and fidelity in monogamous marriages were more popular than they are today. One wonders when that time was: in Puritan New England, whose ecclesiastical records recount seemingly endless trials for fornication and adultery? In England of the Restoration? The France of Louis xiv or xv? The papal court of the Borgias? Rome of the Popess Johanna? Reports of dramatic changes of sexual behavior catch headlines. Editorial writers in left-wing journals can rejoice about the amount of progress away from the benighted legalisms of the past, and editorial writers in right-wing journals can lament the corruption of national morality. All of this, one supposes, is wholesome sport so long as it is not mistaken for serious description of historical processes.

I do not assert that there has been no change in human sexuality in the past several thousand years, or that a change of religious viewpoint has not had a profound and indeed decisive effect on changing attitudes toward sexuality. But the change is rather different than the conventional wisdom would have us believe, and the present relationship between religion and sexuality may also be rather different than the conventional wisdom seems to assume.

Let us begin by acknowledging that this chapter is much more tentative and speculative than previous chapters. Religion is man's view of ultimate reality, a view learned in community and generating community, a view which demands the involvement of the whole man and thus embodies itself in myth and produces, in some form or other, a sense of the numinous or the transcendent. About this there can be little doubt. The conventional wisdom can only argue in response that man does not need an ultimate explanation; once it is conceded that he does, it seems to follow inevitably that such an ultimate explanation would generate community, myth, and the sacred—and, incidentally, that all of these would be enacted in ritual.

But while much has been written on the role of sexuality in the nature religions, rather less attention has been paid to the issue of whether it is possible for religion to avoid being deeply involved in human sexuality, and for sexuality to avoid having powerful religious overtones. As we shall see, all the nature religions of which we have any record were basically fertility cults. Even Judaism, which rose far above fertility cults, nevertheless had a strong fertility element within its beliefs and festivals. Generally speaking, as we shall note later in this chapter, the fertility dimension of the nature religions is explained by the fact that archaic peoples depended desperately on the workings of fertility in nature. If the flock did not reproduce, if the seeds did not grow into harvest, the community starved. It therefore followed that fertility would be considered inevitably a hierophany, a manifestation of numinous power. Man, conscious of the same power within himself, would not merely conclude that his own sexuality was sacred but that it was also intimately linked with the process of animal and plant fertility, and could even in some efficaciously symbolic way produce animal and plant fertility.*

It is also reasonable to argue that since sex is such a power-

---

* Apparently, intercourse between man and woman in a newly planted field has not even today completely disappeared in some rural societies.

ful force in human life, one's view of sexuality will be intimately linked to one's view of ultimate reality, and that therefore religion will shape attitudes toward sexuality (and vice versa) even after man has left the explicit fertility religions behind. However, there remains another possibility: sex may be sacred quite apart from the obvious sexual implications of the fertility cults found in nature religions. Sex, since it participates in the life-producing powers of the universe, may be numinous and hierophantic quite independently of whether man's primary mode of production is agriculture.

However, I am not aware of any careful investigation of the matter. Nevertheless, I think the case for the possibility is put extremely well by the theologian Langdon Gilkey:

> There can be little doubt that the concrete experience in which the power and wonder of existence and of life have most directly manifested themselves to mankind has been in the experience of birth, when through us and to us "being" originally appears. For this reason, fertility has always been one of the primary forms of the sacred in religion, manifesting as it does the unexpected, given, and essential power of life on which man absolutely depends, which he can in part direct, but which he can never originate or completely control by his own powers. This experience of an ultimate, awesome, and yet wondrous power of life on which every value depends is, then, the explanation for a whole range of religious phenomena extending from sexual and birth symbols and rites through vegetation and agricultural symbols and rites, to the universal importance of feminine deities. It also may help explain the strange and awesome power of women in human life.
>
> While postprimitive man knows he institutes the power of life in woman, nevertheless both sexes are deeply aware that it is in and through the woman's being, not in his, that the power of life waxes and appears in space and time. He can, to be sure, feel power *over* other objects from the outside through his finite strength and finite intelligence, and thus is the male sense of power more direct, obvious, but in the end always relative. Woman can feel directly within herself and so from within—and man knows this deeply—the ultimate power of

life by which all creatures come, working through and in her,
and thus in her experience of herself as mother, she enjoys a
closer touch with ultimacy of being, life, and power than he
can ever muster in his own ordinary and secular activities. Any
person who has witnessed the birth of a child has experienced
the wonder, terror, and ultimacy of that event, the strange way
whereby the woman may be said to become a medium or "symbol" of that power, the "place" in time and space where it manifests itself creatively, and a man's quite external relation to this
ultimate wonder. All the aspects of birth bespeak this experience of an ultimate power of life which works *in* and *through*
the mother, not *by* her: the intertwined exultation and pain, the
almost superhuman force that suddenly appears within her to
expel the babe, and the certitude with which every mother
asserts that this was the most wondrous, powerful, and meaningful experience of her life. It is no wonder that women feel such
a crisis for their own sense of reality and of meaning when
this capacity to transmit life, this intensely meaningful role as
a "vehicle" of a transcendent and sacral power, is taken from
them by incapacity or age. The serious impoverishment of the
modern spirit—as opposed to all previous historical *Geists*—
can be seen when we consider that this tremendous experience
of the power and wonder of life, celebrated in all ancient cultures, is almost unavailable to modern men. In modern maternity
hospitals, the woman is generally knocked out by anesthetics the
moment labor begins, the husband is forced by the anxieties
of the medical caste to remain outside, nervously poking butts
in the fathers' crummy waiting room; and the attendants, who
alone are witnesses of the "event," are inwardly technologists
and no witnesses, forced by the requirements of their tasks to
be aware of nothing but the practical medical problems involved
in the delivery. This is not to denigrate the wonders of modern
medicine in preserving both maternal and infant life. It is,
however, to bemoan the almost total absence of this experience
of the depths, power, and grandeur of the life we seek to preserve, an experience most directly present to us when in and
through *us* the wonder of creaturely being appears. In seeking
too desperately to "preserve" our life, and to keep it normal
and unruffled by the incursion of strange experiences and events,
we may easily lose all sense of its beauty and mystery, and so
all real touch with its value. In any case, in numerous experiences of self-affirmation and of joy, and in special "hierophanies"

of birth, our contingency manifests itself to us as a medium or
symbol of that which is sacred; or, to put it another way, it is
suddenly experienced against the horizon of ultimacy and infinity—at first as the creation of that infinity and then as the
medium or symbol of an ultimate being which works in us,
pulsates through us, and creatively realizes itself in our powers
and acts.[1]

If Gilkey's analysis is right—and I suspect it is—then sexuality is by its very nature sacred and by its very nature religious.
Let me once again insist that this is not to say that sex is a religious phenomenon for all men, or even that it has explicitly
and consciously religious overtones for most men at most times
of their lives; but I do suggest that for considerable numbers of
men in many moments of their lives, sexuality *is* religious, and
that an attempt to endow sex with religious meaning is inevitable
in the human condition. The effort to make sex religious and
religion sexual was very explicit in the archaic world. I would
argue that the effort continues, though at the present time it may
not be quite as successful as those who make it would wish.

The oldest examples of human sculpture we have are the female figurines of the Paleolithic caves. Such figurines can be
found in France and Spain, through central Europe and into
Siberia, and even in Alaskan caves. Thus, even before the rise of
agriculture, when man was still a hunting and food-gathering
creature, the woman's sexuality was seen as a hierophany. As
Joseph Campbell says:

human figures of larch and aspen wood are carved to this day
among the Siberian reindeer hunters—the Ostyaks, Yakuts, Goldi,
etc.—to represent the ancestral point of origin of the whole
people, and they are always female. The hut is entrusted to
the little figure when its occupants leave for the hunt; and
when they return they feed her with groats and fat, praying,
"Help us to keep healthy! Help us to kill much game!" "The
psychological background of the idea," Dr. Hančar suggests,
"derives from the feeling and recognition of woman, especially
during her periods of pregnancy, as the center and source of an

effective magical force." "And from the point of view of the history of thought," he then observes, "these Late Paleolithic Venus figurines come to us as the earliest detectable expression of that undying ritual idea which sees in Woman the embodiment of the beginning and continuance of life, as well as the symbol of the immortality of that earthly matter which is in itself without form, yet clothes all forms."

There can be no doubt that in the very earliest ages of human history the magical force and wonder of the female was no less a marvel than the universe itself; and this gave to woman a prodigious power, which it has been one of the chief concerns of the masculine part of the population to break, control, and employ to its own ends. It is, in fact, most remarkable how many primitive hunting races have the legend of a still more primitive age than their own, in which women were the sole possessors of the magical art.[2]

The evidence for the Paleolithic age is, of course, quite thin, and interpretations are based on what we know about the ages that came after. We know more about the early Neolithic times, and here, too, there is a strong suggestion that the female figurines had a religious significance. As Campbell says:

However, no one can speak with certainty of the social and religious place of woman in this period, for the meager evidence of the bones and coarse pottery shards reveals nothing of her lot. One has to read back, hypothetically, from the evidence of the following millennium (4500–3500 B.C.), when a multitude of female figurines appear among the potsherds. These suggest that the obvious analogy of woman's life-giving and nourishing powers with those of the earth must already have led man to associate fertile womanhood with the idea of the motherhood of nature. We have no writing from this preliterate age and no knowledge, consequently, of its myths or rites. It is therefore not unusual for extremely well-trained archaeologists to pretend that they cannot imagine what services the numerous female figurines might have rendered to the households for which they were designed. However, we know well enough what the services of such images were in the periods immediately following—and what they have remained to the present day. They give magical psychological aid to the women in childbirth and conception, stand in house shrines to receive daily prayers and to protect the occupants from physical as well as from spiritual danger, serve to support the mind in its meditations on the mystery of being, and, since they are frequently charming to behold, serve as ornaments in the pious home. They go forth with the farmer into his fields, protect the crops, protect the cattle in the barn. They are the guardians of children. They watch over the sailor at sea and the merchant on the road.[3]

By the time we get to the agricultural tribes and into the historic religions, it is beyond all doubt that we are dealing with fertility cults. So much does man depend upon the fertility of the fields that a religion without strong emphasis on fertility would make no sense at all. In his *Patterns in Comparative Religion*, Mircea Eliade observes:

It is not so long since the custom still prevailed in Eastern Prussia for a naked woman to go to the fields to sow peas. Among the Finns, women used to bring the first seed to the fields in a cloth worn during menstruation, in the shoe of a prostitute, or the stocking of a bastard, thus increasing the fertility of the grain through contact with things connected with persons characterized by a strong note of eroticism. The beetroots sown by a woman are sweet, those sown by a man, bitter. Among the Estonians, flax seed is always brought out to the fields by young girls. The Swedes allow flax to be sown only by women. Again, with the Germans, it is women, and particularly married and pregnant women, who sow the grain. The mystical connection between the fertility of the soil and the creative force of woman is one of the basic intuitions of what one may call "the agricultural mentality."

Clearly, if women can have such influence upon the plant world, ritual marriage and even collective orgy will, *a fortiori*, have the most excellent effects upon the fertility of the crops. . . . Finnish peasant women used to sprinkle the furrows before they were sown with a few drops of milk from their breasts. The custom may be interpreted in several ways: an offering to the dead, a magic way of changing a sterile field into a fertile one, or simply the influence of sympathy between a fruitful woman, a mother, and the sowing. Similarly, we may note, as more than simply a ritual of erotic magic, the role of ceremonial nakedness in the work of agriculture. In Finland and Estonia, they used sometimes to sow at night, naked, saying softly: "Lord, I am naked! Bless my flax!" The object is certainly to make the crop thrive, but also to protect it against the evil eye or the depredations of rabbits. (The sorcerer also goes naked when he is driving off spells and other scourges from the crops.) In Estonia the farmers guarantee a good harvest by doing their ploughing and harrowing naked. Hindu women, during a drought, go out naked and pull a plough through the fields. And also in connection with this erotic farming magic, we may note the fairly common custom of sprinkling the plough with water before its first ploughing of the year. Here the water does not only symbolize rain, but also has a seminal significance. In Germany the ploughmen are often sprinkled with water, and also in Finland and Estonia. An Indian text makes it clear that rain fills the same role here as does the semen in the relations between man and woman. And as agriculture became more developed, it tended to give man a more and more important role. If woman was identified with the soil, man felt himself to be one with the seeds which make it fertile. In Indian ritual grains of rice personified the sperm which made women fruitful.[4]

While the Jewish religion would develop far beyond the fertility cultists, it still had unmistakable fertility components. As Walter Harrelson points out in his *From Fertility Cult to Worship*, it could not have been otherwise.

In the ancient world the gods gave life and fertility. Practices in the acts of worship enabled the human partners to set forth and take part in the process by which the soil was made fertile again, after the long summer drought. The fertility of the flock as well could be portrayed in acts of worship. Each of these acts was a means of sharing the fecundity of the gods, reliving that primordial experience in heaven from which fertility derived.

The Israelites certainly gave large place in their thinking and in their worship to the motif of fertility. They were no less in need of means to ensure that the crops would provide food for the coming year than were other peoples. Israelite religion was also a religion of fertility; it had to be, or it would have been of no consequence for the people. If Yahweh did not provide the grain and oil and fruit, the people could not live.

The rivalry between Baal and Yahweh is amply testified to in our Old Testament literature. It will not suffice to say that the Israelites worshiped a god of history while the Canaanites worshiped a god of fertility. Yahweh was both the God of history and the God of fertility.[5]

Harrelson notes that the feast of the unleavened bread (at the time of the barley harvest), of weeks (at the time of the wheat harvest about seven weeks later—i.e., Pentecost), and the fruit festival in early fall were all nature festivals practiced by peasant people of Canaan long before Moses and Joshua. All three festivals became historicized and were celebrated as symbols of Yahweh's covenant with his people. But the covenants representing God's historical interventions did not eliminate the fertility motifs from the feasts however much the fertility theme may have been transmuted.

For the Israelites, these festivities were just as much occasions of joy as they were for their neighbors. And they did not merely remember God's historical deeds on such occasions. They praised God the creator of life, the giver of food, the provider for his people. They may indeed have had some way of tracing back to the story of creation the process by which the earth produced fruit. But if our literature can be relied upon to reflect general Israelite understanding, they could not go back beyond the act of divine creation of the world. This is to say, the growth and maturing of a barley crop were traceable to the divine goodness in making an earth that would yield grain, appointing rains to rain upon the earth and bring its powers to birth, holding plagues of locusts, blight, mildew, and other scourges of the grain at a distance so that the grain could come to harvest time unscathed. God was the giver of fertility, but Israel could not coerce fertility or even participate in the process through cultic acts. The task of man was radically secularized. Man was to till the soil, remove the rocks, and clear additional acreage. He was to fight the recalcitrant forces of nature in a world twisted by his own sin, wresting food from the earth. This was his part.

The rain came at God's behest; the earth produced because God had arranged in its creation that it should do so. All fruits of the soil, all fruit of the womb, were gifts of God—for Israel as much as for her neighbors. What was eliminated was the necessity or even the possibility for Israel—faithful Israel—to strike some bargain with God, to induce the earth to produce, or even to participate cultically in the earth's renewal.[6]

However, overt fertility rituals were removed from the Jewish religion and, as Harrelson points out, both the theologians and historians of ancient Israel tended to demythologize fertility by emphasizing that it, like all else, was subject to Yahweh's power.

The theologians of ancient Israel came to understand Yahweh to be the creator of all fertility, providing within the natural order for a continuing appearance of life. It was Yahweh who at the time of creation had provided plants that produced their own seed, and animals and men who could procreate. The mystery of fertility was not eliminated, but the ritual acts and mythological explanations of those acts were slowly demythologized and fertility was drained of much of its numinous power in this way. God's good earth teemed with the power to produce living plants. On this good earth, means were provided for the birth and sustenance of animals and men.

Fertility was related to the history of Yahweh's salvation also. The prophet Hosea depicted Israel as the bride of Yahweh, but this bridal imagery was connected with the covenant made between God and people (Hosea 2), a covenant once made in the wilderness and thenceforth binding upon all the people. The Deuteronomistic historian was bitter in his opposition to the practices associated with fertility (Deuteronomy 23:17–18). But this historian and the tradition out of which he came saw in Yahweh's promise of a good land, flowing with milk and honey, rich in all the goods that made life full and complete, clear indication of Yahweh's control over the powers of fertility. This historian too, in his way, demythologized the mystery of fertility, relating it directly to the promise of Yahweh made to the fore-fathers, a promise in process of fulfillment awaiting the End appointed by Yahweh when the entire earth would be transformed into a veritable paradise.

It must be admitted, however, that in later Judaism, once

the ritual practices associated with sacred prostitution, the sacred marriage of god and goddess, and other fertility rites had been eliminated, motifs deriving from fertility religion were permitted to stand within the ceremonies connected with the feast of Booths. The altar was decorated with willow branches; the people marched about the altar bearing other branches. Water was poured upon the altar as a drink offering (see Zechariah 14:17). It seems evident that ancient ritual acts from practices designed to enable worshipers to participate in God's renewal of the earth at the end of the summer have been preserved in certain post-biblical texts from the Talmud. But if such practices were observed in biblical times, the authors and collectors of traditions eliminated all such references from the Hebrew Bible.[7]

Nor are explicit fertility symbols absent from Christianity, though here too they have been demythologized, or to use a somewhat more appropriate word, "soft-pedaled." Still, in the Easter Vigil liturgy of the Roman Catholic church a lighted candle is plunged three times into the holy water; as obvious a symbol of sexual intercourse as one could possibly imagine. It has brought a certain secret joy to my heart to realize how many generations of Roman Catholic monsignors perform symbolic intercourse as part of the Solemn High Mass of Easter—at least it has amused me since I discovered what the Easter candle and the holy water represented, which was a number of years after I had been performing the ceremony myself. I am informed by Herman Schmidt, the distinguished Catholic liturgical scholar, that this fertility rite—and surely it is—is of very ancient origin in the Roman Catholic liturgy, dating probably to fourth-century Rome and almost certainly taken over from the pagan spring festival celebration there. The point, I suppose, is not that the present generation of Catholic clergy, as well as many generations before them, have not understood the obvious sexual imagery of the Easter candle and the holy water, but that those who inserted the ceremony into the liturgy most assuredly knew what it represented.

The nature religions (and presumably their Paleolithic and early Neolithic predecessors) surely considered sex a hierophany; it was a hierophany, like all manifestations of the sacred, both fascinating and terrifying. Woman possessed the power of life and therefore was to be venerated, but this power was a dangerous power and therefore woman was to be feared. One of the citations previously quoted from Joseph Campbell hinted at this fear of woman's fertility. It seems that much of the acts of ritual purification required of women who had given birth or who had completed a menstrual period was based not so much on the notion that sexuality was "obscene" but rather that a woman's sexuality was dangerous.[8] Herbert Richardson in his article "The Symbol of Virginity" notes that in many of the ancient nature religions family was essentially matrilineal and the society matriarchal. The *Männerbund*—the all-male group—was a man's escape from the power of woman and the matrilineal society.

The extreme anxiety before the sexual mana of the female experienced by men in the transition from a matrilineal to patriarchal society is seen in these laws prescribing extreme avoidance of her and hostility directed against her. The male is helped to make the transition to dominance over the female, to independence from the matrilineal family group, by membership in an alternative primary society—the all-male *Männerbund*. A *Männerbund* is a society of males bound together in fraternal loyalty by "spiritual blood ties" (e.g., "blood brotherhood") through their common endurance of an initiatory ordeal and a solemn covenanting together. The initiatory ordeal is also a *rite du passage* whereby the male is "spiritually reborn" into a new primary group which replaces, for him, the biological family. As a sign of his new condition, he often receives a new name, which signifies that his identity is established within the fraternity; hence he is independent from the mothers and female society in general.

In modern societies, boys still go through a *"Männerbund"* stage when, in their early teens, they transfer their identities from their biological family to some peer group, a transfer that even today involves the same type of avoidance and hostility against the mother that was found in the ancient Israelite "amphictyonies." In less evolved societies, however, the *Männerbund* is not simply a stage men go through prior to eventual

membership in an equalitarian heterosexual society, but is itself
the highest stage of social evolution. In such societies, males
live out their entire adult lives within a *Männerbund* and their
behavior conforms to its "covenanting" requirements of absolute
loyalty to the fraternal group as the bearer of all values and
meaning.[9]

Richardson insists that it is only when we understand that the
Jewish religion emerged at a time when the tribes were changing from matrilineal to patrilineal society that we can understand the fact that the "avoidance procedures" of Jewish law were
essentially an attempt on the part of the males to protect themselves from what they saw as the frightening and dominating
hierophantic power of women. Remaining virgin for a period of
time was essential in establishing man's independence of sexuality and an absolutely indispensable test required for admission
into the all-male group.

> We see that, whether in the radical patriarchalism of the Old
> Testament or in the more modified patriarchalism that emerged
> in the Greek world, the decisive institution effecting the transi-
> tion from matrilineal society is the puberty test of the male's
> competence in virginity, a competence in segmenting a sphere
> of voluntary behavior off from the sphere of instinctual bodily
> behavior. This segmenting competence developed by men al-
> lows the differentiation of a nonfamilial public space (governed
> by personal volition) from the private space of the family. In
> this way, sexual intercourse is not absolutely renounced, but
> confined to the internal life of the family group, to nonpublic
> times and places.[10]

But between the writing of the Old Testament and the writing of the New, mankind, according to Richardson, went through
a dramatic change: he entered into the "post-axial period," that is
to say, the period in which he became aware "of the existence
and power of the transcendent and unchanging over the cycle
of nature." It was in this shift, of course, that the great world
religions were born. Sexual abstinence of one sort or another

played a different role after that shift. One is not so much any longer worried about the sexual power woman has, but rather about the limitation the sexual human body imposes on the flowering and flourishing of the spirit. In Richardson's words:

> The *telos* of man is now no longer patriarchal rule over a family and the fathering of biological descendants who shall number a great clan—a notion that makes sex *essential* to human fulfill-ment. Rather, man's *telos* is now the *visio dei,* that "wisdom" whereby a man renounces desire for the pleasures of this world —including a family, sexual pleasure, and progeny of his loins. In this post-axial culture, the earlier *Männerbund* (which incul-cated that sense of male dominance of women necessary for a patriarchy) is replaced by the esoteric eschatological religious community (the philosophers' schools, the Essene sect, the Gnos-tic cult, the early Christian Koinonia, the monasteries).[11]

Through virginity man breaks away, not so much from a feared natural power but through a mortal world to a transcendent world.

> The exercises of this spiritual community help men to develop a sense of the unchanging transcendent world, to renounce alto-gether the world of the flesh and its mortality. Such a *renuncia-tion* of instinctual, bodily behavior is altogether different from the *segmentation* of this behavior from personal, voluntary ac-tivity that was inculcated by the *Männerbund.* Moreover, such a renunciation also implies that in post-axial cultures (where the *Männerbund* is replaced by the spiritual novitiate) the pri-macy of the family is also displaced. For a man's happiness and destiny are now seen to be functions of the religious community of saints—and the family, with its sexual functions, is ultimately incompatible with this. The spiritual community now becomes the primary human institution.[12]

But a second and more important shift in orientation occurred with the discovery of the transcendent. Friendship became possi-ble; possible, indeed, between two human beings who were seen as complete in themselves. Furthermore, this friendship, while

still in the Greek world limited to members of the same sex, did
not require the overt homosexuality which apparently was com-
monplace in the *Männerbund*.

> the ancient world conceived that a personal, voluntary "friend-
> ship" between a man and a woman was impossible; men and
> women were assumed to be different kinds of being. They could
> be related to each other *sexually*, therefore not by the moral
> communion of friendship, for friendship presupposes full equality
> and likeness of humanity in each of the persons united in this
> moral communion. Friendship is not the sexual completion of
> the humanity of one person by another as the two reform them-
> selves into the original androgyne ("one flesh"); rather, it is
> a moral communion between two beings, each of whom is
> hypothetically complete in himself because the fullness of man-
> hood is present in each individual person. The classical Chris-
> tian definition of a person shows this: a person is "an individual
> being with a rational nature."
>
> In terms of the pre-axial perspective, friendship was neces-
> sarily conceived to be a homosexual relation. And it was Socrates
> and the emerging philosophical school in Athens that overcame
> pre-axial sexuality by the institution of Platonic love, or "philo-
> sophical homosexuality." This philosophical homosexuality was
> completely different from the "ersatz heterosexuality" (sodomy)
> that always threatened to break out in the ancient *Männerbünde*
> during their test of abstinence from women—an "ersatz hetero-
> sexuality" which the Old Testament fiercely proscribes. Philo-
> sophical homosexuality was, rather, a new kind of *transsexual
> love*, one that presupposed that every man was not only a sexed
> body, but also a transsexual spirit. Such a spirit might be loved
> through the body, while abstaining from the love of the body
> itself.[13]

But *philia* friendship was quite unthinkable in Greece and Rome
between men and women. As Morton Hunt epigrammatically
puts it: "Men and women accepted sex as a human appetite, considered love a pastime and sometimes a torment, and viewed
marriage as an inescapable social duty." [14] But love—at least in
the sense of friendship—was limited to members of one's own sex.

In Christianity, friendship was possible between men and

women, though it was a nonsexual "spiritual love." Holy men
had women as their companions, and holy men and women engaged in the practice of syneisaktism, or spiritual marriage, in
which a couple lived in the same house, frequently in the same
room, and sometimes even in the same bed, and yet conducted
themselves as brothers and sisters. Richardson describes the
situation:

> Soon monasteries, some including the chaste cohabitation of men
> and women working and praying together, grew up as an in-
> stitutional response to the new understanding of a nonsexual,
> spiritual love. In such religious communities, there was full
> equality between men and women, and occasionally even the
> rule of a prioress over mixed houses. Intimations of such a de-
> velopment appear in the New Testament. Virginity, or the abso-
> lute renunciation of sexual intercourse by women, opened the
> way to this new kind of spiritual community and to the new
> kind of functional equality of men and women which it involved.[15]

The practice was not universally applauded by churchmen,
though it apparently survived through at least the first six centuries of Christianity. Tertullian and Hermas seemed to think it
was very praiseworthy, while men of less sanguine ilk, such as
Jerome, were quite upset about it. "From what source has this
plague of dearly beloved sisters found its way into the Church?
They live in the same house as their male friends, they occupy
the same room, often the same bed, yet they call us suspicious if
we think anything is wrong." And Cyprian, also a somewhat
truculent fellow, gives his opinion of the whole situation—and
thus provides us with interesting historical documentation.

> We have read, dearest brother, your letter which you sent
> to Paconius, our brother, asking and desiring us to write again
> to you and say what we thought of those virgins who, after hav-
> ing once determined to continue in that condition and firmly
> to maintain their continency, have afterwards been found to
> have remained in the same bed side by side with men (of whom
> you say that one is a deacon); and yet that the same virgins

declare that they are chaste. . . . We must interfere at once with such as these, that they may be separated while yet they can be separated in innocence, because by and by they will have become firmly joined by a guilty conscience. . . .

And do not let any of them think to defend herself by saying that she may be examined and proven a virgin, for both the hands and the eyes of the midwives are often deceived, and even if she be found to be a virgin in that particular in which a woman may be so, yet she may have sinned in some other part of her body which may be corrupted and yet cannot be examined. Assuredly the mere lying together, the mere embracing, the very talking together, and the act of kissing, and the disgraceful and foul slumber of two persons lying together, how much of dishonor and crime does it confess! [16]

The Irish—of all people—were apparently the last to give up the practice of the "co-ed monastery," or agapetism, as it was called. One old historical writer comments of the Irish, "They did not scorn to administer and live together with women, because being founded upon the rock they did not fear the wind of temptation." The legend is told about St. Brendan the Navigator (who everybody knows discovered America) chiding a certain holy man named Scuthin because he always slept in bed with two beautiful virgins. Scuthin, displaying the same reluctance to avoid an argument, challenged the sainted Navigator to prove his own virtue by attempting the same feat. Brendan did not turn away from the challenge, and, so the chronicler tells us, was able to maintain his virtue under the circumstances; however, he found it extremely difficult to get any sleep, and therefore cut short the experiment. Only in Ireland!

It is fashionable in contemporary commentaries on Christian sexual ethics to emphasize the negative views of Augustine and other early Church Fathers on sexual intercourse; but these negative views must be understood against the background of the world view of the time. The human body was viewed as a limitation on the human personality, and sex something so obviously corporeal as to be a serious limitation on the freedom and growth of the spirit. Friendship was only possible for those who could become fully human, and to be fully human they had to transcend their bodily passions. The Christian insight was the discovery that women were human too and could transcend the powerful physical force within themselves. In the Christian view of things women were as capable of friendship as were men.

> Following the first axial transition, the possibility of friendship between men and women emerged as a consequence of the discovery that all men possess a spiritual, transsexual soul, or personhood. We have seen, however, that the emergence of this male–female friendship required the renunciation of sexual intercourse—since this sexual behavior was still untransformed, i.e., it was instinctual and aggressive.[17]

In the nature religions women were to be avoided because they were "taboo," that is to say, filled with a sacred power that was both divine and demonic. In Greece, friendship between men became possible without the need for physical homosexuality; and among the Christians, friendship became possible between man and woman with both able to avoid the demonically numinous power of sex. Richardson observes, "The modern discovery that such instinctual behavior can be transformed and integrated within the personal order—a possibility emerging at the 'second axial transition'—opens the way to the integration of sex and friendship." Indeed it does, though that integration is as yet anything but complete. It ill behooves us, who stand rather unsteadily on the shoulders of our predecessors, to criticize them for their failure to have our insights, especially when our insights are still rather confused.

But between the modern effort to integrate sex, marriage, and friendship and the primitive Church there stands the fascinating period of romantic love in the late Middle Ages: a period in which men and women strove for friendship that was indeed sexual but still, in theory at least, quite above the "anomality" of sexual intercourse. Morton Hunt tells the incredible story of the *Minnesinger* Ulrich von Lichtenstein, who pursued his ladylove for fifteen years before winning her "favor." Ulrich engaged in

such activities as going on pilgrimages dressed as Venus or King
Arthur, engaging in numerous tournaments, writing passionate
and poetic love letters to his lady fair. Hunt describes one of
Ulrich's escapades:

> Having completed his epochal feat of love service, Ulrich
> waited for his reward, and at long last it came: the Princess
> sent word that he might visit her. Yet he was to expect no warm
> welcome; she specified that he must come in the disguise of a
> leper and take his place among lepers who would be visiting
> her to beg for alms. But of course this monstrous indignity fazed
> the faithful Ulrich not in the least; nor did he falter when she
> knowingly let him, disguised in his rags, spend that night in
> a ditch in the rain; nor was he outraged when the next night
> he was finally allowed to climb a rope up the castle wall to her
> chamber, only to find it lit by a hundred tapers and staffed by
> eight maids-in-waiting who hovered about her where she lay
> in bed. Though Ulrich pleaded urgently that they all be sent
> out, she continued to be coyly proper, and when she began to
> see that this patient fellow really was getting stubborn at last,
> she told him that to earn the favor he would have to prove his
> obedience by wading in a near-by lake. She herself assisted him
> out the window—and then, bending to kiss him, let loose the
> rope, tumbling Ulrich to the ground, or perhaps into a stinking
> moat. (It is well worth remembering at this point that this
> painful incident was not recorded by any enemy or satirist of
> Ulrich, but by himself, his purpose being to make clear the
> extent of his suffering for love and his fidelity in the face of
> trials.) [18]

What exactly was the reward that Ulrich received? He probably was permitted to kiss her, perhaps even to caress her, and
maybe even to engage in sex play with her while both of them
lay unclothed in bed; but intercourse was, in theory and apparently usually in practice, out of the question between such courtly
lovers, for that was "false love," which destroyed the true love
that men like Ulrich were seeking. Incidentally, Ulrich's friendship with his princess lasted two years, and then he was off in
pursuit of some other ladylove.

Hunt notes that in the midst of his pilgrimage through Europe dressed as Venus,

> he stopped off for three days to visit his wife and children. For the fact is that this lovesick Galahad, this kissless wonder, this dauntless knight-errant, had long had a wife to lie with when he had the urge, and a family to live with when he felt lonely. He himself speaks of his affection (but not his love) for his wife; to love her would have been improper and almost unthinkable. Like the other men of his class and time, Ulrich considered marriage a phase of feudal business-management, since it consisted basically of the joining of lands, the cementing of loyalties, and the production of heirs and future defenders. But the purifying, ennobling rapture of love for an ideal woman —what had that to do with details of crops and cattle, fleas and fireplaces, serfs and swamp drainage? Yet, though true love was impossible between husband and wife, without it a man was valueless. Ulrich could therefore unashamedly visit his wife during his grand tour, proud of what he had been doing and certain that if she knew of it, she too was proud, because *Frauendienst* made her husband nobler and finer.[19]

It is easy for us in the security of our post-Freudian vantage point to dismiss all of this as sick, but to do so would once again miss its historic importance.

> In this cauldron of sustained tension between absolute virginity and erotic gratification, the sexual process was moralized, personalized, and embellished. Most importantly, these courtly lovers were learning, for the first time in human history, how to integrate sexuality with friendship. The express intention of the theoreticians of this late medieval movement was to create a new behavioral possibility: heterosexual friendship (*philia*), the intimate love between men and women as equals, an equality that would not require any renunciation of the sexuality of either. These thinkers noted that friendship (*philia*) existed in Greece only as a homosexual possibility, and they recalled that the spiritual *philia* of Christian love required women to renounce their sexual feelings and their femininity. In courtly love, there was to be something new: a love that could express sexual feeling

and endure sexual differences without being overcome by anxiety and falling prey to aggression. This self-confidence would develop from the gradual exploration, understanding, and appreciation of sexual differences, an exploration that could be continued without danger precisely because, by common consent, the relation was to remain chaste! Notice that, in courtly love, virginity was a moral competence required of both men and women because the pleasures sought were mutual. Unless these pleasures were shared, they could not be enjoyed. A similar mutual competence in virginity is required by American culture and is inculcated by the institutionalization of petting.

In creating heterosexual friendship, courtly love also softened the differences between men and women, differences that were, in the ancient world, the cause of so much sexual anxiety and aggression. This "softening of the differences" was based on the newly developed distinction between sexuality and sex. "Feminine" was distinguished from "female"; "masculine" was distinguished from "male." In the procedures of courtly love, as in the modern petting process, the male could learn tenderness and sentimentality. He learned to "feel feminine," while the female learned to "feel masculine." Each learned to incorporate, by an empathic act, the feeling of the other within the range of his own behavioral possibilities. To manage such feelings is not possible for persons who regard men and women as sexual contraries, who believe that only females "feel feminine" and that only males "feel masculine." [20]

Richardson somewhat testily criticizes as hypocritical those modern theologians who argue the "technical virginity" of those who engaged in long careers of necking and petting before intercourse on their wedding night. He contends, however, such technical virginity has a social function to play in American society not unlike the various previous kinds of virginity played in archaic Greek, early Christian, and medieval society. Preparation for marriage is, in his viewpoint, a time of acquiring the skills in affection and friendship which are demanded by contemporary American culture. To plunge into relationships involving intercourse before these interpersonal skills are acquired by the couple is evidence of a lack of sexual confidence and maturity.

Richardson notes that Harvey Cox and Ira Reiss dismiss such sexual practices as either immoral teasing or unconscious hypocrisy.

What they have not considered, however, is whether

> the simultaneous affirmation of contrary values might be possible on the bases of assumptions other than their own nondevelopmental ones. For the coaffirmation of contrary values may lead not to self-contradictory behavior—at least not during adolescence—but to the sequentialized process of increasing personal and sexual intimacy we have discussed above. The dynamics of this process—a process that furthers experimentation between relative equals, a gradual accumulation of sexual experience, and an eventual integration of sexual behavior into the structure of personal behavior—depend upon the *tension* between these contrary tendencies. The tension forces the sexual process and personal sexual behavior to become increasingly differentiated. In this way a "graded development" supersedes the sharp either/or behavior that Cox and Reiss seem to commend.[21]

It is obviously a long way from the female figurines of Paleolithic man to a lovers' lane in contemporary America. Somewhere along the line it would appear that a bit of the numinous wore off sexuality, though one wonders if archaeologists discovering the remains of contemporary American civilization 5000 years hence would not be inclined to feel that sexuality was an extraordinarily important part of American religion. What would the archaeologist, for example, who had not deciphered our strange language think if he came upon just one bound volume of *Playboy*? He would conclude, I suspect, that we had much in common with the hunting folk who camped around Lake Baikal in Siberia tens of thousands of years ago.

Personal self-fulfillment through sex and family is an integral part of Thomas Luckmann's *Invisible Religion*.

> Another, peculiarly modern, articulation of the themes of self-expression and self-realization is sexuality. In view of the prominent place occupied by sexuality in the modern sacred cosmos,

however, it deserves special consideration. The rigidity with which various aspects of sexual conduct are institutionalized in traditional societies attests to the difficulty in regulating such basic and, in a sense, "private" conduct by external controls— as well as to the importance of such regulation for the kinship system. Wherever the kinship system is a central dimension of the social structure, pertinent norms are typically endowed with religious significance and are socially enforced. With specialization of the primary institutional domains, however, the family and, thus, sexuality lose some of their relevance for those domains and the enforcement of norms regulating the family and sexual conduct *becomes less important*. One may say, with some qualifications, that the family and sexuality recede more and more into the "private sphere." Conversely, to the extent that sexuality is "freed" from external social control, it becomes capable of assuming a crucial function in the "autonomous" individual's quest for self-expression and self-realization. This argument obviously does not imply that sexuality was unimportant or lacked urgency for men before the modern industrial period. Nor does it imply that sexuality did not have religious significance in the traditional sacred cosmos. It does imply, however, that sexuality, in connection with the "sacred" themes of self-expression and self-realization, now comes to play a unique role as a source of "ultimate" significance for the individual who is retrenched in the "private sphere." It is likely that the development which led from the notions of romantic love to what we may call, tongue-in-cheek, the sexual polytheism of the respectable suburbanite, represents more than a short-lived swing of the pendulum from which the weights of Victorian taboos were removed.[22]

Psychoanalytic literature makes clear that much of the emotional disturbance in contemporary America comes from lack of confidence and clarity about one's sexual identity. Both the communes and the left wing of the sensitivity-training movement insist on sexual liberation as a part of the salvation message that they preach. Norman O. Brown advises us that we will become fully human when we are able to be polymorphously perverse, and the theologians of play led by Harvey Cox observe that salvation is hard to come by save by sexuality. In the meantime, of course, the vast majority of us continue to mark such sexual events as birth and marriage with religious rituals. Charismatic prophets periodically arise to announce that salvation can be found if only we will rid ourselves of the outmoded sexual restrictions of the past and give ourselves over to the enjoyment of sex. The differences between the Oneida or New Harmony utopias of the nineteenth century and the mythological utopia envisioned by the *Harrad Experiment* are hard to discover, but both are religious in the strict sense of the word: they provide man with an ultimate explanation for the condition in which he finds himself.

While Richardson's model is extremely helpful in understanding the change in sexuality through the centuries, it ought not to be considered a simple evolutionary model (and is not so considered by Richardson). For example, the *Männerbund* is still very much with us, and in most societies in the world, friendship between husband and wife is not considered a feasible or valuable ideal. Herbert Gans, an astute and careful observer of American working-class life, points out that most life among the working class is still sexually segregated. In the *Urban Villagers,* published in 1962, he notes that the relevant referent group was not one's wife and family (or husband and family) but one's siblings and cousins of the same age. Again, in the somewhat higher-level working class of Levittown the same phenomenon persisted.

> The typical working class family is sexually segregated. Husbands and wives exchange love and affection, but they have separate family roles and engage in little of the companionship found in the middle classes. The husband is the breadwinner and the enforcer of child discipline; the wife is the housekeeper and rears the children. Whenever possible, husbands spend their free time with other male companions, women with other women. Entertaining is rarer than in the middle class, and most social life takes place among relatives and childhood friends. When they are not available, there is occasional visiting with neighbors and also a tendency for husband and wife to draw closer to each other. Even so, it is significant that the first organization to be founded in Levittown was the Veterans of

Foreign Wars, its predominantly working class membership quickly making it a suburban substitute for the city's neighborhood tavern.[23]

Nor has syneisaktism or agapetism or courtly love by any means vanished from the scene—quite the contrary. While some communes (probably a very tiny minority) do practice group marriage, far more of them are attempting to achieve intimate love among all members even though monogamy or even celibacy is practiced. Furthermore, the co-ed dormitory and the co-ed apartment which are quietly but rapidly spreading among the younger generation are evidence that substantial numbers of young people believe that friendship across sexual lines is possible and desirable even if intercourse is not a serious option. Most of the experience with the co-ed dorms indicates that the fornication rate between those who live in the same dorm goes down to practically zero. As one young man observed, "Hell, to sleep with one of them would be incest."

The casualness with which members of the younger generation enter into heterosexual living arrangements astonishes and scandalizes their elders, whether they be the right-wing elders who are afraid the young people will sleep together or the left-wing psychoanalytically oriented who are persuaded that they ought to be sleeping with one another. In some instances, of course, they do; but in others, they do not, and I would gather from what young people tell me there are even instances where the same bed is shared for a substantial period of time without intercourse taking place.

All this reminds one somehow of Scuthin and Brendan the Navigator.

This apparent return—as yet not very carefully studied or documented—to patterns of courtly love or even agapetism may be something rather different. Endorsing strongly the proposition that intercourse, marriage, and friendship can be combined, some of the younger generation may now be experimenting to discover whether intense and intimate sexual friendship can exist without people having to sleep together. It will be an interesting experiment to watch.

Thus while there have been a considerable number of changes in man's attitude toward sexuality since the Ice Age, these changes have not been total or pervasive. It is now believed in theory, at least by certain segments of the population in certain parts of the world, that sex, friendship, and marriage can be combined, though attempts to achieve this combination in practice have not been universally successful—to put the matter mildly. Furthermore, one suspects, from some of the historical accounts of marriages in years gone by as well as what can be observed in primitive tribes today, that however the theory and practice of cultures may have militated against friendship between husband and wife it still managed to occur. Whether such occurrences were more frequent or less frequent than at the present time is difficult to say; probably they were less frequent. But the principal difference between our time and any previous age is that now we have categories of thought and analysis which lead us to expect and demand friendship in our marriage relationships. Indeed, as Luckmann points out, the demand for self-fulfillment in relationships has become part of "the invisible religion."

The theme of individual "autonomy" found many different expressions. Since the "inner man" is, in effect, an undefinable entity, its presumed discovery involves a lifelong quest. The individual who is to find a source of "ultimate" significance in the subjective dimension of his biography embarks upon a process of self-realization and self-expression that is, perhaps, not continuous—since it is immersed in the recurrent routines of everyday life—but certainly interminable. In the modern sacred cosmos self-expression and self-realization represent the most important expressions of the ruling topic of individual "autonomy." Because the individual's performances are controlled by the primary public institutions, he soon recognizes the limits of his "autonomy" and learns to confine the quest for self-realization to the "private sphere." The young may experience some difficulty in accepting this restriction—a restriction whose "logic" is hardly obvious until one learns to appreciate the "hard facts

of life." Content analysis of popular literature, radio and television, advice columns and inspirational books provides ample
evidence that self-expression and self-realization are prominent
themes, indeed. They also occupy a central position in the
philosophy, if not always the practice, of education. The individual's natural difficulty in discovering his "inner self" explains,
furthermore, the tremendous success of various scientific and
quasi-scientific psychologies in supplying guidelines for his
search.[24]

The modalities of the relationship between sex and religion
have changed. In the Western world we no longer have sacred
prostitution, nor do we, save on rare occasions, engage in ritual
intercourse to make sure the fields are fertile. Most forms of
"ritualistic avoidance" of women have been abandoned. But
sexuality is still something about which we are highly ambivalent.
We eagerly seek its delights, and yet we are afraid of our inadequacies. We believe that it will bring us self-fulfillment and salvation, yet frequently we find it frustrating and unsatisfying. We
insist that married sex involve friendship, and invoke both formal
and informal religious norms to justify this pursuit of friendship;
and yet we still find friendship with members of our own sex
considerably less demanding and frightening. We vigorously
insist that sex is something "natural," yet we spend tens of millions of dollars on literature which purports to tell us how to
make this natural behavior successful. If sexuality is not, then,
a *res tremendens et fascinosans,* nothing else is.

It is not my intention to argue that the churches as they
presently exist have been successful in integrating sexuality into
their version of the explicitly numinous; quite the contrary, they
have failed to do so. Nor is it my intention to contend that all
men at all times in their lives view their sexual instincts as something "other." All I am asserting is that for most human beings
there are times in life when sexuality becomes distinctly numinous—at marriage and childbirth in particular, but other times as
well. There are attitudes and behavior when we are dealing with
sexuality that indicate quite forcefully we know we are dealing

with a power that is mysterious—a power that for all our rationality, all our confidence, all our assertions of naturalness we are not able to completely understand or completely control. In this respect I argue we are very little different from our Paleolithic ancestors who also knew that they did not understand it or control it, and that it represented a power which in some fashion was "totally other."

The connection between sex and the sacred, then, is not accidental. It is part of the human condition as we have used the term in this book. The style of the connection may have changed from the past, but it has probably changed less than the purveyors of the conventional wisdom would have us believe. The connection itself, however transformed, seems as persistent as it ever was.

8. Religion and Ethics

IN CHAPTER THREE we quoted Clifford Geertz as arguing that ethos was merely the other side of the coin of world view. Our meaning system tells us not only what reality is but how the good man behaves. It delineates for us what kinds of behavior are appropriate if we are to be in accord with the way things "really are." Ethics, then, in primitive societies is inseparable from religion. The ceremonies of the sacred rituals, the appropriate mode of behavior toward other members of the tribe, the incest taboo, the complex system of relationships with one's mother's family and one's father's family, the norms about which groups one may choose a wife from and which ones it is forbidden to seek a wife from, the appropriate behavior in specified circumstances toward members of one's own sex—all of these are not merely intimately linked up with one's belief system but frequently inculcated in the very ritual ceremonials themselves.

Not everyone in such societies obeys the laws, of course, and some societies are much more tolerant than others of violations of the moral code, nor are these implicit ethical systems so detailed as to provide solutions for every specific problem which may arise in life. But one's meaning system does provide one with certain overarching myths which lay down broad, implicit guidelines for appropriate behavior. In such tribes mythological explanations for ethical norms suffice. However, we have argued in this volume that an explanation's being mythological does not mean that it is superstitious or irrational, but merely that it is comprehensive and poetic. The ethical myths, of course, reflect what actually goes on in the culture, because the relationship between a culture and its meaning system is reciprocal: the meaning system shapes the culture and the culture shapes the meaning system. Some men may systematically violate most of the norms of the culture and most men will occasionally slip from virtue—indeed most will probably frequently slip from virtue— but the ethos of the society remains the model and the template for how one *ought to live*.

When rational and abstract thought began to separate itself from myth in the first and second millenniums before Christ, legal and ethical systems began to emerge as distinct from the myths. The first legal codes were rooted in mythology, and the great ethical edifices of a man like Aristotle occasionally nodded to the myths. Both legal codes and systems of philosophical ethics—to say nothing of the morality and the moral systems later developed by the Christian church—purported in one way or another to be rooted in the nature of things. The Mosaic law and the principles of Aristotle's ethics were taken to have an overriding moral vigor precisely because they reflected either the wishes of the deity or the nature of reality—which meant practically the same thing. Both Artistotle's ethics and the Mosaic law were simply moral conclusions of a vision of the ultimate nature of reality.

The conventional wisdom argues that morality has now been desacralized—that is to say, it is no longer rooted in a religious view of reality; and it has also been personalized—no longer consists of abstract principles but rather is based on the free decisions that individuals make in the circumstances in which they find themselves. Ethical decisions are made by intelligent "loving" human beings who exercise free options instead of being constrained by the juridic obligations of "traditional moral pieties," to use Kenneth Keniston's phrase.

That moral decisions are separated from religion is not demonstrated by the purveyors of the conventional wisdom. They take it as established beyond all doubt that the sacred is no longer a relevant dimension of human life.

There are three different forms of argumentation against "absolute" moral traditions which I will call, for want of better labels, the political, the theological, and the social-scientific situationisms.

"Political situationism" was argued persuasively in the 1950's by such writers as Paul Nitze and Walter Lippmann, mostly, one suspects, in response to what they took to be the horrifying moralism of John Foster Dulles. Their basic premise was that the international society is so complicated and the problems and difficulties facing political decision-makers so many and varied, that it was practically impossible for such a decision-maker to decide that a given decision was morally "right" and all its alternatives morally "wrong." The decision-maker, then, had no choice but to fall into a self-righteousness that was not merely deceptive but could be dangerous, because if one's own decisions were morally "right," it followed that one's critics or one's enemies were morally "wrong," and that by resisting them, even if necessary to the death, one was engaging in a virtuous act. There was, according to such writers, no more room for religious crusades. Foreign policy (and analogously, one supposes, domestic policy, though there were no domestic problems in the Eisenhower Administration) could at best be the product of pragmatic thought and decision-making.

The "theological situationism" is to be found in the writings of such men as Bishop John Robinson, Paul Lehmann, Joseph Fletcher, and Frederick C. Wood.[1] While the casual reader may suspect that situation ethics is nothing more than a moderately serious attempt to rationalize fornication, adultery, and homosexuality in terms that are vaguely Christian, there is an effort at theoretical justification in the theological situationism that purports to protect it from charges of ethical anarchy. Lehmann, for example, opposes his situation contextualism to an absolute ethic: "Ethically speaking, an absolute is a standard of conduct which can be and must be applied to all people in all situations in exactly the same way." Fletcher argues that there are three ethical approaches: the legalistic (which is virtually the same as Lehmann's), the antinomian (a lawless or unprincipled approach), and "the situational." According to Fletcher:

> The situationist enters into every decision making situation fully armed with the ethical maxim of his community and its heritage and he treats them with respect as illuminators of his problems. Just the same, he is prepared in any situation to compromise them or set them aside in a situation if *love* seems better served by doing so. [Italics mine.] [2]

The situationist, then, does not wish to eliminate completely absolute moral principles. He simply wishes to see them applied in practice in a context of "loving decision-making." However much lip service the situationists pay to traditional moral principles, and however sincere they may be in their desire to avoid antinomian morality, their concern with sexuality, their claim that their morality is "new" (and "scientific," "progressive," and "rational"), has led many of their disciples to conclude that one can do pretty much what one wants so long as one can make a persuasive case when one's actions are motivated by love.

There are two kinds of social-scientific situationism. The first and more simpleminded is of the Kinsey Report variety which argues in effect that in a society where traditional moral principles have no validity and where ethics are free at last from the rigid bonds of the sacred, one discovers what morality is by a public opinion poll. The ethical is what most people do.

A more sophisticated approach to morality from the social-scientific viewpoint is that of Lawrence Kohlberg and W. Perry. They see moral reasoning developing through a series of stages until the young person is "free from convention" and makes "his own" moral decisions.

Kohlberg, for example, distinguishes the preconventional stage "which involves relatively egocentric concepts of right and wrong as that which one can do without getting caught, or that which leads to the greatest personal gratification." Then follows the conventional stage during later childhood in which the standards of good and evil are the standards of the community and/or the concept of law and order. Morality is perceived as objective, as existing "out there." The essential moral question is not what is right but whether to do what one knows to be right or not to do what one knows to be wrong. There are two "postconventional" phases. In the first, morality is seen as evolving from the "social contract" as the result of an agreement entered into by members of the society for their common good, and therefore subject to emendation, alteration, or revocation. Social-contract reasoning sees rules as "convenient" and therefore changeable. Finally, the second post-conventional phase and the last stage is the acquisition of "personal principles." Those who are fortunate enough to reach such a stage make their decisions on principles that transcend not only conventional morality but even the social contract. "In this stage certain general principles are now seen as personally binding though not necessarily 'objectively true.'"

It is certainly not my intention in the present chapter to engage in a detailed critique of the three different forms of the "nonabsolute" morality; but some comments are in order.

While political decisions of our public officials are admittedly made in an extraordinarily difficult context, and while—as the United States has ample reason to know—moral self-righteousness on the part of political leaders is extraordinarily dangerous, it does not follow that there are no certain general imperatives which may govern political decision-making. Thus, when John Kennedy rejected a sneak attack on Russian missile sites in 1962, he did so quite explicitly in terms of an abstract and absolute principle: sneak attacks were foreign to the American tradition. It could well be that such absolute principles will be for the most part negative. They will tell a political leader what not to do instead of what to do. They will say, for example, *Thou shalt not systematically deceive the public,* or *Thou shalt not let mil-*

*lions of people starve to death without doing all in one's power
to prevent it*. Alas, absolute moral principles do not dictate practical programs for Biafran relief, or for healing a credibility gap,
or even for coping with missiles intruded into Cuba.

The theological situationists claim to have discovered a "new"
morality in which the circumstances of moral acts are taken into
account. The claim is historical nonsense. The most orthodox
Jesuit moral manual written in either the seventeenth or the
twentieth century (and in fact there wouldn't be much difference
between the two) would insist on the importance of circumstances determining the morality of the action and would also
insist on individual conscience being the ultimate norm for moral
decision-making. Furthermore, the Jesuit moralist would also
have certainly argued that moral decisions must be influenced by
love. The whole tradition of Jesuit casuistry, which it is currently
fashionable to ridicule, was evolved precisely because the Jesuit
moralists were very much aware of how difficult it was to make
concrete moral decisions. The only claim to novelty that the so-
called new moralists can make is that they are willing to push an
investigation into the circumstances affecting ethical decision into
areas which the Jesuits were somewhat reluctant to explore—
principally, sexual morality. The Jesuit reluctance, one suspects,
to consider in detail the circumstances affecting sexual decisions
was based on a fear that all hell, ethically speaking, would break
loose if sexual norms were relativized even in the slightest.

Yet I can remember in the seminary learning from a Jesuit
moralist about certain advice that could be given privately to
couples who were practicing birth control. This advice could not
be preached, and those who were told such private recommendations were also bound not to make them public.°

The theological situationists, like their Jesuit predecessors,

---

° The advice was that if one's marriage partner insisted on using contraceptives and the marriage would be under serious threat if the other
partner did not permit marital relations with contraceptives, then these
relations could be engaged in without sin, though it was implied that it
would be better if they were not enjoyed too much. This is, I would suggest, contextualism with a vengeance.

realize that there is an inevitable strain between ethical principles and individual decisions. Whether one calls oneself a situationist or an absolutist one must still honor both elements of the strain if one is not to end up denying all morality or denying all moral responsibility.

The weakness of the Kohlberg position ° is that abstract personal moral principles, as Kenneth Keniston says, "are intimately —perhaps inevitably—related to the development of moral self-righteousness, zealotry, dogmatism, fanaticism, and insensitivity." [3] Keniston goes on to say:

> In pursuit of his own personal principles, a man will ride rough-shod over others who do not share these principles, will disregard human feelings or even destroy human life. During the period when the "end of ideology" was being announced on all sides, when instrumental and consensus politics was being extolled, we learned to identify abstract personal principles with dogmatic and destructive moral zealotry. How are we to combine these two perspectives? Do we see in Brewster Smith's findings confirmation of the view that student activists are dangerous moral zealots? or do we adhere to Kohlberg's implication that such individuals are more likely moral heroes than despots? [4]

Keniston adds, "whether the highest stages of moral reasoning lead to destructive zealotry or real ethicality depends upon the extent to which moral development is *matched by development in other sectors*. The critical related sectors of development, I submit, are those which involve compassion, love, or empathic identification with others." [5] Then:

> Many moral zealots, bigots, and dogmatists are of course describable, in Kohlberg's terms, as conventionalists, while others are perhaps permanent regressees to the Raskolnikoff Syndrome. But there are at least a few whom we know from personal experi-

---

° Other than the rather basic weakness that comes from the fact that his research was based on the highly unethical practice of deceiving subjects into thinking that they were giving electric shocks to other subjects.

ence or from history who seem truly post-conventional in moral reasoning, but whose genuine adherence to the highest moral values is *not* matched by compassion, sympathy, capacity for love and empathy. In such individuals, the danger of breaking human eggs to make a moral omelet, of injuring people in order to advance one's own moral principles, is all too real. . . . Thus, neatly to identify even the highest levels of moral reasoning with human virtue, much less with mental health, maturity, and so on, would be a serious mistake. What we might term "moral precocity" in youth—high moral development not attended by comparable development in other sectors of life—may indeed be dangerous. The danger lies not in high levels of moral development in themselves, but in the retardation of other sectors of development. What is dangerous is any level of moral development, be it post-conventional, conventional, or pre-conventional, in the absence of a developed capacity for compassion, empathy and love for one's fellow men.[6]

All of which is surely very true, and anyone who knows Professor Keniston knows that he is personally a superb example of compassion, love, and empathy. But what is one to say of an alleged pattern of moral development which produces principles without necessarily producing compassion, love, or empathic identification? Professor Keniston himself admits:

Yet what is true for most is not true for all; and historically, many crimes have been committed in the name of the highest principles, sincerely held. In the end, the findings of developmental psychology in the context of youthful political activism may merely return us to ancient truisms—compassion without morality is sentimental and effusive, while morality without compassion is cold and inhumane.[7]

Indeed yes, one is forced to say, but then compassion is at the very core of morality. The moral system which does not demand compassion is an inadequate moral system. One wonders why the academy is discovering compassion so very late in the radical game.

However, and here we turn Professor Keniston's own words

against him, the cry for compassion and empathy and love is at the very core of the traditional moral conventions which moral development is supposed to transcend. If the ancient truisms "Thou shalt love thy neighbor as thyself" and "Thou shalt be compassionate" are raised to the position of moral absolutes, then one seems to have absolute morality all over again, if it be only through the back door and in the last paragraph. And here is the ultimate dilemma of the moral relativists. They are all highly moral men, and in the final analysis, require some sort of "absolute" moral dictum in which to root their own moral sensitivity. For Professor Keniston, love, compassion, and empathy seem to be required "by the nature of things." It is perhaps not too unfair to ask him why. What is there in the nature of things that makes compassion—an extremely difficult, messy, complicated virtue—necessary? Paul Tillich once remarked that love without the knowledge of how to love is empty, but knowing how to love is an extraordinarily difficult task. The exercise of the art of love grows more complicated and confusing the longer we are at it. If it is an absolute, then there must be something in the nature of things that makes it an absolute. Ethics or compassion is rooted ultimately in one's ultimate interpretive scheme, in one's concept of what the really real is.

Similarly, unless there is such a thing as absolute morality, it is difficult to justify moral outrage, yet moral outrage is abroad in the land now more than it has been in a long, long time. If one's own principles are binding personally but not objectively, what right do we have to insist that they be binding on others? If each one must decide in his own context what love means, then who is to criticize Mayor Daley for making a different decision than Abbie Hoffman; Lyndon Johnson for making a different decision than J. W. Fulbright; Martin Luther King for making a different decision than George Wallace; Marshal Ky for making a different decision than Chairman Ho? Denunciations of war, racial injustice, political oppression, pollution, and other moral evils can be justified merely in terms that these things are dysfunctional for a society; it hurts American society to be engaged in a war in Vietnam. But most moral outrage is not of this variety at all. It is based on the assumption that aggressive warfare is wrong, and that the needless killing of women and children is wrong, that atrocities committed by the military are wrong, that racial discrimination is wrong, that cheating the young out of an education is wrong, that polluting the water and the air is wrong. But, one is forced to ask, why are they wrong? Are they wrong simply because we have certain personal principles which have transcended social convention, and these principles say they are wrong? Are they wrong because in the context in which we make our decisions we judge them to be wrong? Are they wrong because the conventions on which society has agreed declare them to be wrong? If any of these is the justification for denunciations of current public immorality, then moral outrage is scarcely appropriate. The only reason that we can judge our moral decision to be superior to someone else's is that we are able to argue that our decision is more in keeping with the moral principle that is rooted in the nature of things: killing, stealing, cheating, lying, polluting the air, defrauding the weak, exploiting the young are taken to be wrong in themselves. They are wrong because they are wrong. The moral outrage of the protestor makes no sense at all unless it is a *religious* outrage; that is to say, an outrage which views an evil as a violation of the way things ought to be, and things *ought* to be that way because the norms of oughtness are part of the basic and ultimate nature of reality. Unless one's ethical principles take on at least an implicitly sacral character, then moral outrage makes no sense at all.

Man is a norm-fashioning creature. He arranges the patterns of relationships with others in structures so that much of his behavior is routine, and he is thus freed to devote his attention and energies to matters of substance and not of process. Similarly, he elaborates normative structures for himself so that many of his decisions become routine. It is not necessary to invoke ultimate moral principles every time a decision is required. These norms turn eventually into ethical systems; and just as the structure of human interaction can become obsolete and atrophied, so the normative systems can lose their vitality and become juridic and legalistic. Furthermore, if they are rigidly followed without any regard to the circumstances in which the moral agent finds himself, they can defeat their own purposes.

There is an inevitable tension between codifying and revivifying normative structures, as well as between general principles about the way things should be and practical decisions in concrete circumstances. Emphasis will inevitably shift back and forth, but a shift from system to act and from norm to circumstance is a shift and not unidirectional evolutionary progress. If the situationism of the 1950's may have at times gone too far in one direction, the rigid moralism of the 1960's goes too far in the other. The attempt in one decade to proclaim the end of ideology seems to have generated in the next decade a resurgence of an extraordinarily rigid and doctrinaire ideology. The denial of the validity or relevance of absolute moral principles has produced a situation in which the most rigid and irrational absolutism is riding high. It might be much better if the intellectual leaders of the society acknowledge that strain between theoretical principles and practical application is inevitable, and that it is not a sign of evolutionary progress for a man to argue that he no longer needs theoretical principles rooted in the nature of reality in order to make moral decisions.

Most men and women, of course, do not question the relationship between religion and ethics. It is only among the liberal elite that the rejection of "conventional" or "absolute" moral principles has become popular. The sad experiences of the 1960's have made it clear that even among these groups, moral outrage requires a return to absolute morality—that is to say, morality that is rooted in the view of the nature of things and in, at least implicitly, "religious" perspective.

But one can go further. Some of the most "religiously" moral people of our time are precisely those who in theory reject the link between religion and morality and denounce "conventional," "traditional," and "absolutist" moralities and insist that they are not bound by propositional morality. But when it comes to war and race, for example, they yield to no one in their capacity to be outrageously—that is to say, religiously—moralistic; for war and injustice are absolutely evil and violate the nature of things as they ought to be.

Langdon Gilkey argues that there is a final reason why ethics and religion cannot be separated. We need the religious myths to warn us of our own inadequacies and limitations as moral agents, for however high and noble our principles, it is easy for us to become narrow, selfish, and blind when it comes to the application of those principles. The religious mythologies warn us of our own weakness and sinfulness and of the dangers of thinking that we are so rational and so "in control of our emotions" that we can make moral decisions independently of feedback and checks and balances either from our community or from our ethical tradition. The "new" morality, though it claims to be scientific, does not recognize at all what the social scientists tell us about the power of the human unconscious, and the "new" morality— in any of its forms—is not able to cope with human sinfulness largely because it believes that sin is something that has been left behind in the evolutionary process. Alas, would that it were.

In Gilkey's words:

In history men appear to have little control over what they do, for they cannot fully determine the ultimate direction and integrity of their own wills, much less the course of the history in which they are immersed. We can through technology wreck the entire country of Vietnam; but we cannot, whatever we will, achieve our goals there, nor can we even, were the will to do so there, extract ourselves from that guilty and suicidal morass. We controlled by decision our entrance into that portion of history; but all our technological and political experts cannot seem to direct an exit! The great increase in man's ability to control what is outside of him through technology has not led to any corresponding increase either in man's control over himself or over his historical fate. Rather, it is still true that in the political arena, an increment of power—of "freedom" in that sense—ironically tends to increase a man's bondage to his own self-concern, and thus to add to the fated destiny of what was unintended that he will bequeath to his children.[8]

The assumption of the conventional wisdom, then, that ethics can be divorced from religion and that men can make moral judgments without any reference to principles or powers outside themselves seems to be both unreal and too optimistic. The profoundly religious outrage of some segments of the young against what they take to be the moral abuses of the adult society is based on the implicit assumption that there is not only evil in the world but sinfulness. Why else be angry at a man for doing evil unless you think he is responsible for his evil? Why else demand that people be moral, save if you believe they are capable of giving up their immorality? Why else try to reform society unless one believes that there are certain absolute social principles which ought to characterize human behavior? And if they are obsolete, whence comes this absolutism? Here the conventional wisdom is able to provide no answer; but then it can't even explain—not at least as long as it is following its own principles of rational and scientific progressivism—why there should be either immorality or outrage when both are profoundly nonrational activities.

9. Religious Leadership

UNTIL THE SECOND VATICAN COUNCIL, the Roman Catholic priesthood was one of the most powerful religious leaderships in the world. In addition to its strictly cultic role, the Catholic priesthood led its people intellectually, socially, politically, morally—in varying degrees at various times and places, indeed, but still almost always with considerable strength and power. In many of the northern European countries and in the United States the priest was an object of singular personal affection. He was immune from traffic tickets, he received discounts in most stores, his ineptitudes as a preacher were excused, and his faults were overlooked or ignored. "Ah, poor Father isn't feeling well this morning" became a code sentence to convey the fact that Father had entirely too much to drink the night before.

There are a number of reasons for this combination of power in the priesthood and affection toward it. In many countries the priest served as a leader of his people against foreign oppression. In the United States he sustained the immigrants through the painful transition to a new society. In other countries he led cooperative economic and social movements. While in some of the Latin countries the role of the priesthood was rather narrowly defined, in many others the range of priestly activity and influence was extremely broad.

In the wake of the Vatican Council, however, many young priests all over the world (especially, it would seem, in the

United States) are doing their best to relinquish their leadership position. In their view, the priest is merely the cultic leader; he presides over the liturgy, and that is the end of his function. It is argued that all other leadership roles ought more appropriately to be filled by whoever in the community has the talents for these roles.* So eager are some of the young clergy to escape from their pervasive leadership roles that they will not exercise their own talents even if it turns out that they are, indeed, the one in the community best qualified to perform a specific leadership function. Needless to say, such behavior seems odd to their parishioners, many of whom are now beginning to wonder what in the world they pay clerical salaries for if it is not to moderate scout troops ´and teen-age clubs.

The crisis in the Catholic priesthood is merely a somewhat belated replication of the crisis that has gone on in the Protestant ministry for a long time. The clergy, influenced by the conventional wisdom of the universities, are persuaded that their sacral roles are minimal. Most of the laity, only vaguely influenced by the conventional wisdom, still demand religious leadership and, as has been typical of Americans since the very beginning, define that religious leadership in a very broad sense.

It is hardly necessary in this chapter to argue that religious leadership is still demanded in the modern world, nor do I propose to contend that every society we know has had a well-developed religious leadership class. In Joachim Wach's words:

> Such *specialists*, both individual and group, are known in a great number of primitive tribes. The esteem in which primitive society holds those who perform the necessary ceremonies to propitiate [the Gods] varies. With some tribes and groups they enjoy great prestige; in others less respect is accorded these individuals. We do not find specialization everywhere and certainly not monopoly.[1]

---

* It should be noted that this view of the priesthood is rejected both by Conciliar documents and by the writings of prominent theologians. It is, however, widespread among the young clergy.

However, whatever is to be said of the most primitive tribes, religious leadership is certainly well developed in all the historic civilizations, with the possible exception of China.

My contention in this chapter will be twofold: (1) The primary role of religious leadership is "interpretive." (2) In contemporary society the need for interpretation is such that most important leadership positions take on a sacral or quasi-sacral dimension. It is ironic that many of the clergy are eager to give up their sacral roles precisely at a time when the New Left is looking for charismatic leaders, and the neomystics are looking for gurus and holy men.

The most primordial religious leader is the shaman; a man with "a high degree of nervous excitability" (frequently an epileptic). His psychological and physiological oddity is taken to be an intrusion of the sacred, and such an individual is seen as an organ or mouthpiece of the divine. The religious leadership of the shaman is characteristic of nomadic people in Asia and in Africa and among the American Indians. While the shaman's ability to go into trance or ecstasy may be the result of psychological or physical abnormality, that ability is nonetheless one which he is careful to develop and which he frequently combines with the study of properties of herbs and other plants, the changes of the weather, and the habits of animals. Such knowledge reinforces his claim to be in special contact with the deity.

Many archaeologists argue that some of the figures depicted on the walls of Stone Age caves represent shamans, an argument which is justified in part by the fact that the culture of many of the nomadic peoples is thought to be fairly similar to the culture of some Paleolithic tribes. Thus it is probable, though not absolutely certain, that the nomadic hunter and food-gatherer looked to a shaman-like member of his tribe for special contact with reality.

Most past religious leadership has had charisma, that is to say, the special power which gives them the right to exercise authority over others. Max Weber, who analyzed the role of

charisma in society, speaks of religious and nonreligious charisma, though all charisma is to some extent religious in that it
represents a power that is "uncanny" or "out of the ordinary."
He also distinguishes between personal charisma and the charisma of office. Personal charisma is probably the original one, but
as human organizations become more complex and the religious
dimension of society more elaborate, official charisma becomes
extremely important. Wach comments on the differences between
the two:

> No doubt, there is something elementary and irresistible in per-
> sonal charisma, in contrast to which official charisma appears
> less efficacious. The latter may be more clearly defined than the
> vague, often indescribable, personal type, but it is narrower, shal-
> lower, and more limited. There is an additional important differ-
> ence. Charisma of personal character appeals more to the emo-
> tions; official charisma is more "rational." Whereas the former
> claims complete loyalty, even personal surrender, the latter
> usually demands a circumscribed or "tempered" obedience.[2]

There are many different forms of the religious charisma, but
they all represent some sort of special contact with the sacred,
some kind of extraordinary relationship with the transcendent
that enables the possessor of the charisma to stand as a go-
between, mediating between the sacred and the rest of the tribe.
In addition to the shaman, Wach distinguishes nine other forms
of religious leadership:

1. THE FOUNDER. This, of course, is the most important
religious leader: the one who begins a religious tradition.

> In analyzing the various activities of the founders, we find
> in nearly every case preaching and teaching. To convey to others
> the message of salvation and perfection and to lead them to the
> acceptance of the truth revealed to them in their basic experience
> are primary concerns of the founder. This activity may be im-
> plemented by miraculous acts, such as healing, feeding, trans-
> forming matter, etc. It is on this that tradition and hagio-
> graphical development rely and on this basis that they expand.

These acts are meant to illustrate the specific personal charisma which designates the man of God in an unmistakable and un-interchangeable way.

The awareness of his mission comes to the chosen one upon the occasion of his "call." Characteristic of such a mission is the close association of the message with the personality of its pro-mulgator and the permanent endowment with power. The idea of a mission implies consciousness of its mandatory character.[3]

2. THE REFORMER. While the reformer is not a man of the magnitude or the importance of the founder, and while he does not begin a new religious tradition, he does introduce tremendous new energies and quite possibly a new direction into old religious traditions.

In times of threatening decay or disintegration leaders arise in religious groups who are difficult to classify in the traditional historical schemes. They are not on one level with the founders; their creative religious power does not match that of the origi-nator of a great faith. They somewhat resemble the founders in the power, and possibly even in the magnetism, of their per-sonality, in their energy and endurance; but the sociological effect of their activity cannot be compared to that resulting in the emergence of the great faiths.[4]

3. THE PROPHET. The prophetic charisma, according to Wach, implies "immediate communion with the deity, the intensity of which is more characteristic than its continuance."[5] The prophet is preeminently a man who speaks, who interprets, though his interpretation, unlike that of the founder, does not introduce a new or vastly renovated tradition.

The consciousness of being the organ, instrument, or mouthpiece of the divine will is characteristic of the self-interpretation of the prophet. The prophetic authority is distinctly secondary, a derived authority, more distinctly so than the authority of the founder. Furthermore, a certain natural disposition, which many consider to be the basic psychological characteristic of prophecy, belongs to the prophet, who is distinguished by an unusual sensitiveness and an intense emotional life. Visions, dreams, trances, or ecstasies are not infrequently encountered, and by these the prophet is prepared to receive and interpret manifestations of the divine. He shares this privilege with other types of religious leader like the seer, etc. His interpretation, however, is "authorized," a fact which distinguishes him and the seer from the magician and the augur.[6]

4. THE SEER. The principal difference between the prophet and the seer is that the seer's interpretation is likely to be delivered to a group of men who surround him as he sits under a tree, while the prophet's is likely to be delivered to a crowd which follows him down the road or which stands in awe as he storms into the marketplace. As Wach puts it:

> Whereas the prophet is an extremely active figure, the seer is usually an individual of a more passive type. His charisma, like that of the prophet's, is derived from a genuine but less creative religious experience. The seer is granted communion with the deity and is credited with knowing intimately the spirits or gods and with being acquainted with their will and intention. He is able to interpret their tangible and intangible manifestations. In contradistinction to the augur, the seer accomplishes this by intuition rather than by methodical and systematic interpretation of certain specified phenomena. The seer draws more from his inner experience than the augur, who observes exterior objects. His attitude is different from that of the prophet in that, according to the passive character of his state, he is less concerned with developing norms of judgment and rules of action than the prophet. Furthermore, the seer deals usually with individual situations and rarely commits himself to general statements and judgments as does the prophet.[7]

It is worth noting, however, that both the seer and the prophet *interpret* for their followers. The meaning of the ultimate interpretive schemes is not always clear in special sets of circumstances, and one must seek out someone who has "the words of life."

5. THE MAGICIAN. The magician is a man who can get things

done for you. You approach him not so much when you are interested in finding interpretation or an explanation but when you want someone who understands how things go in the spirit world, to get results for you from the spirits. According to Wach, the term "magician"

> invariably implies the command of power due to communion with the unseen or the spirits. This power may be bestowed once and for all, or temporarily and repeatedly, either as a free gift or as a reward for special training and ascetic practices. The authority of the magician is proportionate to his fulfillment of the expectations of his clients. In other words, his prestige is less firmly established and more dependent upon his professional "success" than that of the prophet or seer.[8]

However, the magician's role is still an interpretive one. It is precisely his ability to interpret sacral, that is to say ultimate, reality that enables him to satisfy the requirements of his clients.

6. THE DIVINER. The diviner is also a more practical man, but his concerns are more with what is going to happen than with producing results for clients.

> The charisma of the diviner is originally personal but easily and regularly becomes institutionalized. The diviner shares with the seer a "passive" character but differs from him in having to rely on objects which he uses as mediums for the interpretation of the will of the gods. . . . The magician is not usually very much interested in the theoretical aspects of his craft; his function is predominantly a practical one. The diviner, on the other hand, bases his interpretation on a general scheme or "theory" of the cosmos, which claims a correspondence between the human and the divine realms (microcosm mirroring macrocosm, etc.). The scheme is not so much a spontaneous creative expression of individual religious experience, as in the case of the "prophet," but is rather the tradition of a normative discipline. Even in primitive society this discipline reaches a high degree of perfection and complexity.[9]

The diviner, then, is something of a "scientist" in that he has an elaborate methodology for developing his interpretive scheme.

7. THE SAINT. The saint, on the other hand, interprets the ultimate for people not so much by what he knows but by who he is. The saint is the guru, the holy man.

> In distinction from other types of religious authority, the saint's prestige depends not so much on achievement as upon his personal nature and character. As he is not especially bound by professional ties, he does not necessarily excel in intellectual or in practical talents. His guidance, and it is characteristic of the saint to guide and direct the lives of others, is eagerly sought. Whereas the prophet, with whom the saint shares in exercising such influence, arouses the people by the vigorous impulse of his powerful preaching, the saint may exert his influence quietly but constantly and intensively, though the fierce and fiery temperament of some saints reminds us of the prophet. The saint influences others more by the indirect effect of example than by precept.[10]

8. THE PRIEST. The priest is, of course, preeminently the cultic man: the man who presides over worship. But the cultic function is merely the core of an extremely elaborate role, much of which involves interpretation, and some of it extremely elaborate and abstract interpretation.

> The main function of the priest, as has been pointed out, is cultic. It is here that the real difference between the priest and the other types, such as the magician, diviner, and conjurer, becomes apparent. Worship, as the very expression of religious experience, however primitive or rudimentary its form may be, is the main concern of the priest. He guarantees the right performance of formalized acts of worship. The priest is the guardian of traditions and the keeper of the sacred knowledge and of the techniques of meditation and prayer. He is the custodian of the holy law, which corresponds to the cosmic moral and ritual order, upon which the world, the community, and the individual depend. As an interpreter of this law, the priest may function as judge, administrator, teacher, and scholar, formulate standards and rules of conduct, and enforce their observance. Contemplation and action are intimately interwoven

in his life. Since he performs the sacred rites, he creates and fosters the arts of sacred song, writing, literature, music, dance, sacred painting, sculpture, and architecture. The priest lays the foundation of theology, history, philology, law, medicine, mathematics, and astronomy. As a theologian he becomes the primary factor in the formulation of theology as the theoretical expression of religious experience. . . . The systematization of myths and doctrine, the formulation of creeds, and the collection, redaction, and codification of the sacred writings are his affair.[11]

9. THE RELIGIOSUS. Finally, there is a man (or woman) who derives a kind of unofficial or quasi-official religious authority from his (or her) commitment to a special life of communion with God.

There have always and everywhere been men and women who have been compelled by their religious experience to live a life of closer communion with God than that of ordinary people and, without withdrawing entirely from the world, order their lives according to special religious rules. Various methods have been followed. The individual may try to live an isolated life, form a community, or cultivate privately a contemplative or active religious life, with or without special vows or consecrations. A certain "prestige" results from the charisma of such an existence, and it seems correct to say that it has a stimulating and integrating influence on religion in society. Those in the monastic life in all its variety (hermits, anchorites, monks, and nuns, tertiaries, sodales), ascetics and consecrated persons, and those who care for the sick and the poor and the destitute, prompted by religious motives, fall within the range of this type of religious authority. In practically all religions we find groups and individuals engaged in such activity and in the pursuit of the "good life," particularly in higher and more complex civilizations and societies.[12]

It will be noted that here, too, there is an interpretive role, though sometimes only an indirect one. For the *religiosus* by the very example of his "good life" shows others how they ought to be living if they are to honor the ultimate interpretive scheme.

All nine of Wach's categories involve interpretive functions. The founder and the reformer explicate the ultimate nature of reality in terms of their own religious experience, and collect followers around them precisely because their religious experience seems to be a normative interpretation of the ultimate. The seer, the prophet, and the diviner are explicitly concerned with interpretation; and the priest must interpret the cultic lore, which is merely an elaboration of the ultimate meaning system of his people. The saint and the *religiosus* interpret reality for us by serving as exemplars of the "good life" which is the "ethos" side of one's ultimate world view. While it is possible for societies to dispense with interpreters of their world view, these societies have to be quite primitive. Once social reality becomes complex, interpretation is inevitably required. The religious leader is, in the final analysis, the man who understands the meaning system better than others. If the basic contention of this volume—that meaning systems are required today as much as they ever were—is valid, it would follow that sacred leadership is every bit as important as it ever was. The conventional wisdom, of course, denies such a conclusion and argues, rather, that the clergyman ought to find his validation in being "relevant": engaging in political or social action or becoming a bargain-basement psychoanalyst. Interpreting the Ultimate, it is alleged, is no longer pertinent, because men no longer need the Ultimate. One can only respond that such an explanatory model has a very hard time coping with the emphasis of charisma in the New Left and with the search for holy men among the new mystics. May it also be noted in passing, it ignores the quasi-sacral role of some of the great charismatic leaders of the twentieth century, for some of whom the modifier "quasi" could easily be eliminated: De Gaulle, Churchill, Roosevelt, Hitler, Mao, Adenauer, Fidel, Ho, John Kennedy, Martin Luther King, John XXIII. These leaders were all men who spoke of "the nature of things" and who attracted vigorous, enthusiastic followers precisely because they were able to tap the deep roots of the ultimate convictions of their people.

But one need not search for charisma at such an exalted level. One need only turn on Station XERF, the world's most powerful radio station, broadcasting from Mexico (where it is immune from FCC regulations), just across the American border, with 250,000 watts, which enable its religious message to go from Argentina to Canada. On this station one can hear such people as Brother Al, the Reverend Frederick B. Eikerenkoetter II, C. W. Burpo, Catheryn Kuhlman, A. A. Allen, and Garner Ted Armstrong; also such lesser figures as J. Charles Jessup, David Terrell, and Bill Beeny.[13] In his article on the "God hucksters," William Martin asks, "Who listens to these evangelists, and why?"

No single answer will suffice. Some, doubtless, listen to learn. Garner Ted Armstrong discusses current problems and events— narcotics, crime, conflict, space exploration, pollution—and asserts that biblical prophecy holds the key to understanding both present and future. C. W. Burpo offers a conservative mixture of religion, morals, and politics. Burpo is foursquare in favor of God, Nixon, and constitutional government, and adamantly opposed to sex education, which encourages the study of materials "revealing the basest part of human nature."

Others listen because the preachers promise immediate solutions to real, tangible problems. Although evidence is difficult to obtain, one gets the definite impression, from the crowds that attend the personal appearances of the evangelists, from the content and style of the oral and written testimonials, from studies of storefront churches with similar appeals, and from station executives' analyses of their listening population, that the audience is heavily weighted with the poor, the uneducated, and others who for a variety of reasons stand on the margins of society. These are the people most susceptible to illness and infirmity, to crippling debts, and to what the evangelists refer to simply as "troubles." At the same time, they are the people least equipped to deal wih these problems effectively. Some men in such circumstances turn to violence or radical political solutions. Others grind and are ground away, in the dim hope of a better future. Still others, like desperate men in many cultures, succumb to the appeal of magical solutions. For this group, what the preachers promise is, if hardly the Christian gospel, at least good news.[14]

In other words, the radio evangelists who keep XERF going for fourteen hours every day provide explanations and interpretations in time of stress, of strain, indeed, in Geertz's word, of bafflement. Martin describes the interpretive scheme of Brother Glenn Thompson:

> Brother Glenn Thompson, who also names God as his co-solicitor, claims that most of the world's ills, from crabgrass and garden bugs to Communism and the bomb, can be traced to man's robbing God. "You've got God's money in your wallet. You old stingy Christian. No wonder we've got all these problems. You want to know how you can pay God what you owe? God is speaking through me. God said, 'Inasmuch as you do it unto one of these, you do it unto me.' God said, 'Give all you have for the gospel's sake.' My address is Brother Glenn, Paragould, Arkansas." [15]

But it isn't just money that is involved, or the promise that if one contributes money one will find health and wealth. As Martin says:

> Despite the blatantly instrumental character of much radio religion, it would be a mistake to suppose that its only appeal lies in the promise of health and wealth, though these are powerful incentives. The fact is that if the world seems out of control, what could be more reassuring than to discover the road map of human destiny? This is part of the appeal of Garner Ted Armstrong, who declares to listeners, in a tone that does not encourage doubt, that a blueprint of the future of America, Germany, the British Commonwealth, and the Middle East, foolproof solutions for the problems of child-rearing, pollution, and crime in the streets, plus a definitive answer to the question, "Why Are You Here?" can all be theirs for the cost of a six-cent stamp. On a far less sophisticated level, James Bishop Carr, of Palmdale, California, does the same thing. Brother Carr believes that much of the world's ills can be traced to the use of "Roman time" (the Gregorian calendar) and observances of religious holidays such as Christmas. He has reckoned the day and hour of Christ's second coming, but is uncertain of the year. Each Night of Atonement, he awaits the Eschaton with his followers, the

Little Flock of Mount Zion. Between disappointments, he con-
structs elaborate charts depicting the flow of history from Adam's
Garden to Armageddon, complete with battle plans for the latter
event. Others deal in prophecy on more of an *ad hoc* basis, but
are no less confident of their accuracy. David Terrell, the End-
time Messenger, recently warned that "even today, the sword
of the Lord is drawed" and that "coastal cities shall be inhabited
by strange creatures from the sea, yea, and there shall be great
sorrow in California. . . . God has never failed. Who shall deny
when these things happen that a prophet was in your midst?
Believest thou this and you shall be blessed."

To become a disciple of one of these prophet–preachers is,
by the evangelists' own admission, to obtain a guide without
peer to lead one over life's uneven pathway.[16]

James Bishop Carr, Chairman Mao, Meher Baba, Martin Luther
King, Bishop Fulton Sheen, Timothy Leary—all are, of course,
vastly different men, but they have all claimed to offer a system
of meaning, a basic interpretation, an explanation of what is
going on and why. It takes an exceptional brand of dogmatism to
write such men off as a residue of an unenlightened past, and a
special brand of snobbery to assume that they do not speak to a
basic need of the human condition.

In other ages great leaders of the people enjoyed sacral or
quasi-sacral positions. A king or an emperor was anointed. He
was thought to enjoy special healing powers. A crime against his
person was close to blasphemy. He frequently thought of himself
as the leader of his church, and on a number of occasions was the
one who must reform it despite his clergy. If he led a relatively
moral life he might even be officially "canonized" after his death.
The political leader of the nation was seen as a special kind of
religious person, in part, of course, because it suited his purposes
to be thought of as divine or quasi-divine, but also in part because his followers liked to believe they possessed a leader of
extraordinary powers and of special understanding of the way
things really were.

As Max Weber has pointed out, however, this kind of charismatic and quasi-sacral authority was eventually replaced, first

with traditional authority and then with rational authority—the authority of competence, expertise, and bureaucratic order. We are now, conventional wisdom assures us, to be governed by the technocrat, the intelligent, well-educated man who, if he is not a scientist, at least will be smart enough to fill his staff with them. In our rational, desacralized world it is the man of competency, not charisma, who is the appropriate leader for human organizations—and never mind the overwhelming evidence that people still seem to want charisma. They are, alas, really a little bit belated in their evolutionary development.

However, the criticism of an authority based purely on competence and expertise is heard today not only from the romantic conservatives (such as there may be; in American society most conservatives are as technocratic as liberals) but also from the New Left, which is arguing vigorously for a new kind of authority. Modern authority is in severe crisis precisely because the vast and bureaucratized authority which Max Weber saw evolving is not able to cope with the human problems in the modern world. Rationality, efficiency, and technology as the basis for the legitimacy of authority are no longer persuasive for an increasingly large number of human beings, in part because pure rationality and pure efficiency seem to end up with monstrous irrationality and demonic inefficiency. Not only are the youthful protesters fed up with the bureaucratic society but so is the silent majority. The man who entered the Employment Security Building in Olympia, Washington, and tried to murder a computer merely represents in caricature the feelings of most of us who have, for example, tried to cope with change-of-address notices. (Incidentally, the computer didn't die, because its brains were protected by a bulletproof steel plate.) John Schaar sums up the situation which frustrates old and young alike:

> Our familiar ways of thinking prepare us to imagine that a society must have "someone" in charge, that there must be somewhere a center of power and authority. Things just would not work unless someone, somewhere knew how they worked

and was responsible for their working right. That image and experience of authority has almost no meaning today—as the people in power are the first to say. Modern societies have become increasingly like self-regulating machines, whose human tenders are needed only to make the minor adjustments demanded by the machine itself. As the whole system grows more and more complex, each individual is able to understand and control less and less of it. In area after area of both public and private lives, no single identifiable office or individual commands either the knowledge or the authority to make decisions. A search for the responsible party leads through an endless maze of committees, bureaus, offices, and anonymous bodies.

The functions of planning and control, and ultimately of decision making, are increasingly taken away from men and given over to machines and routine processes. Human participation in planning and control tends to be limited to supplying the machines with inputs of data and materials. And still the complexity grows. Modern man is haunted by the vision of a system grown so complex and so huge that it baffles human control. Perhaps the final solution to the problem of human governance will be to make a machine king.

This is what I mean to suggest by the autonomy of process. The system works not because recognizable human authority is in charge, but because its basic ends and its procedural assumptions are taken for granted and programmed into men and machines. Given the basic assumptions of growth as the main goal and efficiency as the criterion of performance, human intervention is largely limited to making incremental adjustments, fundamentally of an equilibrating kind. The system is glacially resistant to genuine innovation, for it proceeds by its own momentum, imposes its own demands, and systematically screens out information of all kinds but one. The basic law of the whole is: because we already have machines and processes and things of certain kinds, we shall get more machines and processes and things of closely related kinds, and this by the most efficient means. Ortega was profoundly right when a generation ago he described this situation as one of drift, though at that time men still thought they were in command. That delusion is no longer so widespread.[17]

The cult of rationality and efficiency has therefore led to a situation in which the social and ecological problems which face a complex society may not be capable of solution because no one has caused these problems and no one has the power to modify the situation that has created them.

Schaar sees the problem rooted in the scientific and technological concept of reality:

> Bureaucrats still cannot quite believe that the human objects of "urban renewal" see themselves as victims. . . . When thought is so defined, the roles once filled by human leaders wither, and computers can perform them better than men. . . . In some remarkable way, Eichmann was no more responsible than a computer. Bureaucratic behavior is the most nearly perfect example . . . of that mode of conduct which denies responsibility for the consequences of action on the grounds that it lacks full knowledge of the reasons for action. All bureaucrats are innocent.[18]

Schaar's analysis is not strikingly different from that of many of the younger radical critics. The principal reason for citing his analysis, however, is to be able to report on his solution, which strikes me as being extraordinarily interesting from the point of view of the Christian church. Schaar comments:

> the basic opposition is not between charismatic and rational authority, but between what can best be called "natural" and human authority on the one side and bureaucratic–rational control and coordination on the other. . . .
> Rather, what is missing is humanly meaningful authority and leadership. For this the age shows a total incapacity. Establishment officials and hippies alike share the conviction that the only alternatives to the present system of coordination are repression or the riot of passion and anarchy. Both groups, the high and the low, are unable to escape the crushing opposites that the world presents to us and that Weber taught us to believe are the only possible choices. Both groups conceive of authority almost exclusively in terms of repression and denial and cannot imagine obedience based on mutual respect and affection. Confronted with the structures of bureaucratic and technological coordination, the young fear all authority and flee

into the unreason of drugs, music, astrology, and the *Book of Changes,* justifying the flight by the doctrine of "do your own thing"—something that has never appeared on a large scale among any populace outside Bedlam and the nursery, where it can be indulged because there is a keeper who holds ultimate power over the inmates. When those in high positions are confronted with challenges, their first response is to isolate themselves from the challengers by tightening the old rules and imposing tougher new rules. When the managers do attempt reforms in a "humanistic" direction, the result is nearly always a deformity: to humanize leadership—institute coffee hours, fabricate human interest stories to show that the powerful one is a human being after all, and bring in the makeup artists when he has to go on television; to humanize bureaucracy—institute T-groups and ombudsmen; to humanize the law—introduce the indeterminate sentence, special procedures and officials for juvenile offenders, and psychiatrists who will put a technical name on any state of mind for a fee. It is always an alliance between "democratic" ideology and expert manipulation, in a hopeless attempt to reconstruct something now almost forgotten—the idea and the experience of genuine authority. In the earlier ages of man, leaders were made by art to appear as more than human: divine or semi-divine personages. Today the ones who stand at the command posts and switching points are made by art to appear as more than mechanical.[19]

It is necessary, therefore, to break out of the trap of Weber's "false opposites." It is not a question of either retreating to charisma or advancing bravely to the rational legal destiny but of developing something different from both.

Schaar then proceeds to see the basis for this kind of leadership:

> Each man is born, lives among others, and dies. Hence, each man's life has three great underpinnings, which no matter how far he travels, must always be returned to and can never be escaped for long. The three underpinnings present themselves to each man as problems and as mysteries: the problem and mystery of becoming a unique self; but still a self living among and sharing much with others in family and society; and finally

a unique self among some significant others, but still sharing with all humanity the condition of being human and mortal. Who am I as an individual? Who am I as a member of this society? Who am I as a man, a member of humanity? Each of the three questions contains within itself a host of questions, and the way a man formulates and responds to them composes the center and the structure of his values.

Humanly significant authorities are those who help men answer these questions in terms that men themselves implicitly understand. The leader offers interpretations and recommendations which resonate in the minds and spirits of other men. When leaders and followers interact on levels of mutual, subjective comprehension and sharing of meaning, then we have humanly significant leadership. The relationship is one of identification and coperformance. The leader finds himself in the followers, and they find themselves in the leader. I am aware that to the rational and objective men of our day, this is mysticism. But it is those same rational men who cannot understand why the rational, objective, and expert administrators are losing authority, if not yet power, in all the modern states. The answer is mysteriously simple: to the degree that the administrative leader achieves the objectivity and expertise which are the badges of his competence, he loses the ability to enter a relationship of mutual understanding with those who rely on him for counsel and direction.

Humanly significant leadership bases its claim to authority on a kind of knowledge which includes intuition, insight, and vision as indispensable elements. The leader strives to grasp and to communicate the essence of a situation in one organic and comprehensive conception. He conjoins elements which the analytic mind keeps tidily separate. He unites the normative with the empirical, and promiscuously mixes both with the moral and the esthetic. The radical distinction between subjective and objective is unknown in this kind of knowledge, for everything is personal and comes from within the prepared consciousness of the knower, who is simultaneously believer and actor. When it is about men, this kind of knowledge is again personal. It strives to see within the self and along with other selves. It is knowledge of character and destiny. Most of the facts which social scientists collect about men are in this epistemology superficial: information about a man's external attributes, rather than knowledge of who he is and what his possibilities are.[20]

I cannot avoid pointing out what should be obvious in that lengthy quote from Schaar. The authority he is describing sounds remarkably "priestly." I believe Dr. Schaar would not want to deny this, particularly when one sees the kind of language he thinks "humanly significant" leadership ought to use:

> The language in which the knowledge appropriate to humanly significant leadership is expressed is also very different from the language of rational and objective discourse. It is a language profuse in illustration and anecdote, and rich in metaphor whose sources are the human body and the dramas of action and responsibility. This language is suggestive and alluring, pregnant, evocative—in all ways the opposite of the linear, constricted, jargonized discourse which is the ideal of objective communication. Decisions and recommendations are often expressed in parables and visions whose meanings are hidden to outsiders but translucent to those who have eyes to see. Teaching in this language is done mainly by story, example, and metaphor—modes of discourse which can probe depths of personal being inaccessible to objective and managerial discourse. Compare the Sermon on the Mount with the latest communiqué from the Office of Economic Opportunity in the War on Poverty; or Lincoln's Second Inaugural with Nixon's first.[21]

Let it be noted carefully what Schaar is saying. He is insisting not merely that this is a humanly desirable kind of leadership, but that it is functionally necessary if large corporate structures (government, business, labor, education, and church) are not going to become monstrous machines running out of control. Schaar thinks that between Abbie Hoffman and Robert McNamara there is a third choice; but let it also be noted that the third alternative is not one for which many models exist.

I now wish to turn to a more detailed description of what I take to be the functions of leadership in a modern religion, or, indeed, in any human organization.

1. Symbolic Leadership

In a recent article in *Commentary,* Midge Dechter suggested
that it was reactionary to wish to be governed by attractive
people, and deduced that the whole Kennedy cult of the 1960's
was basically reactionary. This is the sort of superficial smartness
that one has come to expect from intellectual journals. Reactionary or not, the human need for leaders who incarnate the
goals, values, and élan of an organization is powerful and probably permanent. An effective leader must be "transparent"; that
is to say, his commitment to the values and goals of the organization must be such that the members can see in him the personifi-
cation of what the organization is striving for. What is required,
one suspects, is not a special kind of personal attractiveness but
rather a clear, enthusiastic, and articulate commitment to goals.
The great men of the 1960's, such as John Kennedy and Martin
Luther King, were not Pied Pipers; but they were men whose
convictions and commitments were unmistakable. Man seems to
need in his leaders evidence that they "really believe" the things
they say, and that they really have confidence that the goals they
describe can be achieved. I do not believe that the mass media
can "merchandise" this quality.

There is no room, then, in the symbolic leader for self-pity or
hand-wringing, for indecisiveness or hedging of bets. He must
have courage, wit, hope, and the willingness to take risks. He
must be able to channel energies and enthusiasms instead of trying to restrain them. He must, in Robert Kennedy's words, say,
"Why not?" instead of "Why?" Midge Dechter to the contrary
notwithstanding, it seems most unlikely that either the need for or
the availability of this sort of leader is going to be eliminated
from modern society.

The symbolic leader plays both a prophetic and therapeutic
role, which is to say, he both challenges and comforts. He stirs
his followers out of their lethargy, complacency, and self-satisfac-
tion. He is not satisfied with the way things are, and he demands

of those associated with him that they use the best of their talents. On the other hand, he is not a prophet in the sense of Amos denouncing or Jeremiah sitting on the edge of the city calling down imprecations. He is also able to comfort, to reassure, to strengthen, to support. If he says to his followers that certain things must be done, he also says they are capable of doing them. His prophecy is never such as to make his associates feel inadequate. Quite the contrary, his prophecy is designed to make them feel more adequate than they were before they heard the prophecy.

2. Ideological

Precisely because he is in a leadership position, the leader is forced to see the "big picture," that is to say, he must be aware of both the overall needs of his organization and of the values and traditions which constitute the ideology of the organization. His associates are involved in their own specific tasks and needs and are not normally inclined to look beyond these immediate tasks and needs to the big picture. It is a leader's role, then, precisely to prevent his associates' turning in on themselves and their own immediate problems and preoccupations. He is *not* a man who provides easy answers—a simple and often quite futile task. He is rather a man whose assumption it is to ask the right questions, to point out the relationships between the group's values and the big picture, which will force the other members of the group to think through their beliefs and their obligations. He poses problems, not solutions.

And he also rejects incomplete answers, that is to say, answers which do not take into account either the ideology of the organization or the reality of the problems it faces. Thus, Kennedy rejected an answer to the Cuban missile crisis which would have involved a surprise attack on Cuba precisely because it was false to the American tradition. Similarly, one would suppose that a religious leader would reject any response to contemporary problems of sexuality which would ignore the need to respect human life. But I am suggesting that the leader would ask the question, "What does our insight into the meaning of sexuality imply for our religious beliefs and behavior?" and let his colleagues attempt to arrive at an answer instead of imposing one on his own initiative. It takes no great skill to provide answers, but to ask the right questions, to distinguish between answers that are adequate and answers that are not, requires a great deal of skill.

3. Interpersonal

The leader realizes that in the complex world in which we live he can ill afford to lose any of the talents of the members of his group. He therefore must create an atmosphere in which there is the greatest possibility for his individual colleagues to develop their talents to the maximum. This means not only guaranteeing them the greatest degree of freedom possible within the group but also creating an atmosphere of harmony and social support among his colleagues. Basic to this, of course, is his obligation to protect the rights of members of the group, but, also, he must do all that he can to see that the conflicts and the strains which exist among his various colleagues are honestly and openly worked out. Conflict and tension cannot be eliminated from the human condition, but its negative effects can be minimized both by bringing conflicts into the open and by providing for everyone a sufficient amount of personal security so that every new conflict does not seem to be an attack on the core of one's personality.

The interpersonal skills that are required of the leader might be compared to the socio-emotional role traditionally attributed to the mother of the family. It has been assumed that the mother is the one who has been responsible for harmonizing difficulties, healing hurts, protecting rights, and facilitating the development of talent. I would note, however, that in the best of modern families the father shares in the socio-emotional leadership just as a mother shares in the task-oriented leadership.

4. Organizational

Despite the naive romanticism of our young, and some of our not-so-young, no groups of human beings could function for very long unless there was organizational effort. The leader, then, must either be an administrator or see that administration gets done. Administration may be less important than symbolizing the goals and values in an organization or interpreting its ideology or creating an effective interpersonal environment. This does not mean that it is unimportant. That some ecclesiastical leaders, alas, have equated administration with leadership does not mean that we can now have ecclesiastical groups in which administration is taboo.

The leader must, first of all, obtain the consent of his colleagues for the major decisions that the group makes. Effective authority is, in the final analysis, the ability to obtain consent. Just as it is easy to give answers, so it is easy to give orders. But orders and answers can be ignored, particularly when one does not have a secular arm available to enforce them. However divine one may be persuaded one's power is, it still is a useless power unless it is accepted by those toward whom it is being directed. A leader who is not able to obtain the consent of a very large majority of his colleagues on a given policy matter has failed as a leader, no matter how noble the title he may claim. Not only, then, does the leader propose the right questions, but he also presides over the dialogue which will lead to a response to the questions. He realizes that everyone whose cooperation is necessary for the implementation of the decision ought to have some kind of participation in the making of the decision. If any substantial part of the membership is excluded from the decision making, then the chances of a successful implementation of the decision are minimal.

Second, the leader must preside over the implementation of the decision. He must direct and coordinate the activities of his colleagues in such a way that the maximum result is obtained in the minimum of effort. It is not, for example, necessary to convene a meeting of the whole group to determine whether stamps should be purchased (nor, as happened in one convent I know, have a twenty-minute discussion each day before Mass to decide what hymns were to be sung). The leader must see, in other words, to the "bookkeeping" and "housekeeping" details. It is an onerous and perhaps thankless task, and his colleagues may grumble and complain about the need to be concerned over such details. Nevertheless, they would grumble and complain much louder if the leader failed to arrange for those things in such a way that the organizational climate of the group would provide some stability and order.

Finally, the leader must see that the organization is arranged in such a way as to maximize pluraformity among the various subgroups within it. For just as the talents of the individuals are developed when they have the greatest possible amount of freedom, so the contribution of subgroups will be most effective when they enjoy the greatest amount possible of initiative, responsibility, and structural flexibility. Just as it would be disastrous for an organization if everybody behaved exactly the same, so it would be disastrous if each subgroup within the organization was under obligation to follow one, and only one, model. Pluraformity is messy, inconvenient, and fits poorly on the organizational chart, but in its absence vitality and variety, ingenuity and creativity vanish. Perhaps the worst thing about Max Weber's bureaucrats is that they are so uniform. Given the strain toward routinization and uniformity in the modern world, the leader preserves pluraformity only if he is willing to take positive action to promote, facilitate, and guarantee variety and flexibility. He cannot assume, at least not in the present state in the evolution of the species, that pluraformity will take care of itself, but he can assume that the alternative to pluraformity is apathy.

Jeffrey Hadden in his book *The Gathering Storm in the*

Churches documents the emerging conflict between Protestant laity and clergy. The former become more deeply involved in social concerns and more skeptical of traditional religious belief, while the latter remain more conservative politically and more traditional religiously. Hadden, good liberal that he is, is sympathetic to the liberal position. But one wonders if the whole framework might not be changed. The conventional wisdom says that everything is changing and that religion must change as rapidly as everything else does; most congregation members are seeking religious stability, looking for an interpretive scheme which will provide some sort of framework of permanence out of which they can operate. The implication of his book is that those congregation members may understand more of social reality than do their clerical leaders who are convinced that there is no more fixity or permanence in the world. Furthermore, those congregation members who are concerned with ultimate meaning may have superior insight into the human condition in contrast with their clerical leaders who think mankind has evolved beyond the need for ultimate meaning. Those congregation members who see an intimate connection between religion and the strong personal relationships of their lives, home, family, and neighborhood may understand more about religion than do their clerical leaders who consider religion's principal role to be to destroy the stable relationships of the past. Finally, those members of Christian denominations who look askance at violence and revolution may understand their own tradition better than those eager clerical enthusiasts who seek to evolve religious justifications for revolution, to justify hatred, violence, and destruction instead of trying to heal, unify, and build up. The congregation members, incidentally, may also know a little bit more about the climate of American politics and about the long history of most revolutions making things worse instead of better.

The stereotypical liberal mind will immediately accuse me of assuming a reactionary position, though I would argue, on the contrary, that his position is reactionary because it is so narrow and insensitive to human beings and their needs; also because I suspect he is more interested in taking a vigorous, progressive, liberal, and moralistic stance than he is in persuading his congregation to agree with him. People are not persuaded by those who denounce them or inform them with characteristic liberal moral arrogance, "You simply have to understand that . . ." One persuades people by obtaining their consent.

Churches with a prophetic religious tradition must obviously be in the forefront of any quest for social justice. The clergy of these churches must take the lead in reminding their congregations of their obligations in justice and in charity. The issue is not whether this is an obligation for the churches, but rather how best and how most effectively this obligation may be carried out. The conventional wisdom argues that the typical Sunday churchgoer is benighted, both because he still maintains mythological beliefs out of the past and because he is afraid of social change. The only proper approach to him, then, is to denounce him, since he is obviously an evolutionary anomaly. I am merely arguing that a religious leader who really wishes to obtain the consent of his congregation will investigate the possibility that there might be something authentic and inevitable in the congregation's quest for religious meaning, and that he ought to try to sympathetically understand this fear of social change. I would want to at least raise the possibility that the clergyman who understands both the longing for the sacred and the fear of social change in his congregation is far more likely to be an effective leader for them—and quite possibly may come to understand dimensions of his own personality that he has repressed. But it is possible to go even further. The minister or priest who can relate the quest for social justice explicitly and concretely to the fundamental myths of his own religious tradition and to the fundamental needs of his congregation might just possibly find that he has more enthusiasts than he knows what to do with. To do this, of course, he will have to accept his people for who and what they are, and respect the honesty and authenticity of their religious search, however unsophisticated it may be and however inferior in its articulation and clarity. For a clergyman trained in a modern divinity school and at least a marginal number of the intellectual elite, acceptance of and respect for the white middle and working classes is extraordinarily hard to come by. There is nothing in their training or in the journals they read to persuade them that a typical member of those congregations is anything more than a racist or fascist. Small wonder that such a clergyman begins to ponder the advisability of seeking a post in the campus ministry or on the college faculty where he can once again associate with academics who are, of course, authentic human beings.

Snobbery is not a new development among religious leaders. We are not unaware of what happens when the rank-and-file members of a religion finally have enough of a clergy that alienate themselves by snobbery. The name of the process is reformation.

10. Conclusion

THERE ARE THREE QUESTIONS to which this book does
not purport to give an answer:

1. Is there in fact a transcendent, a reality which corresponds
   in some fashion to man's vastly different descriptions of the
   deity?
2. Can man have religion without a transcendental referent?
   Can an ultimate interpretive scheme be created which
   does not involve any conviction about the Ultimate?
3. Will the churches—that is to say, institutionalized religion
   in its present manifestation—survive?

The answer to the first question is beyond the scope of social
analysis, though the author obviously has an answer of his own—
as does every man, even he who says he doesn't.

The answers to the second and third questions can at best be
tentative. Obviously, there are some very powerful religious
movements in the world which explicitly exclude a transcendental
referent—Marxism, evolutionism, scientism, etc. Yet, the doc-
trines, the ethics, the traditions, the heroes, the ritual, and the
myths of these "worldly" religions in fact take on an aura of the
sacred which is not greatly different phenomenologically from the
sacral elements of the admittedly transcendental religions. Man
makes his ultimate concerns sacred, that is to say, "other," despite
vigorous efforts to prevent them from becoming sacred. The failure of the various "scientific religions" to capture mass support

despite their claim to be more enlightened and progressive than traditional churches suggests at a minimum that the "this-worldly" religions will have a long way to go before they replace the transcendental ones. After all, the Enlightenment was a long time ago, and Voltaire's deists have not exactly become a majority of the population even of the Western world.

Again, let it be clear that I am *not* arguing that every man needs a religion, much less the sacred, much less a church. I am merely contending that there is in the human condition a built-in strain toward evolving an ultimate meaning system and making it sacred. There is no reason to think that agnosticism, atheism, skepticism, and irreverence are any more common today than they were in other societies, and equally no reason to think that faith, devotion, religious commitment, and sanctity were any more common in the past than they are today.

If one means by a "church" merely a human organization concerned primarily with religion, then one would be vastly surprised if a complicated and highly structured world like our own was able to produce a religion that did not turn into "church." To talk about "institutionless" religion is at best naive romanticism. Whether the existing churches will survive or not is, of course, another matter. They may, and then again, they may not, though at least some sort of presumption has to be made in favor of them simply from the sheer fact of their long survival. As we pointed out repeatedly in this volume, one's religion is absorbed in much the same way as one's language; and while one can turn away from one's religion, and while the option of religious choice is more real today than it has ever been, there is nonetheless a strong strain in the socialization process toward maintenance in some form or other of one's basic religious orientation. Thus, the churches have a good deal going for them. That they have survived the assaults of scientism from without and the incredible corruption and ineptitude of their administrators from within should at least give us pause before we cheerfully predict that they are going to be replaced by new religions and new churches.

Much apostasy from religion is strongly related to conflicts with one's parents. Many of those who think they are breaking away from their church in the name of enlightenment and free-dom actually are at least partially working out conflicts with their mother and father. The literature of the sociology and psy-chology of religious apostasy is not extensive; in fact, most of it has been produced by those affiliated with the National Opinion Research Center. My colleague Joseph Zelan, in studying grad-uate students in the late 1950's, discovered that those who abandoned their religious affiliation tended to be "rebellious," "alienated" individuals whose unhappiness and frustration ap-peared in many different sets of human relationships. David Caplovitz and I, following up on Zelan's research, discovered strong relationships between religious apostasy and reports of troubled family background. John Kotre, in *A View from the Bor-der*, discovered that a self-definition of belonging to the Roman Catholic church or not belonging to it among graduate students who had attended sixteen years of Catholic schools was very strongly related to religious or emotional conflict in the family background. Finally, in the NORC study of the Roman Catholic priesthood, fairly high correlations were discovered between a tense family background and resignations from the priesthood.

It is not our intention to explain all apostasy or all of any given decision to apostasy in terms of revolt against family, but our evidence does lead us to suggest that a good deal of the apostasy phenomenon is related to childhood or to familial ex-periences. This is of course what our theory would lead us to suspect, for we have argued that one acquires one's interpretive scheme in the very early phases of the socialization process. If this process is a relatively benign and emotionally satisfying one, a person is much less likely to feel at conflict with his interpretive scheme than he does if he has acquired it in the midst of a stressful and turbulent emotional situation.

However, it might be argued that the churches cannot survive indefinitely on the strength of the universal drift of the socializa-tion processes of generation after generation. At some point, erosion may be expected to set in, and, indeed, there are those who would argue that erosion already has set in, though the data on church affiliation in the United States do not yet support such an assertion.[1]

There are three strategies which one hears being offered to the churches today. The first is that they should refuse to compromise with the modern world. They should remain aloof from the controversies and the fashions of the time, insist vigorously and rigidly on their own traditions, and avoid even the slightest taint of compromise. Such a strategy was, more or less, the official policy of the Roman Catholic church before the Vatican Council. It is still characteristic of many fundamentalist Protestant groups. John XXIII, in officially breaking with such a conservative policy, called those who advocated it "prophets of doom," though there is no reason to think, on the basis of the present situation, that the Johannine Council effectively broke the stranglehold that the prophets of doom have on the Roman Catholic organizational structure.

The second strategy can be called the "social relevance" approach. It argues that "mythological" religion has been permanently defeated, that man has "come of age" and no longer needs faith or the sacred. I have somewhat scornfully dubbed the assumptions of this strategy "the conventional wisdom" in this present volume. According to its proponents, the Church must abandon its mythology, its conventional morality and piety, its basic belief in the transcendent, and become "involved," which usually means committed to left-wing political and social action or to one of a variety of forms of psychiatric activity. Such a strategy has its most enthusiastic supporters in the faculties and students of some of the more elite divinity schools (though by no means all faculty or all students at such schools) and also among the better-educated clergy in the main-line Protestant denominations which are represented in the National Council of Churches. Since Vatican II, a number of Catholic clergy, particularly the younger ones, have also jumped on the social-relevance bandwagon. In the last chapter we raised some questions about the effectiveness of such strategy from the viewpoint of the sociology of religion. The whole book is obviously intended to question the underlying assumptions on which the relevance strategy is based.*

The third strategy, obviously in harmony with the analysis of this book, would argue that the churches should be primarily concerned with reinterpreting their own mythological tradition. In the face of the scientific and historical attack on the *factuality* of myth there have been basically two responses from the leaders of the churches. Either they retreated into absolute insistence on the strict literalness of the myth and adamantly refused to concede any validity in scientific criticism, or they abandoned the myth completely and surrendered to the onslaught of rationalistic science. As time went on, a third approach appeared, in which a scientific world view was generally accepted and religious truths were nonetheless proclaimed as representing an *entirely different kind of truth*. This approach, strongly biblical in its flavor, and enthusiastically proclaimed by the towering personality of Karl Barth, dominated Protestant theology for several decades under the name of "neo-orthodoxy," but, as Langdon Gilkey points out, the neo-orthodox solution ultimately was a failure because it had isolated itself too completely from the world of science and did not attempt to speak meaningfully about the religious implication of scientific activity.

> Thus they sought to build an autonomous structure of Biblical religious truth unrelated to their own scientific world view. What they were unaware of was that in the dark of night that world view of science, which they accepted, had radically changed their own hermeneutic, that is, the meaning, logic, structure, and authority of their own Biblical language about God's activity in the world. For these two worlds of *Heilsgeschichte* and *Historie*, and their appropriate languages, were impossible to keep apart, especially since according to the Biblical view God did enter into nature and into history. And each

---

* I do not by any means question the propriety, desirability, or even the necessity of social involvement on the part of the clergy and people of the churches. One need not abandon faith, myth, or the sacred to become socially involved.

time the two worlds came together in God's "mighty acts," the scientific assumptions held by these modern theologians threatened the meaning and the authority of the Biblical Word that they also wished to affirm for our time. As nineteenth-century science had demolished an older orthodox view of religious truth which had provided "information" about specific space–time events in nature and in man's history, so the influence of twentieth-century science has likewise made unintelligible a neo-orthodox form of religious truth which sought, not to preempt the place of science, but to isolate itself completely from the influence of science.[2]

Men like Gilkey, Paul Ricoeur, and other contemporary churchmen argue for a new approach to the traditional myth which concedes they were not designed to convey precise and scientific history, but which also argues that they do have existential truth relevant to the situation in which modern man, with all his marvelous scientific tools, finds himself.

There can be no doubt that the churches have been so far considerably less than successful in interpreting their myths as pertinent to the present condition of human bafflement. Completely irrelevant they are not, but pertinent and challenging, especially for the more concerned and thoughtful church members, they certainly also are not. Thomas Luckmann suggests why this is the case.

Institutional segmentation of the social structure significantly modifies the relation of the individual to the social order as a whole. His "social" existence comes to consist of a series of performances of highly anonymous specialized social roles. In such performances the person and the personal, biographical context of meaning become irrelevant. At the same time, the "meaning" of performances in one institutional domain, determined by the autonomous norms of that domain, is segregated from the "meaning" of performance in other domains. The "meaning" of such performances is "rational"—but only with respect to the functional requirements of a given institutional area. It is, however, detached from the overarching context of meaning of an individual biography. The missing (or poor) integration of the meaning of institutional performances into a system of *subjective* significance does not disturb the effective functioning of economic and political institutions. As an actor on the social scene the individual does not liberate himself from the control of institutional norms. Since the "meaning" of these norms only indirectly affects his personal identity and since it has only a "neutral" status in the subjective system of significance, however, the individual does escape the consciousness-shaping effect of institutional norms to a considerable extent. The individual becomes replaceable as a person in proportion to the increasing anonymity of specialized roles that are determined by the functionally rational institutions.[3]

One cannot, of course, be too harsh in criticizing the theories of the churchmen of the past. It has taken a long time for us to develop the conceptual tools which enable us to understand that science speaks one language and myth another—both valid in their own way as descriptions of reality. To have said to a congregation of the Inquisition that Galileo was playing one "word game" and the author of the Pentateuch another would have been to use concepts that the inquisitors would not have understood. Nonetheless, one laments the fact that they were not capable of suspending judgment longer than they did, just as one laments the fact that many scientists were not able to contain their enthusiasm for dismissing myths until we became more sophisticated in our understanding of the different modalities of human thought and expression.

The critical problem of the churches with the challenge to "interpret" the myths is that the myths are "broken"; the factual component of the mythological narrative is now subject to review and criticism by science, and, indeed, can in no sense claim to compete with science as a description of what literally happened in the past. But there are two points to be kept in mind in a discussion of the "broken" myth. The first is that the mythmaker was obviously not trying to narrate science or history as we understand the terms today. He was trying to say something about the nature of the ultimate reality in which he and his fellows found themselves. While he may have believed that things "actually happened" the way the story said they did, his primary concern was not with how events actually happened but with the meaning of reality that his narration of events conveyed. In archaic myth there was a clear awareness that the story dealt with events that happened *in illo tempore,* to use Mircea Eliade's words, in time quite different from the time in which the myth-maker lived. In the myths of the historic religions, on the other hand, events are described as happening in historic times, but the events themselves are still secondary to the reality that they symbolized. Thus, the important point about the Exodus story is not how many days Moses spent on Mount Sinai but rather that the Sinai story conveys to those who heard it a world view, an ethical system, a sense of mission and hope rooted in the conviction that God has entered into a covenant with the Israelite people.

In Christian mythology the basic issue is not so much how exactly the events of Jesus' resurrection occurred, but rather the existential truth conveyed in the Resurrection story: through Jesus mankind triumphed over sin and death. In the peculiar atmosphere of the last several centuries of conflict between science and religion, the order of importance has been reversed; the details of the Sinai experience and the death and Resurrection of Jesus have become more important than the interpretive system which these stories are designed to convey. Curiously enough, be it noted, the interpretive scheme stated in the Sinai and Easter experiences is far more marvelous—in the strict sense of the word—than the mere physical facts recounted. That the deity should enter into a covenant with the people is far more splendid and wonderful a notion than that he should speak to Moses in a burning bush; that the whole human race would triumph over death is indescribably more astonishing than that one man should do so. The notion that one could make Christianity palatable to a scientific world view if one abandoned a commitment to the Resurrection of Jesus could only be held by those who failed completely to understand the interpretive scheme that was incarnated in the Resurrection story.

So much time and energy in the past several centuries have gone into arguing over the concrete factual details of the mythological story, that there has been little or no time available to look seriously at the religious and existential truth the story conveys. I am not saying that there are no strictly historical facts in the Jewish and Christian myths. Exegetical scholarship leaves us in no doubt that many of the events in the life of Jesus transpired more or less exactly the way they were described. Certainly in the historical religions some facts must be assumed by the believers of the myth to be literally true or the myth would be empty; but the relevant point is that the myth-makers were far more interested in conveying an interpretive scheme about the nature of ultimate reality than they were in telling a story that would measure up to the strict scientific canons devised only centuries into the future.

Yet our education has been such that if we are told that something is mythopoetic we find ourselves asking the question, "Does that mean it really isn't true?" The only response is no, it simply means that it is a different kind of truth, in its own way more comprehensive than the rationalist truth of science.

For Christians, for example, the question of whether Jesus rose from the dead is not totally irrelevant. However, Christians should be aware that a completely satisfactory scientific and historical account of the events after the death of Jesus is quite impossible. The more basic question is whether the Christian's world view includes the notion that the human race through God's power will triumph over death. Compared to *that* question the precise historical and physiological details of the events after the death of Jesus are relatively unimportant.

In my more cynical moments, I am inclined to suspect that many "religionists" and "scientists" spend so much of their time arguing about secondary questions because they do not want to face the painful, terrifying, and awesome issue about the ultimate

nature of the really real. The second point to be made—and much
more briefly—about the broken myth is that, as we pointed out
in Chapter 3, all of us engage in myth-making activity; we
experience in that activity the awareness that concrete factual
details are much less important than the message we wish to
convey through our narrative. We modify details, rearrange
events, eliminate some aspects of the story, and emphasize others,
all so as to convey our *interpretation* of the *meaning* of the event.
If I am telling a colleague why I fired a research assistant *
I will not attempt to recount scientifically the exact sequence of
events. I will rather arrange my narrative in such a fashion that
I can convey to him my basic interpretation that the research
assistant was incompetent. Details of the encounter between the
two of us which do not fit my interpretation will be eliminated
and details which do will be developed at great length—perhaps
even lovingly. It does not mean that I am trying to deceive my
colleague, that I am trying to tell him something that is not true;
quite the contrary, I am trying to convey to him a truth that is
larger than all the aggregation of factual details would indicate.
I have not tried to deceive anyone, but instead of amassing a
collection of facts, I have tried to describe the *meaning* of an
experience.

It is precisely with the description of the *meaning of an
experience* that the myth-makers in the historic religions are concerned. The experience may be relevant or irrelevant; the meaning may be attractive or repellent; their message may have
validity of meaning or it may not; I may be willing to make
commitments to the "culture system" that they are trying to
convey through their narrations or I may not; but I should at
least understand what they are about and not think that I have
adequately responded to them when I quibble with their factual
details.

The organized churches, I would contend, must engage in
the sorts of creative interpretation of the mythological traditions:

---

* Which, by the way, I have never done, though this should not
necessarily be counted virtue in me.

but they should make clear to their followers what these myths say about the ultimate nature of reality and about the human condition. In an earlier age and for large numbers of people in the present age the myth itself was enough. It was as though the hearers of the myth were poetically receptive to a narrative poetically told. Interpretation was unnecessary because—probably at the preconscious level—they perceived in the narration answers to questions of ultimate meaning that were rarely explicitly articulated. But in our age of explicit articulation the substantive content of the myth must be explicitly articulated, although, be it noted, it is most unlikely that those who have completely repressed the mythopoetic dimensions of their thought processes will ever really be able to understand the myth, even when its substantive content is liberated somewhat from its mythopoetic garb.

In other words, before well-educated and intellectually sophisticated contemporary men are able to appreciate the full emotional, affective range of the mythological story, they must understand how the story purports to provide answers to the basic existential questions about ultimate reality that man asks himself. What does the Sinai myth or the Easter myth say in response to the basic questions about the meaning of life?

The churches may not be able to interpret their own myths. If they don't, so much the worse for them, because man must have his myths. In Langdon Gilkey's words about a scientific culture:

> even in such a culture, the peculiar language of myth and therefore of religion is not only necessary because unavoidable, but even more it is essential if a scientific culture is to deal creatively with its own peculiar problems and so its own destiny.[4]

Without myth, in other words, man is ill-equipped to cope with "the ultimate or existential issues of actual life and the questions of human and historical destiny." If the churches do not provide responses to these critical problems out of their own tradition, then presumably new myth-makers will appear on the scene to hawk their wares. In either case, one suspects the concern with the mythological will increase rather than decrease, a suspicion which, by the way, provides us with a model that is not at all troubled by the recent resurgence of the mythological on the college campus.

To present somewhat schematically our argument: man has historically expressed his interpretive schemes in the form of myths. There is no reason to think he will not continue to do so. Religious myths have been on the defensive because of the misunderstanding of the purpose of myth in the early years (which are just ending) of the scientific revolution. Now that mythology is being freed from misunderstanding, one can expect it to flourish once again, although now it will be necessary for the myth-makers or their disciples to interpret the substantive content of the myth. One can expect myth-making to become particularly vigorous when scientific society faces extreme crises.

But such extreme crises seem to have occurred. I now propose to discuss two such crises and to comment on the pertinence of religion (though not necessarily the churches) in coping with them: *the technology issue and the generation gap.*

There is no doubt that technology is in deep trouble. The New Left school of political and social criticism equates technology with "the Establishment" and argues that technological culture is out of control, destroys the creativity of the human spirit, and eventually will destroy the whole race if it is not prevented from doing so. Authors like John McDermott and Theodore Roszak vigorously insist that "objective consciousness" and belief in the benign effect of technological improvement may mean profit for those who are already wealthy, more power for those who already have power, and destruction for those who question the use of power and wealth; that "objective consciousness" and blind faith in technology will ultimately destroy the race either in a thermonuclear holocaust or by pollution or by so dehumanizing and depersonalizing life that it is no longer tolerable.[5]

The defenders of technology like Emmanuel G. Methnane [6] admit that endless and unquestioned innovation, production, and distribution of goods and services may involve certain extremely serious problems. Yet it is only through further technological developments subject to the control of enlightened science and equally enlightened government that the problems technology has already produced will be brought under control.

On the one hand, then, the romantic critics of technology argue that it is foolish to expect that technology can bring itself under control, because by its very nature it is destined to generate an unending series of new productive innovations. The defenders, on the other hand, argue that while some aspects of the technological processes are out of control, they can be brought back under control through intelligent supervision and further developments in technology itself.

There is a good deal to be said for both sides of the argument. While a man like Roszak is an incurable romantic, clearly in love with his own erudition and powers of articulation, he has been able to strike a responsive chord in many young people precisely because he perceives the absurdity in the destructiveness of unrestrained technological development. However, as Margaret Mead points out in a book review of Roszak's *The Making of a Counterculture,* most of us would starve to death if the technological society was in fact overthrown by a "counterculture." As someone who would have died in infancy in the absence of improved medical technology, I am not prepared to refute Dr. Mead's observation. Furthermore, there is something just a bit ironic about Roszak's denouncing the technological culture in a paperback book, printed by a highly sophisticated printing press, published by a most established publishing house, distributed by efficient techniques of mass distribution, and advertised by the equally efficient advertising techniques of that technological culture. It is also ironic that even though he rejects rationalistic science, Roszak is all too willing to provide his book with very learned, scholarly footnotes.

Still, defenders of technology are quite correct in their observation that realistically the problems of environment will only be solved when we have developed more elaborate and efficient methods of processing—or, more likely, recycling—the waste products of society. However, with Lake Erie dead and Lake Michigan dying, with the air filled with sulphur dioxide, and with enough nuclear weapons to destroy the earth many times over, the scientists and technologists will forgive us if we have some reservations about the benign impact of unrestricted technological development.

The real issue, then, is not whether we can abolish technology; obviously, we can't. The creation of countercultures is not likely to solve the problems of a technological society. The solution is not to be found in more technology, although we must have some technological innovations if only to be able to cope with the waste presently being produced. Nor is some sort of control on production and distribution the answer. Controls of many sorts are already being imposed. The issue is, I think, rather more basic: What is the nature of man and his destiny? Only when we can answer that question can we have some sense of what technology ought to be if it is to be man's servant.

In Langdon Gilkey's words:

> A sense of the mystery and inviolability of the person, both in his personal and political relations, is necessary if we are to understand at all what scientific knowledge means to society both for good and for ill. A scientific culture can become demonic if science is not used by men whose self-understanding and thus whose public action is guided by symbols that transcend the limits of scientific inquiry and illumine the spiritual, personal, and free dimensions of man's being.[7]

Man's creation of his great scientific and technological masterpieces has revealed the power of his intellect, the strength of his will, the courage of his imagination, but it has also revealed the ambiguity of his condition and the disasters which his pride can bring him.

> One of the most vivid, ironical, and frightening examples of this sad truth about history—that even as mature technologists we have little control over our own intellects and wills, over our own acts, and so *ipso facto* over our resulting history —is the history itself of technology. Technology is perhaps the purest symbol of the victory of man's purposes over blind nature, of the victory of human intelligence and freedom over mere chance; it is thus the paradigm for the myth we are discussing. And yet look at technology. Ironically, it illustrates the deep ambiguity of all of man's powers and therefore of his history, combining possibilities for both good and evil, and even overlaying its own essence as an expression of human freedom with the implacability of determining fate. For technology itself has become one of the fates that haunt modern man, mocking his control over himself and even over nature. In fact, it has almost replaced blind nature as the main causative factor in whatever threatens our contemporary existence—it is worse, more hazardous to health and safety, to live in cities than in nature; and the rapid and uncontrolled development of technology is beginning to frighten many thoughtful technologists.
>
> Technology is a powerful modern symbol of the ambiguity of our destiny, if not of fate, for three reasons. Each of these reasons represents the loss of the control by man's rational and purposive intentionality over the technology that man has created. Thus has human freedom, in creating technology, warped *itself* into a fate that has become a threat precisely to that freedom.[8]

Man's actions, Gilkey tells us, "even, and perhaps especially," when he has mastery, power, and knowledge remain ambiguous in basic motivation and tragic in unforeseen consequences.

> When any generation, however secular, finally sees this ambiguity, and the inescapable selfishness that was its cause, they are apt to find their moral nerve cut. An angry helplessness about any creative action anywhere appears—and men withdraw from social history in despair, disgust, and shame, . . .[9]

Theodore Roszak's counterculture, in other words, is the discovery, however contorted and unexpressed, of the ambiguity of human motivations and the tragedy of unforeseen consequences. The making of a counterculture is an attempt, ultimately terribly inadequate, to respond to the crisis. What Roszak and others have discovered—though they would never use the word—is the sinfulness of man.

In every epoch of our history, then, we need to discover not only moral standards by which we may judge ourselves and the social world we live in, but also forgiveness somewhere for what we and our world are, an assurance of the ability to accept ourselves and our world, even in the ambiguity that we know to characterize them when we are aware of the truth. For only thus are we enabled to go on with our worldly work for a better and juster world than we now have. And in order to do *that*, we need to have a faith that something works for good, even beyond and within the mess that we men have made and will continue to make; we need an intelligible ground for hope, a credible "myth" that does not lie to us about ourselves and our future. Finally, if life is in this way made up of ambiguity and frequent conflict, we need to have an urge for reconciliation, with the others whom we have injured and with ourselves too. All of this points beyond the scope and capabilities of our own knowledge and of our own moral powers to the deeper sources of both, the God who is creative of our astounding capacities, who judges our waywardness, and who accepts our repentance; who works in the midst of our evil as well as of our good to further his purposes and fulfil his promises; and who calls us to reconciliation so that we may start again on his and our work for a better and more humane future.

The vast new powers of science do not, in the end, make religious faith and commitment irrelevant; they make them more necessary than ever. And they make of the utmost importance the understanding and the use of the deeper symbols expressive of the real issues and so the realistic possibilities of man's destiny —the symbols of man's potentialities and nature as the image of God, of his waywardness as fallen from grace; of the judgment, the mercy, and the promise of God. For only on these terms can the mystery, the risk, and the hopes of the destiny of a scientific culture be comprehended and borne.[10]

Indeed, modern man has immense power and mastery to display over nature, but increasingly all that power does is to make the ambiguity of the human condition more painful. "Science does not answer the ultimate question of hope; it raises it more poignantly than ever." [11]

In other words, mythology of some sort—that is to say, an interpretive scheme wrestling with the issues of man and reality —is absolutely essential if scientific society is to understand itself and protect itself from self-destruction.

> Thus, however "secular" may be the way in which a scientific culture seeks to understand its past and present, though such secularity of comprehension is never total, such a culture inevitably uses mythical language in understanding its own future destiny. [12]

In the final analysis, then, the neo-orthodox were completely wrong to think they could maintain religion and science in separate compartments of human knowledge and discourse, for religion must speak to and about science, not, indeed, to deny its developments, and surely not to quibble with it about the factual details of past events, but to help it to understand itself, its own destiny, and particularly the destiny of man who has created science.

> But correspondingly, without the transcendent dimensions introduced by religious myths a culture cognizant merely of the factual will understand neither itself nor its destiny. For the shape of "the factual" it believes it understands, and the way it understands its future, will in the end be determined by its own unexamined myths. And such myths, because they are neither factual nor ideal, will fail either to calm its deepest anxieties or to ground its most important hopes. [13]

It is precisely the lack of any systematic interpretive scheme which has enabled technological innovations to rage out of control. It is an interpretive scheme about man and his destiny, most likely expressed in mythological terms, that will enable man to bring technology back under control. If I were in a key position in a church (I am not and never likely to be), I would consider it one of my prime responsibilities to search my mythology for religious truth that would speak to the crisis of science and technology.*

A second problem for which mythology or at least a meaning system is needed is the so-called generation gap. There has been a good deal of nonsense written about the "younger generation," but nothing more nonsensical than Margaret Mead's *Culture and Commitment: A Study of the Generation Gap*.[14] Dr. Mead argues that the present younger generation living in a "prefigurative culture" represents a decisive change in the human evolutionary process. This is the organic evolution model pursued with a vengeance. Ernst van den Haag, reviewing Dr. Mead's book, quotes the following data from Professor Seymour Martin Lipset:

> At Harvard the police had to be called in several times because of violent rioting between 1807 and 1830. Half the senior class was expelled in 1823. In Princeton half the students were expelled in 1806 following a rebellion. . . . Students occupied college buildings while "Nassau Hall resounded to the reports of pistols and the crash of bricks against doors, walls, and windows." Yale fared no better; nor did the University of Virginia, which had to tighten Jefferson's liberal rules. The targets? Anything from examinations and bad food to politics, morals and religion, "compulsory military training, ROTC, stupid courses." In 1922 George Santayana wrote that the students "all proclaim their disgust with the present state of things in America; they denounce the Constitution of the United States, the churches, the colleges, the press . . . they are against everything—but what are they for? I have not been able to discover. . . ."

It is hard to see how Dr. Mead could find "this youthful

---

* One such attempt, not completely successful but still interesting, is Jurgen Moltman in "Christian Rehumanization of Technological Society," *The Critic*, May–June, 1970, p. 10. Moltman quite correctly describes man as a "sorcerer's apprentice" who has unleashed powers that he cannot control. The weakness, from my viewpoint, of Moltman's attempts at interpretation is that he doesn't go nearly deeply enough into the nature of man and his destiny to enable the sorcerer's apprentice to know what he is to do when he puts down the broom.

activism . . . wholly new" except by sharing the historical ignorance of her young subjects, which is pushing empathy too
far.

   Culture and Commitment repeatedly asseverates a "rebellion of youth": it is the proof offered for the existence of the
generation gap to be bridged by "prefigurative" culture. (One
can't always be sure whether prefigurative culture is described,
predicted, or advocated.) Yet there has been a rebellion only
among college students, usually in elite colleges, where the
students are almost exclusively the offspring of the middle classes.
Less than half our youth attend college (a far smaller proportion does abroad). Of this minority of the young less than 10
percent can be said to have even remotely participated in the
rebellion here; fewer abroad.

   In the United States (and elsewhere) lower-class youths—
perhaps more perceptive than Dr. Mead—have seen the antics
of their middle-class age-mates not as "youth rebellion" but as
gratuitous psychodrama staged by spoiled or bored or guilt-
ridden youngsters indulged, or helped along, by a flaming faculty
and smoldering parents.[15]

These are harsh words, but they certainly are supported by
every research project done on young people I have ever seen.
My colleague John W. C. Johnstone, in his study of Webster
Grove High School in Missouri, concluded that there was rather
little difference between the senior high school students in that
well-to-do suburb and their parents. Most of the research done on
the student protesters indicates that they come from families
where radicalism or at least liberalism is part of the environment
in which the young people were raised. In a carefully documented article in the *New York Times Magazine,* Professor Joseph
Adelson, of the University of Michigan, observes, "that there is a
generation gap that is not totally false, perhaps, but false enough.
In politics, in values, in aspirations, and plans, the younger generation has far more in common with its parents than it is different from them." [16]

if we are talking about a fundamental lack of articulation between the generations, then the answer is—decisively—no.

From one perspective, the notion of a generation gap is a form of pop sociology, one of those appealing and facile ideas which sweep through a self-conscious culture from time to time. The quickness with which the idea has taken hold in the popular culture—in advertising, television game shows and semi-serious potboilers—should be sufficient to warn us that its appeal lies in its superficiality. From another perspective we might say that the generation gap is an illusion, somewhat like flying saucers.[17]

How has this illusion been perpetrated? The mass media, with their insatiable hunger for novelty, have been primary contributors.

Thus, the typical TV special on the theme, "What Is Happening to Our Youth?" is likely to feature a panel consisting of (1) a ferocious black militant, (2) a feverish member of S.D.S., (3) a supercilious leader of the Young Americans for Freedom (busily imitating William Buckley), and (4), presumably to represent the remaining 90 percent, a hopelessly muddled moderate. But we have much the same state of affairs in the quality magazines, where the essays on youth are given to sober yet essentially apocalyptic ruminations on the spirit of the young and the consequent imminent decline (or rebirth) of Western civilization.[18]

The generation gap basically is a gap that exists not between parents and their children but between some children and other people's parents.

But the conventional wisdom of the generation-gap model blinds us to a far more serious problem in the youthful segment of society, a problem which the young education editor of the *Saturday Review*, Wallace Roberts, sensitively portrays in his description of New Trier High School in Winnetka, Illinois. It is the problem of despair.

The New Trier students that Roberts describes are not for the most part hippies or left-wing protesters. Some of them smoke pot, but few of them are likely to become addicts. An occasional one may just possibly join a commune. A few of them may experiment with witchcraft or astrology or the *I Ching*, though perhaps not very seriously. And yet, Roberts detects in them a mood of hopelessness and despair. Products of one of the richest communities in the country and one of the best high schools in American secondary education, with everything possible to live for, they seem to lack hope, joy, and confidence in their own future. As one who has spent a decade in a neighborhood not too different from Winnetka on the South Side of Chicago, I can testify that the Irish Catholic adolescents of Beverly Hills are no more immune from despair than their counterparts on the North Shore. It took me a long time to understand the despair and even to realize what it was. It took me an even longer time to realize that the suicide which took place every year or two represented in only a slightly exaggerated form the feeling of many other young people. I was astonished to learn, in fact, how many of them had held the instruments of self-destruction in their own hands. Whether it was Catholic morality or—as seems more likely —the strength of middle-class ego training, most of them did not dispose of themselves, at least not with an abrupt suicidal act. Nonetheless, many, indeed most of them, I would say, felt that they had very little to live for.

I would contend that the rock-music enthusiasts, the drug addicts, the hippies, the communitarians, the witches and warlocks, the protesters, the radicals, the Weathermen, are all but the tip of the iceberg. They reveal in exaggerated form a listlessness, an apathy, a discouragement, and a frustration which is widespread, not to say pervasive, among young Americans. Is this despair a "generation gap"? I would rather think that it is merely an exaggerated variety of a feeling which already exists among the parents of the upper-middle-class young people. It is a frustration and it comes with the realization that abundance and affluence are not enough; that not, indeed, by bread alone does man live.

In other words, the despair, which a perceptive observer of

his own generation like Wallace Roberts has discovered, is despair based on the fact that many modern young people have nothing to believe in, have no interpretive scheme, have no mythology which will give order, coherence, purpose to their lives. They are a caricature of what the conventional wisdom says modern man is. They are young people without a faith, without a sacred, without an interpretive scheme, without a community. They do not know who they are, where they are going, or why they live.

I would suggest that the representatives of the organized religions who think they can establish contact with such a generation of young people by using their language, smoking their drugs, dancing to their rock tunes, marching on their protest lines, or wearing their psychedelic clothes have missed the point entirely. If there is one thing clear in all the deviant streams running through youthful American culture—drugs, rock, protest, communes, superstition—it is that the younger generation quite explicitly wants something to believe in and norms which follow from that belief according to which they can live.

I fear that in the past paragraphs the clerical dimension of my personality has got the best of me, and that I have, on the basis of data which can only be described as systematic impressions at best, proceeded to preach a sermon.

But then, if I am true to my convictions as expressed in this book, I must believe that the social scientist cannot keep his passion or his commitment out of his work. On occasions, I suspect, it is extremely fruitful even for analytic purposes to let that passion show through. In any case, in the previous paragraphs and, I dare say, in many other paragraphs in the book I have not been at pains to hide my passion or my convictions.

To recapitulate, the volume began with that rather bold assertion that fundamental religious needs had not changed since the Ice Age. Modern man, like his archaic predecessor, needs faith, community, myth, ethics which reflect the nature of reality, an opportunity to experience the sacred, and particularly to understand sexuality as sacred, and religious leadership which will facilitate his interpretation of the meaning of life. That conventional wisdom which sees man as evolving away from the need for faith and for the sacred (arguing that "man has come of age") is not based on empirical evidence but on a priori assumptions about the nature of the human evolutionary process, assumptions which simply do not fit concrete historical evidence. The model of the conventional wisdom does not enable us to understand either the persistence of religion among the overwhelming majority of people in the Western world, or the resurgence of bizarre forms of religious behavior among young people, or the religious and mythological coloration allegedly "scientific" value systems quickly acquire. I have not argued that every man must have faith but have suggested, rather, that most men do need faith at least at some times in their lives, and that there is no evidence to show that the need is any less now than it was in the past, or that our archaic predecessors were any more devout than we are today.

When one makes an assertion like that, one is faced with unusual kinds of *ad hominem* arguments. A very distinguished European theologian once remarked to me, "But in the Middle Ages people prayed the Angelus in the fields. Certainly they were more *religious* than we are today." One would, of course, have to know how many people did in fact pray the Angelus in the field, and what religious meaning such behavior had for them. One would further have to know whether medieval society was as really devout as the picture of the farmers praying the Angelus would lead us to believe. There is every reason to think that it was not. But of course the contention in this volume has not been that the modalities of the sacred remain fixed. Quite the contrary, they obviously change as cultures change. The point, rather, is that there is no unidirectional evolutionary movement in this change from the sacred to the secular. Furthermore, I also contend that from one point of view the modern man who does *not* say the Angelus in the field might be more religious than his ancestors who did because he is forced to address himself to explicitly religious questions as they were not.

There have been, as I pointed out in the volume, extremely important changes in man's religious behavior. Even if scientific progress has led to a decline in the number of natural mysteries that religion must explain, growth in human knowledge and self-awareness and the increased complexity of human relationships have increased the number of *human* problems which create bafflement and mystery. However, the three most important changes are:

1. Myths are no longer self-evident, at least for the most sophisticated among us; they must be interpreted and explained. Meaning systems have to be explicit and articulate.

2. Man has many different meaning systems to choose from and a marvelous supermarket of interpretive schemes. Most of us may not in fact exercise an option for an interpretive scheme different from the one we acquired early in our socialization experience. Nevertheless, the very fact that the supermarket exists does create an atmosphere of option which never existed in the past.

3. Finally, while we still acquire religions from a community and generally live them out in a community, we still, relatively speaking, have considerably more freedom from the community in making our religious choice than did our ancestors.

These three changes are of immense importance. In fact, they create a very different ambience than that in which our Ice Age ancestor walked. But all three of them work not to decrease the importance of interpretive schemes but to make them more explicit, more conscious, and probably more necessary.

The conventional wisdom is under assault from all sides—a phenomenon which would have been unthinkable even a decade ago. The young radicals and the New Leftists denounce it for being hyper-rational. Depth psychologists criticize it for ignoring the human unconscious. Students of comparative religion decry its misunderstanding of mythology. Social critics are angry at its passive acceptance of liberal positivism. Existentialists want no part of its bland indifference to the hard ultimate questions that man must ask. And we lowly survey researchers say, "It doesn't seem to be substantiated by the factual data."

And Professor Harvey Cox has made his pilgrimage from the secular city to his festive city on a mountaintop that sounds rather like Camelot, which, be it noted, was a mythological place both in the time of King Arthur and in the 1960's.

Notes

Chapter I: Introduction

1. Eugene Fontinell, *Toward a Reconstruction of a Religion.* Garden City, N.Y.: Doubleday, 1970, p. 19.

2. Martin E. Marty, *The Modern Schism.* New York: Harper & Row, 1969, p. 11.

3. John Cogley, *Religion in a Secular Age.* New York: Praeger, 1968, p. 71.

4. Ramon Echarren, "Communicating the Faith in Present-Day Society," *Concilium,* Vol. 53, pp. 15–16.

5. Peter L. Berger, *A Rumor of Angels.* Garden City, N.Y.: Doubleday, 1969, p. 7.

6. Andrew M. Greeley, *Religion in the Year 2000.* New York: Sheed and Ward, 1969, pp. 32–35.

7. Guy A. Swanson, "Modern Secularity," in Donald R. Cutler (ed.), *The Religious Situation: 1968.* Boston: Beacon Press, 1968, pp. 811–13.

8. Swanson, *op. cit.,* pp. 813–14.

9. Gerhard Lenski, *The Religious Factor.* Garden City, N.Y.: Doubleday, 1966.

10. Martin E. Marty, Andrew M. Greeley, Stuart Rosenberg, *What Do We Believe?* New York: Meredith Press, 1968.

11. "The Religious Behavior of Graduate Students," *Journal for the Scientific Study of Religion,* Vol. 5, No. 1 (1965), pp. 34–40.

12. *Ibid.*

13. David Martin, *The Religious and the Secular,* New York: Schocken, 1969, p. 123.

Chapter II: New Myths and Old

1. David Matza, *Delinquency and Drift*. New York: Wiley, 1964, p. 3.

2. Robert Nisbet, *Social Change in History*. New York: Oxford University Press, 1969.

3. Robert Nisbet, *The Social Bond*. New York: Knopf, 1970.

4. Nisbet, *The Social Bond*, p. 318.

5. *Ibid.*

6. *Ibid.*, p. 304.

7. *Ibid.*, p. 305.

8. *Ibid.*, p. 306.

9. *Ibid.*

10. *Ibid.*

11. *Ibid.*, p. 308.

12. *Ibid.*

13. *Ibid.*

14. *Ibid.*, p. 303.

15. *Ibid.*, p. 309.

16. *Ibid.*, p. 331.

17. *Ibid.*, p. 332

18. *Ibid.*, pp. 334–35.

19. *Ibid.* p. 358.

20. *Ibid.*, pp. 360–61.

21. *Ibid.*, pp. 362–63.

22. *Ibid.*, pp. 105–6.

23. John Schaar, "Reflections on Authority," *New American Review*, Vol. 8 (1970), p. 671.

24. Friedrich Heer, *The Intellectual History of Europe*, trans. by Jonathan Steinberg. London: Weidenfeld and Nicolson, 1966, p. 57.

25. *Ibid.*, pp. 59–61.

26. David Martin, *The Religious and the Secular*. New York: Schocken Books, 1969, pp. 65–66.

27. *Ibid.*, p. 71.

28. Martin E. Marty, *The Modern Schism*. New York: Harper & Row, 1969.

29. William Stahlman, "Global Myths Record Their Passage," *Saturday Review*, January 10, 1970, p. 101.

30. Gerald Hawkins, *Stonehenge Decoded*. New York: Dell, Delta, 1966, paperback.

31. Claude Lévi-Strauss, *The Savage Mind*. Chicago: University of Chicago Press, 1969, pp. 13–15, paperback.

32. *Ibid.*, p. 22.

33. Nisbet, *The Social Bond*, p. 388.

34. *Ibid.*

35. *Ibid.*, p. 372.

Chapter III: Religion and Faith

1. Clifford Geertz, "Religion as a Cultural System," in Donald Cutler (ed.), *The Religious Situation: 1968*. Boston: Beacon Press, 1968, p. 641.

2. Clifford Geertz, "The Impact of the Concept of Culture on the Concept of Man," in John R. Platt (ed.), *New Views of the Nature of Man*. Chicago: The University of Chicago Press, 1965, p. 112.

3. *Ibid.*, pp. 112–14.

4. *Ibid.*, pp. 116–17.

5. Clifford Geertz, "Ideology as a Cultural System," in David E. Apter (ed.), *Ideology and Discontent*. New York: The Free Press, 1964, pp. 62–63.

6. Geertz, "Religion as a Cultural System," p. 667.

7. *Ibid.*, p. 668.

8. *Ibid.*

9. Geertz, "Ideology as a Cultural System," pp. 71–72.

10. Geertz, "Religion as a Cultural System," p. 668.

11. *Ibid.*, p. 643.

12. *Ibid.*, p. 653.

13. *Ibid.*, p. 654.

14. *Ibid.*, p. 655.

15. *Ibid.*, p. 656.

16. *Ibid.*, p. 663.

17. *Ibid.*, p. 669.

18. Clifford Geertz, "Ethos, World-View and the Analysis of Sacred Symbols," *The Antioch Review*, Vol. 17 (December, 1957), p. 424.

19. *Ibid.*, p. 422.

20. Clifford Geertz, *Islam Observed*. New Haven: Yale University Press, 1969, p. 95.

21. *Ibid.*, p. 101.

22. *Ibid.*

23. *Ibid.*, p. 97.

24. Geertz, "Ethos, World-View and the Analysis of Sacred Symbols," p. 422.

25. *Ibid.*, p. 426.

26. Geertz, "Religion as a Cultural System," p. 669.

27. *Ibid.*, p. 677.

28. Geertz, *Islam Observed*, p. 17.

29. *Ibid.*, p. 18.

30. *Ibid.*, p. 114.

31. *Ibid.*, pp. 103–4.

32. Robert Nisbet, *The Social Bond*, New York: Knopf, 1970, pp. 239–40.

33. *Ibid.*

34. *Ibid.*, p. 241.

35. Thomas Luckmann, *The Invisible Religion*. New York: Macmillan, 1967, p. 113.

36. Peter L. Berger, *A Rumor of Angels*. Garden City, N.Y.: Doubleday, 1969, pp. 67–68.

37. *Ibid.*, p. 74.

38. *Ibid.*, p. 80.

39. *Ibid.*, p. 81.

40. *Ibid.*, p. 87.

41. *Ibid.*, p. 89.

42. Langdon Gilkey, *Naming the Whirlwind*. Indianapolis: Bobbs-Merrill, 1969, pp. 363–64, paperback.

43. *Ibid.*, p. 362.

44. *Ibid.*, p. 361.

45. *Ibid.*, pp. 362–63.

46. *Ibid.*, p. 397.

47. *Ibid.*, pp. 402–3.

48. Geertz, "Impact of the Concept of Culture on the Concept of Man," p. 116.

Chapter IV: Myth and Man

1. Alan W. Watts, *The Two Hands of God*. New York: Braziller, 1963, p. 2.

2. *Ibid.*

3. *Ibid.*, p. 16.

4. Charles Long, *Alpha: Myths of Creation*. New York: Braziller, 1963, p. 13.

5. *Ibid.*

6. *Ibid.*, p. 16.

7. Mircea Eliade, *Patterns in Comparative Religion*. New York: Sheed and Ward, 1958, p. 455.

8. *Ibid.*, pp. 455–56.

9. Mircea Eliade, *The Sacred and the Profane*, trans. by Willard R. Trask. New York: Harcourt, Brace, 1959, p. 95.

10. *Ibid.*, p. 99.

11. Henri Frankfort, Mrs. H. A. Frankfort, John A. Wilson, Thorkild Jacobsen, *Before Philosophy*. Baltimore, Md.: Penguin, 1949, p. 15, paperback.

12. *Ibid.*

13. *Ibid.*, pp. 24–25.

14. *Ibid.*, pp. 19–20.

15. Paul Ricoeur, *The Symbolism of Evil*, trans. by Emerson Buchanan. Boston: Beacon Press, 1967, p. 163, paperback.

16. Claude Lévi-Strauss, *The Savage Mind*. Chicago: University of Chicago Press, 1969, pp. 268–69, paperback.

17. *Ibid.*, p. 269.

18. *Ibid.*

19. Charles Long, *op. cit.*, p. 172.

20. Watts, *op. cit.*, pp. 16, 17

21. *Ibid.*, p. 31.

22. *Ibid.*, pp. 45, 46.

23. Joseph Campbell, *The Hero with a Thousand Faces*. New York: Pantheon, 1949.

24. Giorgio de Santillana, *Hamlet's Mill*. Boston: Gambit Press, 1969.

25. Joseph Campbell, *The Masks of God: Primitive Mythology*. New York: Viking, 1959, p. 42.

26. *Ibid.*, pp. 33–34.

27. *Ibid.*, p. 34.

28. Joseph Campbell, *The Flight of the Wild Gander*. New York: Viking, 1969, pp. 54–55.

29. Watts, *op. cit.*, pp. 13–14.

30. *Ibid.*

31. Especially as contained in *The Sacred and the Profane*.

32. Campbell, *The Flight of the Wild Gander*, p. 191.

33. *Ibid.*, p. 192.

34. *Ibid.*, p. 226.
35. Eliade, *The Sacred and the Profane*, p. 204.
36. *Ibid.*, p. 205.
37. *Ibid.*, p. 207.
38. *Ibid.*, p. 213.
39. Ricoeur, *op. cit.*, p. 349.
40. *Ibid.*, p. 351.
41. *Ibid.*, pp. 352–53.
42. Campbell, *The Flight of the Wild Gander*, p. 164.
43. Lawrence S. Kubie, *Neurotic Distortion of the Creative Process*. New York: Noonday, 1968, paperback.
44. *Ibid.*, p. 31.
45. *Ibid.*, pp. 34–35.
46. Robert N. Bellah, "Civil Religion in America," *Daedalus*, Winter, 1967, pp. 1, 19.
47. Quoted from David Bidney, "Myth, Symbolism, and Truth," in T. A. Sebeck (ed.), *Myth: A Symposium*. Bloomington, Ind.: Indiana University Press, 1958, p. 23.
48. John F. Hayward, "The Uses of Myth in an Age of Science," *New Theology*, No. 7, Martin E. Marty and Dean G. Peerman (eds.). New York: Macmillan, 1970, p. 71.
49. Langdon Gilkey, *Religion and the Scientific Future*. New York: Harper & Row, 1970, pp. 36–37.
50. *Ibid.*, p. 47.
51. Michael Polanyi, *Personal Knowledge*. London: Routledge & Kegan Paul, 1958.
52. Thomas Kuhn, *The Structure of Scientific Revolutions*. Chicago: University of Chicago Press, 1962.
53. Stephen Toulmin, *Foresight and Understanding*. New York: Harper & Row, Torchbooks, 1963, paperback.
54. Gilkey, *Religion and the Scientific Future*, p. 50.
55. *Ibid.*, p. 51.
56. *Ibid.*, p. 66.
57. *Ibid.*, p. 73.
58. *Ibid.*, p. 26.
59. *Ibid.*, pp. 76–77.
60. *Ibid.*, p. 78.
61. *Ibid.*, p. 80.
62. Herbert W. Richardson, *Toward an American Theology*. New York: Harper & Row, 1967, p. 52.
63. *Ibid.*
64. *Ibid.*, p. 53.

65. *Ibid.*

66. Harvey Cox, "Religion in the Age of Aquarius," *Psychology Today,* April, 1970, p. 47.

67. *Ibid.,* p. 64.

Chapter V: Religion and Community

1. Émile Durkheim, "Search for a Positive Definition," in Louis Schneider (ed.), *Religion, Culture and Society.* New York: Wiley, 1964, pp. 32–33.

2. Bronislaw Malinowski, "Death and the Reintegration of the Group," Schneider (ed.), *op. cit.,* pp. 113–14.

3. Will Herberg, *Protestant, Catholic, Jew.* Rev. ed. Garden City, N.Y.: Doubleday, Anchor, 1955, paperback.

4. *Ibid.,* p. 77.

5. *Ibid.,* pp. 78–81.

6. *Ibid.,* pp. 263–65.

7. Robert A. Nisbet, *The Sociological Tradition.* New York: Basic Books, 1966, pp. 47–48.

8. Thomas Luckmann, *The Invisible Religion.* New York: Macmillan, 1967, p. 45

9. *Ibid.*

10. *Ibid.,* pp. 48–49.

11. *Ibid.,* p. 51.

12. *Ibid.,* p. 53.

13. *Ibid.,* p. 52.

14. Andrew M. Greeley, "Religious Intermarriage in a Denominational Society," *American Journal of Sociology,* Vol. 75, No. 6 (May, 1970), pp. 949–51.

15. Herbert Gans, *The Levittowners.* New York: Pantheon, 1967, pp. 264–65.

16. Clifford Geertz, *Islam Observed.* New Haven: Yale University Press, 1969, p. 94.

17. *Ibid.,* p. 100.

18. Gans, *op. cit.,* p. 365.

Chapter VI: Religion and the Sacred

1. Mircea Eliade, *The Sacred and the Profane.* New York: Harcourt, Brace, 1957, p. 11.

2. *Ibid.*, pp. 20–21.

3. William James, *The Varieties of Religious Experience*. New York: New American Library, Mentor, 1958, p. 67, paperback.

4. F. C. Happold, *Mysticism*. Baltimore, Md.: Penguin, 1963, p. 55, paperback.

5. Philip Ennis, "Ecstasy and Everyday Life,"' *Journal for the Scientific Study of Religion*, Vol. 6, No. 1 (1967), p. 42.

6. *Ibid.*, p. 43.

7. Clifford Geertz, "Religion as a Cultural System," in Donald R. Cutler (ed.), *The Religious Situation: 1968*. Boston: Beacon Press, 1968, p. 655.

8. Edward Shils, "Ritual and Crisis," in Donald R. Cutler (ed.), *The Religious Situation: 1968*. Boston: Beacon Press, 1968, pp. 746–47.

9. *Ibid.*, p. 748.

10. David L. Miller, *Gods and Games*. Cleveland: World Publishing, 1969, p. 138.

11. *Ibid.*, p. 140.

12. Sam Keen, *Apology for Wonder*. New York: Harper & Row, 1969, pp. 211–12.

13. Robert E. Neale, *In Praise of Play*. New York: Harper & Row, 1969.

14. John B. Orr and F. Patrick Nichelson, *The Radical Suburb*. Philadelphia: Westminster, 1970.

15. *Newsweek*, May 11, 1970.

Chapter VII: Religion and Sex

1. Langdon Gilkey, *Naming the Whirlwind*. Indianapolis: Bobbs-Merrill, 1969, pp. 317–19, paperback.

2. Joseph Campbell, *Masks of God: Primitive Mythology*. New York, 1959, pp. 314–15.

3. *Ibid.*, p. 139.

4. Mircea Eliade, *Patterns in Comparative Religion*. New York: Sheed and Ward, 1958, pp. 332–34.

5. Walter Harrelson, *From Fertility Cult to Worship*. Garden City, N.Y.: Doubleday, 1969, pp. 12–13.

6. *Ibid.*, pp. 13–14.

7. *Ibid.*, pp. 68–69.

8. In this and subsequent paragraphs I will rely heavily on the brilliant analysis of the theologian Herbert Richardson in his arti-

cle "The Symbol of Virginity," in Donald R. Cutler (ed.), *The Religious Situation: 1969.* Boston: Beacon Press, 1969, pp. 775–811.

9. *Ibid.*, pp. 779–80.

10. *Ibid.*, pp. 781–782.

11. *Ibid.*, p. 783.

12. *Ibid.*, pp. 783–84.

13. *Ibid.*, pp. 784–85.

14. Morton Hunt, *A Natural History of Love.* New York: Knopf, 1959, p. 127.

15. Richardson, "The Symbol of Virginity," p. 787.

16. Quoted in Hunt, *A Natural History of Love,* p. 99.

17. Richardson, "The Symbol of Virginity," p. 790.

18. Hunt, *A Natural History of Love,* p. 138.

19. *Ibid.*, p. 137.

20. Richardson, "The Symbol of Virginity," pp. 800–1.

21. *Ibid.*, p. 806.

22. Thomas Luckmann, *The Invisible Religion.* New York: Macmillan, 1967, pp. 111–12.

23. Herbert Gans, *The Levittowners,* New York: Pantheon, 1967, p. 25.

24. Luckmann, *op. cit.*, pp. 110–11.

Chapter VIII: Religion and Ethics

1. Some of those writings are: Fletcher, *Situation Ethics: The New Morality,* Philadelphia: Westminster, 1966; Robinson, *Christian Morals Today.* Philadelphia: Westminster, 1964; Lehmann, *Ethics in a Christian Society.* New York: Harper & Row, 1963; and Wood, *Sex and the New Morality.* New York: Association Press and Newman Press, 1968.

2. Fletcher, *op. cit.*, p. 26.

3. Kenneth Keniston, "Moral Development, Youthful Activism and Modern Society," *Youth and Society,* Vol. 1, No. 1 (September, 1969), p. 124.

4. *Ibid.*, p. 124.

5. *Ibid.*, p. 125.

6. *Ibid.*

7. *Ibid.*, p. 126.

8. Langdon Gilkey, *Religion and the Scientific Future.* New York: Harper & Row, 1970, pp. 91–92.

Chapter IX: Religious Leadership

1. Joachim Wach, *Sociology of Religion.* Chicago: University of Chicago Press, 1944, p. 334.
2. *Ibid.,* p. 337.
3. *Ibid.,* p. 343.
4. *Ibid.,* p. 344.
5. *Ibid.,* p. 347.
6. *Ibid.*
7. *Ibid.,* pp. 351–52.
8. *Ibid.,* p. 354.
9. *Ibid.,* p. 356.
10. *Ibid.,* p. 358.
11. *Ibid.,* p. 365.
12. *Ibid.,* pp. 368–69.
13. William C. Martin describes the adventures of these radio evangelists in the article "The God Hucksters of Radio," *Atlantic,* June, 1970.
14. *Ibid.,* p. 52.
15. *Ibid.,* p. 54.
16. *Ibid.,* pp. 54–55.
17. John C. Schaar, "Reflections on Authority," *New American Review,* Vol. 8 (1970), pp. 66–68.
18. *Ibid.,* pp. 71, 72.
19. *Ibid.,* pp. 73–74.
20. *Ibid.,* pp. 75–77.
21. *Ibid.,* pp. 77–78.

Chapter X. Conclusion

1. There was some evidence of erosion in American Protestantism shown in Martin E. Marty, Andrew M. Greeley, Stuart Rosenberg, *What De We Believe?* New York: Meredith Press. 1968. See also John Kotre, *A View from the Border.* Chicago: Aldine, 1971.
2. Langdon Gilkey, *Religion and the Scientific Future.* New York: Harper & Row, 1970, pp. 32–33.
3. Thomas Luckmann, *The Invisible Religion.* New York: Macmillan, 1967, pp. 95–96.
4. Gilkey, *op. cit.,* p. 65.

5. Theodore Roszak, *The Making of a Counterculture.* Garden City, N.Y.: Doubleday, Anchor, 1969, paperback.

6. Emmanuel G. Methnane, *How Technology Will Shape the Future.* Cambridge: Harvard University Program on Technology and Society, Reprint No. 5, 1968.

7. Gilkey, *op. cit.,* p. 89.

8. *Ibid.,* pp. 92–93.

9. *Ibid.,* p. 97.

10. *Ibid.,* pp. 97–98.

11. *Ibid.,* p. 99.

12. *Ibid.,* p. 134.

13. *Ibid.,* p. 136.

14. Margaret Mead, *Culture and Commitment: A Study of the Generation Gap.* Garden City, N.Y.: Doubleday, 1970.

15. Ernst van den Haag, "One Man's Mead, Another Man's Poison," *Atlantic,* June, 1970, pp. 118–20.

16. Joseph Adelson, "What Generation Gap?" *New York Times Magazine,* January 18, 1970, p. 10.

17. *Ibid.,* p. 35.

18. *Ibid.*

Index